TYSON FURY

TYSON FURY

GYPSY KING
OF THE WORLD

NIGEL CAWTHORNE

First published in 2020 by Ad Lib Publishers Ltd
15 Church Road
London, SW13 9HE

www.adlibpublishers.com

Text © 2020 Nigel Cawthorne

ISBN: 978-1-913543-93-8

A CIP catalogue record for this book is available from the British Library.

Every reasonable effort has been made to trace copyright-holders of material
reproduced in this book, but if any have been inadvertently overlooked the
publishers would be glad to hear from them.

Printed in the UK

10 9 8 7 6 5 4 3 2 1

CONTENTS

PROLOGUE **UNFINISHED BUSINESS** VII

INTRODUCTION **THE HOLY HAND** XV

CHAPTER ONE **BORN TO FIGHT** I

CHAPTER TWO **INTERNATIONAL AMATEUR** II

CHAPTER THREE **TURNING PROFESSIONAL** 17

CHAPTER FOUR **TITLE SHOT** 31

CHAPTER FIVE **BRITISH AND COMMONWEALTH CHAMP** 59

CHAPTER SIX **CLIMBING THE WORLD CHAMPIONSHIP LADDER** 87

CHAPTER SEVEN **THE ULTIMATE FIGHTING MACHINE** 121

CHAPTER EIGHT **MADISON SQUARE GARDEN** 163

CHAPTER NINE **WORLD CHAMPION** 191

CHAPTER TEN **BREAKDOWN** 215

CHAPTER ELEVEN **COMEBACK** 229

CHAPTER TWELVE **SHOWDOWN AT THE STAPLES CENTER** 249

CHAPTER THIRTEEN **JOSTLING FOR POSITION** 259

CHAPTER FOURTEEN **REMATCH** 287

UNFINISHED BUSINESS

Billed as 'Unfinished Business', the Tyson Fury–Deontay Wilder rematch on 22 February 2020 was the most eagerly awaited fight since Lennox Lewis bludgeoned Mike Tyson into submission in 2002.

Others went further back, comparing it to the fight between Muhammad Ali and Joe Frazier in 1971. Both Fury and Wilder were undefeated and the rematch had been agreed immediately after the controversial split-decision draw of their fight in December 2018. The rematch would be decisive, as both men claimed to have been at less than peak form in their first bout. Fury was overweight and had been out of the ring for nearly three years, while Wilder claimed that he had broken his arm during training.

Since their first fight, Wilder had fought twice, winning by a knockout on both occasions. Not a great technical boxer, he had been behind on points on all three judges' scorecards in the second fight until he delivered the KO. Fury had also fought twice, with unanimous points decision and one TKO (technical knockout). He had also taken to wrestling, beating WWE champion Braun Strowman at the World Wrestling Entertainment Crown Jewel. However, Fury had been injured along the way. In his fight with Sweden's Otto Wallin in September 2019, he had sustained a cut on the face which needed forty-seven stitches. Wilder would be aiming to open it up.

Wilder held the coveted WBC belt, defended nine times by Muhammad Ali. But Fury retained the lineal title. There was everything to play for. At the weigh-in there was the usual pre-fight banter with Fury's fans booing Wilder. The pair were barred from the standard face-off after pushing and shoving each other at an earlier press conference.

'Look how small you are, you little midget,' screamed Fury. 'Busted, one hundred per cent. I've never been so sure of anything in my life, you big dosser.'

As the rival camps stepped in to separate the two unbeaten heavyweights, Wilder taunted Fury about his two knock-downs in their first fight, fourteen months earlier.

'I was the one standing over you, I was the superior one,' Wilder said. 'How many times have you dreamt about the twelfth round? You know the story of David and Goliath? You know what happened? That's going to happen again. Timber! It's going to happen again and, this time, I promise you won't get up.'

In response, Fury ramped up the insults, saying: 'You're a pussy. Look at you, your knees are shaking, you're terrified!'

For Wilder there was also a racial element to the fight.

'I'm looking forward to providing my service to my greatness on black history month,' he said, 'making Tyson Fury a black history trivia question.'

Fury refused to be billed at the 'great white hope'. He responded: 'I'm not into all this racial thing. White man versus black man. And black history month. I refuse to get into that. This is not a racial war! We're all human beings, it doesn't matter if you're black, white, pink or green, we all share the same blood. This isn't a racial war between blacks and whites, it's a fight between the two highest performing heavyweights on the planet, there's nothing racial about this fight. I have nothing against Wilder as a man and neither does he against me, but we want to give it to each other.'

Though it was generally thought that Fury could out-box Wilder, the 'Bronze Bomber' had one of the most lethal right hands in boxing history – the 'Alabama hammer'. His trainer, Jay Deas, said Wilder hit as hard as anyone who ever put on gloves. But Fury's camp insisted that the Gypsy King had developed the power to knock Wilder out – with Fury himself predicting he would do it in round 2. Still, on the eve of the fight the odds were 10/11 in Wilder's favour.

'You have to be perfect for thirty-six minutes to beat me,' he told Fury. 'I just have to be perfect for a second.'

Fury dismissed Wilder and his big right hand as a 'one-trick pony' and believed he had figured out how to defuse the champ's one and only weapon. For the rematch, he changed trainer, dropping Ben Davison, who had coached him since late 2017 and helped him shed the weight he had gained since he dropped out of the fighting game two years earlier. Instead, he took on Javan 'SugarHill' Steward, nephew of the late Hall of Fame trainer Emanuel Steward, and returned to Kronk Gym in Detroit, where he briefly trained in 2010. This marked a change in tactics. Davison had encouraged Fury to go the distance, figuring that he would always win on points. But Fury believed that the Americans would not give up the heavyweight crown easily and the three US judges at the rematch would find a way to mark him down. This time he would have to go for a knockout and SugarHill was the man to give him it. After all, Wilder had a weakness.

'He might be able to punch, but I know he's got a glass chin. All big punchers can't take one back,' Fury said. 'So let's see if he can really do the talking when it comes to fighting a proper heavyweight champion of the world. It's all right fighting bums, you big dosser. But when you fight a real man, you know to sit down.'

The fight was a sell-out. With a capacity of 17,000, tickets for the MGM Grand Garden Arena, Las Vegas, were changing hands for up to $11,000 and pay-per-view buys were expected to top two million. Fury was promised at least a £30-million-pound payday.

'This is the biggest fight of the last fifty years in the heavyweight division, with two men putting it on the line,' he said. 'The fans will be the winners because we both have a lot to lose. It's going to be an entertaining fight.' Fury claimed that this was his date with destiny. 'This is my time in the stars, time in the sun, five minutes of fame, whatever you want to call it. This is what I live to do. I've lived and breathed this since I was fourteen and I couldn't think of being in any better place in the world. Even if you gave me ten million pounds to spend and sent me to the Bahamas with eight strippers and a load of alcohol, it would be no good to me because I'd rather be here getting punched in the face by Wilder. That's what turns me on.'

For Fury, dethroning the WBC champ would complete his collection of titles. 'After I beat Wilder I will have achieved everything and won every single belt there is – English, Irish, British, Commonwealth, European, a whole lot of international and intercontinental belts, every single world title belt and two *Ring* magazine belts,' he said. 'The only belt I didn't win, which I'm pretty pissed about, is the Central Area title. I think it's vacant. I'll have completed the game. When you get a computer game and you complete it, you get to the end, it's all easy then. On Saturday night I will complete the toughest sport in the world. Finished it.'

He was pumped up. Leaving his dressing room with his corner team, he roared: 'We are Sparta!' Ever the showman, Fury began the entertainment with his ring walk – or rather, in this case, ring ride: he was carried into the arena on a throne, propelled by beautiful women dressed as glamorous gladiators. Dressed like a Poundland king, wearing a Burger King crown befitting Las Vegas, he left no one in doubt that he intended to be the king of heavyweight boxing once again. On the way to the ring, he lip-synced along to Patsy

Cline's 'Crazy', perhaps a nod to his much-publicised mental-health issues.

By contrast, Wilder went gangsta, wearing an all-black costume with latest hip-hop sensation D Smoke rapping him to the ring. The *Sun* said he looked 'like *Teenage Mutant Turtles'* enemy Shredder had been dragged through a diamond mine and was fuming about it'. This would be the eleventh consecutive defence of his WBC heavyweight title. And it would possibly be his last.

From the start of round 1, Fury demonstrated his new tactics. He came bounding from his corner to take on the champ. Throughout the fight he moved forward, forcing Wilder on to the back foot. He attacked steadily, never letting his opponent breathe. He threw three times as many punches as Wilder, never giving him the room to deploy his deadly right. Fury landed one punch to the side of Wilder's head in the early rounds that cut open his ear. In round 3, he knocked him down. It was the first time Wilder had hit the canvas in ten years. He was on his back again in round 5, bleeding from the mouth and the ear.

Wilder was never in the fight, and his corner threw in the towel in the seventh when it was clear that their man was clean out of punches. The self-styled 'baddest man on the planet' had been comprehensively beaten. This time there was no doubt about the result. The Gypsy King was now king of the world. He celebrated by leading the crowd in a spirited rendition of Don McLean's 'American Pie'.

Now Fury had the WBC belt, he wanted to get on with the long-awaited fight against Anthony Joshua, the man who held the other heavyweight title. Fury wanted to unify the titles again, as they had been back in 2015, when he dropped out of the ring. But first he needed that WBC belt, which is why his first stop on the comeback trail had to be the defeat of Deontay Wilder.

THE HOLY HAND

In the twelfth and final round of the WBC heavyweight championship fight at the Staples Center, Los Angeles, on 1 December 2018, Tyson Fury hit the canvas for the second time. A furious right-left combination from Deontay Wilder dumped him flat on his back with just over two minutes to go in the fight. Everyone thought that Fury's bid for the title was over. The right hand and left hook that Wilder landed cleanly put Fury flat on his back. It looked like they would finish Fury for good.

'I saw his eyes roll into the back of his head. I was like it's over,' said Wilder.

Fury lay motionless on the canvas. As the count hit five, Fury still looked unconscious. BBC boxing correspondent Mike Costello said that if you had seen him being pounded to the canvas, you could not believe that any man could rise to his feet after that colossal right hand from Wilder. But Fury showed a huge heart. Those at ringside – who included boxing greats Floyd Mayweather, Evander Holyfield, Lennox Lewis and James 'Buster' Douglas, as well as actress Hayden Panettiere and footballer Zlatan Ibrahimović – could barely believe their eyes and were asking the same question after the fight: how did Tyson Fury get up? Wilder, too, was stunned to see his rival come back for more. So was Fury. Fury later said he was not sure how he got back up but, as a practising Catholic, he believed that God had put him back on his feet.

'I had a holy hand upon me that brought me back and I've got a fighting spirit and I never say die, I get back up,' he said. 'I was brought back. I rose to my feet from the brink of defeat. I can't tell you how because I don't know. I don't know what happened.'

Fury barely beat referee Jack Reiss's count. Before the fight the referee had promised the Gypsy King that he would not stop the fight if he was knocked down. Reiss had told Fury, 'I'll tell you to step to the left and step to the right. If you can do that and you tell me you're all right then I won't stop the fight.'

Reiss got to a count of six before Fury showed any sign of recovering. But within three seconds, he was on his feet. Fury went on to land right hands that made a tiring Wilder retreat.

'That round should probably have been a draw,' he said. 'It was a great fight.'

As much as Wilder tried, he couldn't land another power shot on Fury before the final bell sounded, to a roar of appreciation from the crowd. Fury then climbed up on the ropes and raised his arms, claiming victory to the cheers of his fans. The two fighters hugged.

Many judged Fury to be the winner on points. But the two knockdowns ultimately cost Fury a fight because only one judge – Canada's Robert Tapper – scored the fight for Fury, Tapper giving him 114–112. Mexico's Alejandro Rochin made it 115–111 for Wilder, and 113–113 was the score from British official Phil Edwards. The result was a draw with the referee raising both men's arms. It meant that Wilder retained the title while both men remained undefeated.

'I thought I won,' said Fury afterwards, 'but two men tried their guts out. I'm not going to scream *"Robbery!"* I'm not going to take anything from Wilder. Great fighter, a hell of a champion. He kept coming all night.'

But Wilder had knocked the big man down twice.

'I think with the two knockdowns I definitely won the fight,' Wilder said. 'We poured our hearts out tonight. We're both warriors, but with those two drops I think I won the fight.'

Fury clearly disagreed.

'We're on away soil,' Fury said. 'I got knocked down twice, but I still believe I won that fight. The Gypsy King has returned. I'm a professional athlete who loves to fight. He is a fearsome fighter. The world knows the truth.'

A man who knows a thing or two about heavyweight title fights, Lennox Lewis, agreed, tweeting, 'The #WilderFury judging takes me back to my first fight with @holyfield Just goes to show how hard it is for a Brit to come to America and take someone's belt even tho that's what we clearly saw. Big up to @Tyson_Fury who never ceases to amaze me. Hold ur head high!'

WBC president Mauricio Sulaiman said, 'I think the draw

is well taken. It could have gone either way. It was a great fight. The two knockdowns were the defining factor of the fight. Several rounds were very close – a few punches makes the difference.'

Wilder and Fury both said they were open to an immediate rematch. Fury would have owed it to Wilder if he had dethroned the other man, but now it would be up to Wilder to determine who he wanted to fight next. 'We gave the fans a great fight tonight,' Wilder said. 'We're the two best in the world and we proved it tonight. When you get two warriors, you get a great fight. That's what we proved tonight and I'm ready to do it again.'

Fury agreed. 'We're the best two heavyweights on the planet,' he said. 'There is another certain heavyweight who is a chicken. Joshua, where are you?' It looked likely that there would be a rematch between Fury and Wilder, with unified champion Anthony Joshua hoping then to take on Wilder for the right to become the undisputed heavyweight champion of the world.

Though he has failed to seize the WBC heavyweight title, Tyson Fury remained boxing's lineal heavyweight champion, having not lost the four titles he won from Wladimir Klitschko in the ring. Fury vacated those crowns in October 2016 to seek treatment for alcoholism, cocaine addiction and depression, and didn't box for two and a half years. His weight ballooned to over 28 st. Back in training, he lost nearly 150 lbs, weighing in at 256.5 lbs.

'I hope I did you all proud after nearly three years out of the ring,' Fury told his fans. 'I was never going to be knocked out tonight. I showed good heart to get up. I came here tonight and I fought my heart out.' He described his performance as 'the best comeback in boxing history . . . a year ago, I was 400 lbs and in terrible shape. I was so, so terrible,' Fury said. 'Two and a half years out of the ring, living like a rock star, and a very low time. I fought back from suicide, mental health [problems], anxiety, and I wanted more than anything to show the world that it can be done. Anything's possible with the right mindset . . . I ain't just going to stay down because I got punched in the face and knocked back down. I'm not the champion for nothing. Every time the lineal champion has come back from years out he's been destroyed, so I set a precedent. It was a great experience in my journey in life.'

Despite only achieving a draw, Fury rightfully was proud of his performance against an opponent commonly considered boxing's most dangerous puncher. Wilder had, up to that point, won thirty-nine out of his forty bouts with a knockout. By clambering back on his feet, Fury remained convinced he had won.

Promoter Frank Warren and the British Boxing Board of Control (BBBC) complained to the World Boxing Council over the scoring that robbed the British fighter of the title and knew that Fury was determined to prove his point at the earliest opportunity. 'I thought he had won it by three rounds,' said Warren. 'When you think of what he has come from to be here. It is the art of hitting and not getting hit. I didn't think he was going to get up, but at the end of the round he was pushing him back. It is a draw but everyone knows he won it and we will want to do a rematch. How could a fight like this not be a rematch? It is unfinished business. He won that. He won that fight and everyone knows it. The best fought the best, but it was not the best decision.'

Wilder, too, felt that there was more for him to prove. 'I did not sit still, I was too hesitant, I started overthrowing the right hand. I was forcing my punches too much,' he said. 'When I rush my punches like that I'm never accurate. The rematch I guarantee I'm going to get him.'

Fury's trainer was Ben Davison. He said, 'I told Tyson before the fight he would beat him with his left hand. We didn't come here for money to get through the fight. We came here to win and I'm sick and gutted.'

But in Los Angeles Davison was told to hold his tongue. In the Staples Center, Fury's supporters included thousands of members of the travelling community and, amid criticism of scorecards, Fury said: 'I was telling my brothers and family to keep quiet. There were about 10,000 travellers and Brits from around the world. They probably would have smashed this arena up if I'd instigated it – I mean to the floor.' Outside the ring, Tyson Fury now knew how to keep the peace and let cooler heads prevail. 'I'm going to go home, enjoy Christmas with my family, sit down with Frank in January and see what we'll do next,' he said. Besides, he had an audience with whom he shared a greater concern.

'For all the people out there with mental health problems,' he said, 'I did it for you guys.'

BORN TO FIGHT

Tyson Fury was born to fight. It was in his blood.

Fury came from a well-known family of fighting travellers that included former professionals Peter and Hughie Fury. Most of the fighting Furys though had scrapped without gloves in fields and fairground booths. Tyson's father, 'Gypsy' John Fury, made the transition from bare-knuckle boxer to the licensed ranks, losing an eliminator for the British heavyweight title to Henry Akinwande in 1991.

Tyson's maternal grandfather was Ticker 'Tiger' Gorman, one of nine children who came over from Ireland, and had sixty heavyweight bouts as a journeyman in the 1940s and 1950s. Tiger's nephew Bartley Gorman was the undefeated bare-knuckle boxing champion of the UK and Ireland and was often referred to as King of the Gypsies. Between 1972 and 1992, he reigned supreme in the world of illegal gypsy boxing. He fought down a mineshaft, in a quarry, at horse fairs, on campsites, in bars and clubs, and in the street.

Tyson's paternal grandfather and great-grandfather were also boxers.

Fury's grandmother was born at Nutts Corner near Antrim while his mother was born in Belfast. From Galway, his father was a cousin of Irish former WBO middleweight champion Andy Lee, former British light heavyweight champion Hosea Burton and British heavyweight champion Hughie Fury, who challenged for the WBO heavyweight title in 2017. Tyson and Hughie told the press in 2013 that they aimed to become the new Klitschkos. His nineteen-year-old half-brother Tommy also entered the ring as a light heavyweight.

'Boxing is a key element of the travelling culture,' said Tyson. 'Before anything else, you learn how to fight. Whereas in other cultures little kids will kick a ball about, we're punching hands. When we have a dispute we're not supposed to go to the police, we're supposed take our shirts off, go outside and sort it out with fisticuffs. To be a good fighting man is one of the best things you can ever be in life. But you go outside now and people are pulling swords out. You've got little men wanting to be big men but they can't, so they pull out a gun and let five bullets go instead.'

The chances of Tyson following in the family's footsteps seemed slim at first. Born nearly three months early, he weighed little more than 1 lb. 'The doctors told me there was not much chance of him living,' said his father. 'I had lost two daughters in the same way who had been born prematurely. They told me there was not much hope for him. A doctor said, "What are you going to call him?"

'It was 1988, Mike Tyson was in his pomp as world

heavyweight champion, and so I said, "Let's call him Tyson." The doctors just looked at me and smiled, but I always hoped in my heart that one day my lad might be world champion, too.'

And, of course, Tyson Fury was the perfect name for a boxer. Fury Sr said he wanted to see his son achieve what he himself could not. 'I had no education, I came from a large working family,' he said. 'So what did you do for money? Fought among travellers. Prize fights, pick-up fights. It was a brutal business. Brutal. You could have got killed. I had me jaw broke, teeth missing. When you are out there you are a gladiator, my friend. It's you and him. It's the worst thing in the world and all you want to do is be safe and win and get paid.'

Back in the home country of Ireland, there was a simple reason for the name 'Fury', which didn't have anything to do with boxing. The Irish form of Fury or Furey is Ó Fiodhabhra, which means 'the man with bushy eyebrows'. This was abbreviated to Ó'Fiura. Another variant was Fleury, which is from County Longford in the centre of Ireland. Tyson's father and grandfather were from Tuam in County Galway. At an early age, John Fury moved with his family to Lancashire in England where they continued to live the traveller life.

'Our lifestyle has been around for a thousand years – and now we still live in the 1800s,' said Fury. 'We don't move in normal time. You go back to my great-great-grandfather and we are still doing the same stuff. It is still fighting talk. If you want to fight, you take your shirt off, you go outside and you have a knuckle-up, and the best man shakes his hand and they go off for a drink. That is how things are sorted out in our culture. If you have a dispute, you don't go to the police or else you are known as a grass, an outcast, and nobody wants to know you. So we settle it our way. We don't get laws involved. And we marry our own people. There are exceptions, of course. But mainly we marry our own. A travelling man goes out to work – buying, selling, whatever he is going to do. It has always been that way. We aren't an educated race. We don't go to school.'

They were still steeped in an old-fashioned macho ethos.

'We still think it is a man's world. In our culture it is all about the men,' said Tyson. 'The men can do everything, and women just clean and cook and have children and look after that man. They should be happy with that lifestyle, really. There are no rights for women in a travelling community, not at all.'

Fury's destiny was set even before his father named him Tyson. Apparently Fury's great-uncle Uriah Burton once made a prophesy to Fury's Uncle Pat, who later became his trainer. 'He said to my uncle, "You know, when your brother gets married to my niece she is going to drive him insane,"' Fury explained, 'but a fighting man will come out of those sons he has. He predicted my future a year before I was born. I know it sounds stupid to talk about breeding and classing human beings like animals. But I am fighting royalty. Uriah is on my father's side and Bartley Gorman, the other undefeated champion, is on my mother's side. I have gypsy kings on both sides of the family.'

Gypsy John's fighting life took a darker turn in 2010 when he was sentenced to eleven years for gouging a man's eye out in a brawl after a twelve-year grudge erupted in bloody violence at a car auction. The forty-six-year-old Fury boasted that he was the country's toughest man before trying to blind Oathie Sykes. When the incident ended up in court, Sykes said he had gone to a car auction to buy his son his first van when John Fury approached him with his 'chest up'. The two men had once been friends, but had a violent bust-up over a trivial matter during a trip to Cyprus in 1999. When they met at auction, Sykes said, Fury asked him, 'What about me and you finishing that fight?'

Sykes claimed that he replied, 'I don't want no trouble.' He said Fury replied, 'I'm the best man here in the auction, I'm the best man in the country.' Sykes explained that he took it to mean that he could beat any man at the auction, 'he's the best man at fighting'.

A fight broke out between the two between the cars, before Fury was said to have grabbed Sykes by his hair. 'He was pushing his hand in my face,' Sykes said when he was in court. 'It was his finger, it went in my eye, in the corner and he wouldn't stop. He was like gouging and poking and twisting and poking. All of a sudden, I heard this sound, a clicking like, a popping noise and when he took his hand away I realised blood was on his hand, a lot of blood. It was like he was trying to pull his finger into my brains through my socket. I was screaming, "Please stop, you're hurting me." After that he tried to take my other eye – he tried to blind me, sir, not once he tried to blind me, twice.'

Fury claimed that he meant Sykes no harm, saying the brawl was a fair 'fight between travelling people'. Sykes denied that it had been a 'straightener' – an organised fight between two grudging parties. Fury denied that he had meant to deliberately blind the other man. 'If I was going to do what he said I done to him it would have been a lost worse than that,' Fury said. 'I'm not a feather-duster man.'

Tyson's father admitted wounding Mr Sykes with intent to cause grievous bodily harm and said, 'I'm worried about my son. His boxing career is on the line. If I could give my own eye to him to get back to my children I would do – I'm begging you for my life.'

John Fury went to prison and Tyson said, 'I'm gutted, it was self-defence, but the law's the law and he pleaded guilty.' While his father was in jail, Tyson visited him three or four times a month. 'It's hard seeing him in there but I'm hoping any success I have will help him get through it 'cos it was me dad who made me what I am. I was born and bred to be a fighter,' he said.

Tyson himself avoided fights outside the ring. 'I stay away from all that,' he said. 'I don't go to travellers' fairs and horse-racing dos. Or anywhere that people get drunk and challenge me to a fight. Me being a boxer, they get a few beers inside them and they think they're Mike Tyson and Muhammad Ali rolled into one and start brawling. I'd get me licence taken off me if I got involved. I'm not a troublesome person. I've never had a fight outside the ring in my life.'

* * *

Tyson Fury was born in Wythenshawe, Manchester, and brought up in Styal outside Wilmslow in Cheshire. His family had been living on permanent sites for years by the time he was born. 'I'm proud of what I am, and that's a traveller,' Fury says. 'I have got Irish descent, I was born in Manchester but I'm not Irish or English, I'm a gypsy. I'll tell you what makes a traveller: you're born one, like you're born black. To me it is irrelevant whether I live in a house, a caravan or a tent.' Fury used his upbringing to his advantage. 'I like the feel of being a gypsy. The traveller background gives you that ultimate fighting steel, the determination and will to win, to dig deep. There's no loser in me. As a traveller you never regret anything. You do what you have to do and move on. No ifs, buts or whys.'

But he did encounter prejudice. 'I get it every day. "You gypsy bastard, you fat gypo." All sorts of stuff. It's mainly the Facebook warriors. I know I could savage them like a pit bull if I wanted but I don't because I know every time I win it hurts them more inside. Travellers will be discriminated against for the next thousand years. Nothing will change. It's the world we live in . . . You can't change people's opinion on travellers. Maybe one or two, but not millions. That's not up to me. I really don't care what they think of us. Look. If the blacks can make it out of slavery, I'm sure we can do something.'

For the first few days of his life, the prematurely born Tyson was barely hanging on at all. But he pulled through and not only survived but grew into a strapping lad who was determined to become a boxer from the age of ten.

'I've never encouraged Tyson to fight,' said his father. 'In fact, I've tried my best to discourage him from being a boxer, but it's in him, he wasn't interested in anything else. He's been in the gym since he was twelve.'

His uncertain start in life did not help. 'I remember always being a weakling,' Tyson said. 'I was tall and thin – scrawny. I was about three-and-a-half, four stone at ten years old. I never thought I'd be a fighter. I was always very shy and timid, I'd cry over anything. I still will now, actually. I'm very soft when it comes to talking about families or old times and that sort of stuff. I can cry like that. Watching movies. I can cry over *The Notebook*.' This is a 2004 movie where a poor yet passionate young man falls in love with a rich young woman, giving her a sense of freedom, but they are soon separated because of their social differences. It was a world away from Tyson's own life. As a child he was not much of a scrapper.

'I never used to fight in school,' he said. 'I used to get beat up a bit sometimes and I wouldn't fight back. I don't know what happened to me. I got to about fourteen or fifteen and I wasn't timid any more. I was like a man.'

Tyson's first job was working for his dad, a used-car dealer. Tyson would wash the cars and clean them out. 'I would do stuff for him pretty much every day, it was quite a good job, to be honest,' he told the *Guardian*. 'I did it all the way through school, from about the age of ten until I was sixteen. I was always quite good at fixing and working with cars. My dad's always dealt cars and I've always been brought up around them. They're one of the things I've always been interested in. Having said that, there wasn't any particular model and make I favoured. I would liken it to working in a sweet shop; for me it was a bit like that, being surrounded by them all.

In that kind of situation, a car's just a car really. While we were cleaning them out we used to find occasional things that people had left behind, usually CDs or the occasional mobile phone. But if we could get them back to the people, we always did.'

Tyson could drive from the age of nine. His dad had his car pitch at the family home in Wilmslow, so the young Tyson used to drive the cars around the land, take them up to the tap, wash them and reverse them back. 'By the time I was seventeen, I could drive like [rally driver] Colin McRae,' he said. He was working with cars throughout the time he was first getting into boxing. 'It was great for me because it gave me discipline. I know how to work for money and I know how to appreciate it when I've got it. It also kept me out of trouble and kept me off the streets, drinking and all that stuff. A lot of my friends when I was fourteen or fifteen, they were all up and down, wanting to go out on a Friday night, and my dad had me working really late on Fridays and Saturday mornings and even on Sunday mornings. And when I'd finished all that, we used to spend the rest of the time talking about boxing.'

When he started fighting at amateur international level, Tyson had to spend most of the week on a training camp in Sheffield, so he got less time with the cars. It was a passion he could indulge more fully in later life.

INTERNATIONAL AMATEUR

Tyson Fury started his amateur career at the age of sixteen. He was six-foot-five and weighed 15 stone. Already calling himself the Gypsy King, he had a mean layer of stubble that would burgeon into his now famous beard – which he shaved off on the eve of the Wilder fight. This cost him £1,000 after he struck a bet with his trainer Ben Davison and fighting cousin Isaac Lowe to see who could grow the longest whiskers.

'The legend is back, I didn't need a big beard,' he said. 'I think I look fifteen years younger without it and my wife says she likes me better without the beard – she said she fancies me more.'

As an amateur, his first opponent was sixteen-year-old Duncan Lee from Great Missenden in Buckinghamshire. Fury towered over him by at least six inches. Lee had won his first fight and succeeded in putting Fury on the ropes. But

Fury was fast with his fists and light on his feet. His power shots were well-timed and he regularly split his opponent's guard with uppercuts. His work rate was too much for Lee, who struggled to land a significant shot.

'I was not worried going into the fight because I won my previous one,' Lee recalled. 'I remember growing some stubble in an effort to look a bit meaner but then I found that Tyson had grown a big beard!' The fight was stopped in the third round due to excessive bleeding from Lee's face. 'I wasn't really hurt because of the adrenaline. The fight was stopped because I had a lot of blood. At the age of sixteen, they don't encourage knockouts so I had no problem with the decision to stop the fight. I remember Tyson had a very big reach and that he was a gentleman in that he came and shook my hand in the changing room. He was a true gent.'

For Fury, it was a significant victory. 'At the time, there were only three junior super-heavyweights active in England and Duncan had already beat the other fella,' he said. 'When I stopped Duncan in round three, I instantly became the best junior super-heavyweight in the country after just one fight!' He had shown no sign of being nervous. 'I was a natural who enjoyed every minute of it.'

Lee's father had filmed the fight and uploaded it to YouTube after Fury defeated Wladimir Klitschko in Düsseldorf to take the unified world heavyweight title in 2015. 'Please excuse the poor filming from my Dad,' said Lee. 'He was too busy watching me getting beaten up.' The fighter later had to give up fighting due to a wrist injury and became a musician.

Fury said his victory came from an unstinting belief that

it was his destiny to become world champion. 'There was that expectation after my first amateur fight,' he told the *Manchester Evening News* in 2013. 'Everybody thought I would be a champion top boxer – my dad, my uncles, everybody after one fight. I see myself as the unified heavyweight champion of the world, making two defences of my titles every year in luxurious places like Monaco and Las Vegas. I see all the sacrifice and hard work, all the days away and training camps all paying off to the ultimate goal of being heavyweight champion and having plenty of money in the bank. I don't see myself getting punch-drunk in boxing. I don't see myself staying too long and getting injured or hurt. I can see a clear path and that is not going to happen.'

He already had role models fixed in his mind. 'When I was sixteen, I admired only two fighters: Rocky Marciano and Uriah Burton. Everyone had heard of Marciano, the world heavyweight champion who never took a backward step and never lost a fight. But Burton was known only in the secretive world of the travellers, a name uttered in hushed tones. He was an ogre, they said. He had the strength of five men. He beat opponents two at a time. He would stop at nothing and fight to the death. He sounded like something from the dark ages, more myth than man. Only when I came to know him did I realise the stories were true.'

At seventeen, Fury won a bronze medal in the AIBA (International Boxing Association) Youth World Boxing Championships. As an amateur, Fury represented both England and Ireland three times at international level. At first he was based at the Holy Family boxing club in Belfast,

Northern Ireland, and later switched to the Smithboro club in County Monaghan in the Republic of Ireland. The Irish team took on Poland in 2007, losing twelve matches to six. However, Fury won both of his fights, which were staged in Rzeszów and Białystok. Early on, he got used to fighting on foreign soil. He also boxed for Ireland against the USA, winning both bouts by knockout. But he was forced out of the Irish national championships after protests about his eligibility. Although both his parents were born in Ireland, it was not the custom of travellers to register births with the authorities.

'When Dad was born, the tradition was to get the child baptised but not registered,' said Fury. 'I've employed a genealogist to work on my case. I've been a regular visitor to my grandfather's grave out west. I know what I am. All I need is proof.'

At the English senior championship, Fury represented Jimmy Egan's Boxing Academy and came up against David Price, who was bigger and five years older. 'When I fought him I was a raw seventeen-year-old kid. He was twenty-three, or something like that,' said Fury. 'I'd had ten bouts and he'd had seventy. He was a Commonwealth champion and had won all sorts while I was a novice. He was the only one who ended up on the floor and I was trying to catch him with big hooks, while his style was totally suited to the amateurs.'

Price recalled, 'At the time, Fury was pretty inexperienced and I remember getting in the ring and I could see that he was young. He didn't look quite ready. The occasion might have got to him a little bit. He kind of froze in the first couple of rounds. And in the amateurs then the tactics were getting the lead in the first round and protect your lead. If you started fast you had a great chance of carrying on and winning the fight. I think I was well up after two rounds and then he started to warm into it. He clawed a few points back.

'There was a knockdown – he used to say he knocked me down but it didn't get ruled a knockdown. I fell in over my front foot and he pushed the back of my head to the floor. That happened and then the last round I coasted it. It was an all right fight. But at that time I thought he was a little bit young, I was a little bit long in the tooth. But you could tell he had talent.'

Price won 22–8 and continued bragging about the victory when he turned pro, saying that he was the last and only Englishman to beat Fury. But Fury was not impressed. 'As somebody said to me after – if I was a double ABA champion, a Commonwealth champion with seventy fights and I could only do that to a ten-fight novice, I'd pack the game in,' he said.

Fury's trainer Steve Egan had never had any doubts about his young protégé. 'He was only fourteen when he came to us. He was a big lad and from the moment I saw him I said he was going to be a heavy champion of the world,' Egan said. 'I still say his best performance was when he won the ABA championship. He was world-class that night and should've gone on from that. I thought he'd stay with me and develop, but we parted after winning the English title. He's a born fighter. He won't lie down. He will fight to his last breath.'

Representing England, Fury won the EU Junior

Championship in May 2007, but lost to the Russian Maxim Babanin in the final of the European Junior Championships. As a junior he was ranked No. 3 in the world behind Babanin and fellow Russian Andrey Volkov. Nevertheless, as early as 2006 – when Fury was just eighteen – Egan had confidence that his boy could conquer all before him. With amazing vision, he predicted: 'The 2008 Beijing Olympics, 2010 Commonwealth Games, 2012 London Olympic Games, 2013 British champion, 2014 European champion, 2015 WBC champion and 2016 undisputed heavyweight champion of the world. He will be,' Egan said.

However, Price was selected over Fury to represent Team GB at Beijing where each country was restricted to one competitor per weight division. The decision rankled further when Price returned from Beijing with a bronze medal at superheavyweight – Fury insisted he would have come home with a gold. Instead, Fury became holder of the Amateur Boxing Association superheavyweight title of 2008. By then, he was six-foot-eight and weighed 18 stone.

In December 2008, Fury decided to turn pro. His amateur record was an impressive thirty-one wins – twenty-six by knockout – and four losses.

TURNING PROFESSIONAL

Tyson Fury made his professional debut in the Nottingham Arena on 6 December 2008. He was twenty. His first bout was against the Hungarian Bela Gyongyosi on the undercard of Carl Froch versus Jean Pascal for the vacant WBC super middleweight title. This brought Fury to a wider audience in the UK as the fight was broadcast on ITV4.

It was not much of a match. Fury weighed in at 261 lbs, Gyongyosi just 191.75 lbs. The Hungarian was a good six inches shorter and had lost five of his last six bouts. A cruiserweight, he had had nine defeats in his fourteen fights. It was noted that Fury, wearing high white trunks, looked a little flabby around the middle. He had just returned from his honeymoon. His new bride, Paris, was Scottish, but came from a similar traveller background. The couple had met at the wedding of a mutual friend in London when she was just fifteen.

'Even though Tyson was a similar age to me, he looked

about twenty-five as he was so big,' she recalled. 'He had all this facial hair and a beard and these big sideburns. I remember seeing Tyson as soon as my friend and I got out of the car to go into the wedding and I have to admit I did refer to him as "Farmer Giles" and have a laugh at his expense. Then his aunt, who I had known all my life as she was my mum's friend, told me she wanted to introduce me to her nephew. I was wearing a hat for the wedding and I remember being hardly able to see Tyson from under my hat as he was so tall. We only saw each other for a split second and I didn't really give him another thought.' At five foot eight, she was no midget either, but still small beside Tyson.

'We didn't actually get together until a night out when I was living in Doncaster,' she told the *Doncaster Free Press*. 'The night was to mark my sixteenth birthday. Tyson happened to be there by fluke. He was my first boyfriend as I was not allowed a boyfriend until the age of sixteen. He is the only boyfriend I have had.'

This was very much in the traveller tradition. Fury admitted that his prevailing views on women were not exactly in fashion, but he couldn't care less for the opinion of settled society. 'We are outsiders. But that is our way. Just like the Muslims have their ways, we have our ways,' he told the *Irish Times*. 'There are these girls who want to open their legs to every Tom, Dick and Harry. But they are looked upon as rubbish in our community. We don't do stuff like that. If I had a sister who did that . . . I'd hang her. She would bring disgrace on the family. It is a very, very bad thing to do. We don't do that. Women have to be pure and respectful. They can't go out drinking down the town and doing whatever they want to do. Just doesn't happen.' He asked for tolerance of travellers' ways. 'People have got to understand that our lifestyle is totally, totally different. We may be the same colour, and we may speak the same language, but deep inside we are not alike. We are aliens. What is it? Our goals are different to other peoples. We want different things.'

This was not alien to Paris. 'Tyson would train in boxing during the week and then come and see me at the weekend,' she said. 'I would always be so excited at the thought of seeing him. Even after we got engaged, Tyson would sleep in a caravan in the yard of my parents' home while I slept inside the house. We didn't sleep together until after we got married. That is the traveller's way and the gypsy way of life.'

She, too, was proud of her roots. 'You are what you are. It is a way of life and is like being Asian or black or Jewish,' she said. '*My Big Fat Gypsy Wedding* gave a very bad image of what travellers are like and most travellers are not like that, just a very small minority. People from a travelling background have big families and it is quite old-fashioned and everyone looks out for each other. It is like a community.'

They dated for three years before getting married when she was almost nineteen. 'Tyson never actually proposed to me,' she said. 'He just told me we were getting married. We were having a picnic and chatting about his future as a boxer and he turned to me and said, "First, I am going to turn professional, then win the English title then the British title, then I'm going to marry you." I was a bit shocked, but also very happy.'

The couple married in December 2008, at a church in Doncaster followed by a reception at a nearby hotel called The Stables – and, indeed, it wasn't at all like *My Big Fat Gypsy Wedding*. 'What you see on the show does happen,' Fury told the *Daily Star*. 'There are gypsies who do have weddings like this. But by no means is it what every gypsy does. The people in the show are from a certain part of the travelling community. They are from a lower class. I'm not having a go at anyone, I'm just saying how it is. If you go to a wedding of a couple from a rough council estate, it will be different than a wedding of a couple from a middle-class area. That's the way it is. It's the same in every community. And the travelling community is no different. Us travellers call the kind of people on the show Kippians. They wear bright colours and want to be noticed. They are the chavs of the travelling community.' Fury thought that the TV show gave the wrong impression. 'If all you knew about the traveller community was from watching that show then you would be well off the mark. For starters, it only shows a particular set of travellers and it's all fake. They're all putting on an act for the cameras. The travellers on that show you see going into trailers probably all have houses. Those crazy wedding dresses you see on that programme, they just know they're going on TV so they're pushing the boat out. It's just a big put-on.'

He even took a swipe at one of the stars of the show, a former bare-knuckle fighter. 'Even the resident hardman of the show, Paddy Doherty, admitted he exaggerated his tough-guy image,' Fury said. 'He hasn't had a fight in thirty years. These people are the lowest of the low in my book. We settle things among ourselves in the travelling community. Men like that are scum and God deals with them in his own way.'

But he did not dismiss *My Big Fat Gypsy Wedding* out of hand. After all, it pulled in an audience of more than eight million a week. 'The show is popular and gets huge viewing figures,' he said. 'It's popular because it is interesting and gives people an insight to a world that they know nothing about. And that's a good thing for the travelling people. But the show has only focused on a small part of that world. It wouldn't be half as popular if it followed me around. But people don't like average Joes as much as those who are a bit more extravagant. But it's a bit like a gypsy watching *Shameless* and then believing everyone in the general public is like Frank Gallagher. It's not that simple.'

At their wedding, Paris and Tyson had 400 guests, though it was a surprisingly modest affair compared to the ones that aired on the TV programme that had so incensed Fury. 'I've never been to a wedding like the ones on the show,' Fury said. 'But I know people who have. They look like fun. Everyone is entitled to have any kind of wedding they want. My wife looked beautiful and we had a great day. That's all that matters to me.'

Later, as his fame grew, Fury would go on to find that he was attacked on social media for his gypsy heritage. 'I've had discrimination and abuse on Twitter. There's loads of discrimination on Twitter against travellers,' he said. 'If a travelling man went round saying the same about black people or Asians, whatever race, colour or creed they are, they'd get into deep trouble. But nobody seems to be bothered just because we are travellers. I'm not here to be abused. I'm six-foot-nine and nearly eighteen stone. I will not be bullied. I'm a human being, I can't be told what I am and what I do to my mother and sisters and cousins and brothers without responding. I'm not just going to take that and I will crack sometimes. But I've got to be the big man and I've got to stand up and represent my people. The way to do that is in the ring, by becoming a world champion.'

When Paris first met Tyson, she had no interest in boxing, but became fascinated by the sport and began to surprise herself with the boxing knowledge she picked up. 'I have a very extensive knowledge of boxing now as I have picked up a lot from hearing Tyson talking with friends about boxing,' she said. 'I like watching heavier weight boxing, but I can't bring myself to watch lighter weight boxing. Seeing men who weigh the same as me boxing just doesn't seem right. It is like watching children fighting.'

Back in Fury's world of work, the honeymoon may have left him out of shape, but in his 2008 bout against Gyongyosi he delivered a left hook to the body that put his opponent down after 2 min 1 sec of round 1. Bela did make it back on to to his feet, but as he was grimacing and favouring his right side, referee Howard John Foster waved an end to the bout after just 2 min 14 sec.

Over the next seven months, Fury had six more fights. He faced the thirty-five-year-old German Marcel Zeller at the Robin Park Centre in Wigan on 17 January 2009. Nicknamed 'Highlander', Zeller wore a Scottish kilt instead of trunks. By then, Fury had lost some of this honeymoon fat and came in

8 lbs lighter than at his debut just a month earlier, though he was still 10.5 lbs heavier than his opponent. Zeller was only six-foot-one.

In round 1, Zeller, a rough-house fighter, backed himself into a corner and repeatedly motioned Fury to come on. Fury responded with a pair of uppercuts and a few body shots that slipped through Zeller's guard. Showing no fear, Zeller went on the attack, trying to upset Fury's rhythm. He was battered back by accurate shots from Fury who mixed his attack on the body as well as his head.

In round 2, Zeller started bleeding from the nose. The fight was paused 47 sec into round 3 when Zeller went down from what referee Howard John Foster determined to be a low blow. A warning was issued to Fury and Zeller was given time to recover. But 2 min 50 sec into the round, Zeller was backed into a corner and was absorbing punches while making no effective response. That was it. Foster stepped in and waved an end to the bout.

At the Norwich Showground on 28 February 2009, Fury faced the thirty-five-year-old Russian Daniil Peretyatko, a.k.a. Daniel Peret or 'Shrek'. He was eight inches shorter than Fury, but 4 lbs heavier. Peretyatko had started his career as a cruiserweight, tipping the scale at under 15 stone. He had since ballooned and he had lost eight of his last eleven bouts.

It was easy for Fury to control this fight, using his superior height and reach to land telling punches, while remaining out of range of his opponent. He connected with several solid shots to the ample midsection of Peretyatko, as well as landing a couple to the head that slipped past his guard.

Midway through round 2, Peretyatko developed a cut over his left eye. Following the round, referee Ken Curtis went over to check with Peretyatko's corner and view the cut. He immediately turned and waved an end to the bout, though Peretyatko wanted to continue.

Next came thirty-two-year-old Lee Swaby, previously known as the man who had knocked out Enzo Maccarinelli in 2000. But his early promise soon faded. He lost every time he stepped up a class and had lost nine of his last ten bouts. Fury had a weight advantage of 20.75 lbs. They met at the Aston Events Centre in Birmingham in a bout that was aired on ITV4's *Fight Night* on 14 March 2009, where Fury was seen punching himself in the face following an uppercut that had failed to connect with Swaby 1 min 43 sec into round 4. At 3 min Swaby retired in his corner, leaving the battlefield to Fury. The extraordinary video clip of Fury hitting himself went viral with over two million views. Fury explained later, 'In my fourth professional fight, I threw a big right uppercut against Lee Swaby, completely missed him and ended up hitting myself between the eyes. It stunned me for a bit, more out of surprise than anything else. The punch would have knocked out a lot of boxers.'

By then, David Price had turned professional and, on 28 March that same year, 2009, he knocked out David Ingleby in round 3 of his first pro fight. He saw himself as a rival to Fury, after beating him as an amateur, and said he was none too impressed with Fury's professional fights.

'He's beaten three bums and suddenly thinks he's some kind of superstar,' said Price. 'He hasn't beaten anything like the competition I did in the amateurs and hasn't achieved even half of what I did. I'm not impressed with the physical shape he is in or his punching power. He's boxing live on ITV4 and yet he can't be bothered to get his body into any kind of shape.' Although it was a bit harsh to characterise the opponents Fury had defeated as 'bums', he was finding it difficult to find any serious competition of any kind. Before his fight against thirty-five-year-old 'Magic' Matthew Ellis from Blackpool at the historic York Hall in Bethnal Green, London, on 11 April, Fury complained about the difficulties he had in finding suitable sparring partners, let alone someone to fight him for real. He said that he would treat the Ellis bout as a sparring session as he needed to get some rounds in.

The *Daily Mail* said, 'It's "Magic" for British Tyson as heavyweight aims to extend unbeaten run.' Yet, beyond his youth and size, the newspaper thought Fury had little going for him. Promoter Mick Hennessy put them straight. 'I purposely ignored all the British Olympic boxers to concentrate on signing up this boy,' he said, 'and it's frightening to think how good he could be.'

During their pre-fight build-up, Matthew Ellis suggested that Fury was taking a step up to cruiserweight too soon. But the warning fell on deaf ears. Egged on by the crowd, Fury changed his strategy and went out looking for the quick knockout. Ellis chose to stand back in front of the much bigger and taller man, allowing Fury to tee off on him while offering next to nothing in the way of a challenge.

Putting his fast left jab to work, Fury also fired out right hands from the jab and sent Ellis down with a combination that consisted of two right hands and a left hook to the head. Ellis beat the count, but hit the mat for a second time within the first minute, this time after a right hand to the side of the head. Still conscious, Ellis chose to remain on his knees as referee David Parris counted him out. The official time was just 48 sec into round 1. As a spectator sport, this bout in no way provided value for money, but there was no booing from the crowd who were already caught up in the Tyson Fury hype machine. Both the fighter himself and promoter Mick Hennessy claimed that none of the Top 10 heavyweights in Britain wanted to fight him and continued to have trouble finding opponents.

Even when Fury got a spot on the undercard of the Carl Froch–Jermain Taylor world super-middleweight title fight in Connecticut, USA, on 25 April, there was no one to be found to face him. His next outing was on the undercard of the Darren Barker–Darren McDermott Commonwealth middleweight title clash on 23 May. Three days before the bout, his opponent Scott Belshaw, from Lisburn in Northern Ireland, said he was planning on gatecrashing the heavyweight title picture by ending the unbeaten run of Tyson Fury in their 'battle of the big prospects' at the Watford Colosseum. At six-foot-seven, twenty-three-year-old Belshaw was just two inches shorter than Fury. Their combined weight tipped the scales at just under 500 lbs while their records were just as impressive. The two of them had won all but one of their sixteen pro contests with a dozen knockouts between them. Belshaw had just one defeat as a pro (which was later avenged) and on his eleven fight pro record, with seven of his ten wins having come inside the distance. He had also been Irish amateur champ five times.

'I know I've got the power to knock guys out,' he said. 'My record proves that and I'm confident that I can do that to anyone I get in the ring with. I have the dynamite in my fists but I don't think he has and I believe that will be the difference.'

Fury said that a win would take him another step closer to British and Commonwealth title fights, but Belshaw wasn't paying any attention to anything that his opponent said. 'Fury has a bit of a gob on him and he likes to talk but none of that makes any difference when you get in the ring,' he said. 'I'm not one for making predictions, I'll let my fists do all my talking.' Belshaw, talking in the last few days before the fight, also said the timing could not have been more perfect. 'I'm really fired up for this. I was due to fight in Belfast last weekend and I had worked so hard for that one so when it fell through I was gutted. Thankfully this opportunity came out of the blue and I jumped at it. I believe this is destiny for me and it's my time.'

And he was ready. 'I've been training very hard since Christmas and it's a massive chance for me. Tyson is the one with all the hype, everyone is talking about him and he's calling everybody out but I'm the first person to step up to the plate and I'm very confident. We sparred together a couple of years ago and it was a good, tough spar. I felt I was stronger in there and I know I've improved a lot since then, although I'm sure he has as well.'

Fury's only worry was that Belshaw would not show up on

the day. 'My promoter's offered Belshaw the fight and all his demands have been met so let's hope he doesn't chicken out now,' he said. 'His team have said that he's up for it and he's got everything he asked for so the only thing I need to know now is that he's going to turn up on Saturday night.'

Promoter Frank Maloney – who later transitioned to become Kellie Maloney – hailed Belshaw as the second coming of George Foreman, but Fury didn't take that assessment too seriously. 'I don't expect to be buying a Scott Belshaw grill any time soon but I can promise him a roasting on Saturday night,' he said. 'Some people seem to think he's a top prospect but we'll find out who the real deal is at the weekend. I'm up for fighting any of these other so-called prospects because there's no point in me going around saying I'm the best young heavyweight out there unless I'm willing to back it up. I'll be ready to make a move on the British or Commonwealth titles this year and what I saw in Belfast on Saturday night [15 May] with Sam Sexton taking the Commonwealth title from Martin Rogan backs that up. I offered to take on Sexton in his backyard in just my third pro fight but he didn't want to know so he's already running scared.'

Fury had taken a trip to the European mainland where he got in some sparring ahead of the contest on Saturday 23 May. 'I've been finding it hard to get sparring in the UK let alone opponents so it was good to travel over to Germany where most of the top guys are based these days,' he said. 'It was great to get some quality sparring under my belt over there and I thoroughly enjoyed the experience and, hopefully, it will show in my performance on Saturday.'

In the ring, Fury wore a pair of shorts that combined the Union Jack with the Irish tricolour. He was comfortable fighting a man his own size. It meant he could jab straight with his arm at ninety degrees to his body. Fury had been working on that jab, perfecting ramrod accuracy and adding a nasty snap. In the event, Belshaw had no answer to it and was stopped 52 sec into round 2 after a third knockdown.

Fury returned to York Hall in Bethnal Green to box against Latvian fighter Aleksandrs Selezens on 18 July. After dealing out some minor punishment in the first two rounds, Fury began to let his hands go in round 3. A flurry of body shots sent Selezens crumbling to the mat. A few moments later his corner threw in the towel. It marked the first stoppage loss for Selezens.

Despite the easy victory, Fury was not at his best. He had temporarily split from Egan and was training while also suffering from a injury. 'I was disappointed with my last fight because I know I can box a lot better than that,' he said. 'I'm my own worst critic. I always set high standards and if I don't perform to them I give myself a lot of stick. I had a bad back for two months. I got punched in the back and couldn't train or do anything. Selezens was a spoiler, but he'd never been stopped or put down and I was the first to do it.'

It might not have been the ideal result for the boxer but it was also true that Tyson Fury had won all seven of his professional fights in under four rounds.

TITLE SHOT

Fury took on the holder of the BBBC's English heavyweight title John 'Big Bad John' McDermott, who had taken the vacant title in April 2008 in a bout against Pelé Reid. His claim to fame was that he had knocked out Vitali Klitschko in a kickboxing match in 1992.

Klitschko and Reid met at the European championships in Bulgaria, where the Ukrainian was the man to beat. 'Vitali was the full-contact champion and his poster was everywhere,' Reid said later. 'But this was point scoring. It was all about hitting as much as you can without getting hit. You weren't supposed to knock each other out, but you could hurt each other.' Reid, who said he never intended to become a fighter, was not intimidated. 'Vitali was a big guy and when I saw him before the final, I remember him smirking at me. But I was confident I could go in and out and beat him.'

In round 2, Reid did what he wasn't supposed to do. He

put Klitschko flat on his back with a spinning back-kick to the jaw. 'They were going to disqualify me,' said Reid. 'I remember the officials talking about it. But they decided my technique was good and there was no intention to knock him out, so they gave me the win. What I achieved that day was my greatest achievement in my competitive sporting career. It never got any better than that. Even now, people, young people who weren't even born when it happened, ask me about knocking out Vitali. You should see how people react to me after they've seen it on YouTube. I was told Vitali was denying it happened, so someone put it on there and now just about every day, someone comes up to me and says, "I never knew you fought Vitali."'

But as it turned out, Reid was not a match for Big Bad John, who knocked him out in round 2. McDermott went on to fight Danny Williams in July 2008 for the British title but lost, even though Williams had three points deducted – two points for low blows and pushing in round 11, one for ejecting his gum shield in round 12. 'Allah was watching over me and I got the decision despite the referee trying to take it off me,' Williams said.

McDermott disagreed, but the rematch in May 2009 went the same way. He seemed to be on a losing streak and now Fury was eager to take his English heavyweight title. 'I've been looking for John McDermott for a while now,' said Fury. 'He's been offered the fight before, but turned it down. But now the fight has been ordered by the board he surely can't back out.' Fury reckoned that McDermott was scared of him. 'I'm bringing that fear factor back into boxing like Mike Tyson did. I'm looking at my opponents in their corner and they're scared of me before I even fight. Watch McDermott and see if he's not scared. I think he'll be in a shell for five rounds before he even wakes up. But he'll wake up on the floor. I've got a hundred per cent knockout record and I don't want to lose that.'

Fury had reunited with trainer Steve Egan and was still having trouble finding sparring partners, yet they had set their sights on going for both the British and Irish titles before the end of the year. The English title was to be merely a stepping stone. Fury taunted the twenty-nine-year-old McDermott about his weight, calling him 'McDoughnut', 'McMuffin' and 'Big Mac'. It was all brushed aside by his opponent's camp.

'This kid is a good talker, but he is heading for a painful fall and when that happens he will realise the trouble that his big mouth has got him in,' said McDermott's promoter Frank Maloney. 'We still don't know if he can fight. Hopefully, when Big Bad John hits him on the chin, we will find out.'

But Fury was convinced he had the ability to back up the hype and promised a performance that would secure him a shot at Danny Williams' British title. 'It's boxing, it's a business. I'm not going to be nice to him,' he said. 'If I'm any good I'll win. It's no good me saying I'm going to be a champion and then getting beaten by McDermott. Every fight I have, I put pressure on myself.'

On 11 September 2009, Fury travelled to the Brentwood Leisure Centre in McDermott's home county of Essex for the fight. The clash was hyped a real grudge match. Fury put McDermott, who was shorter, under early pressure with his solid jab, but the title holder responded well by getting inside Fury's long reach and got a number of clean rights to Fury's chin. He even dropped his hands near the end of round 1 to taunt Fury. Fury paid him back by rubbing his head in his face. After the bell the two men had to be separated and the referee warned them both at the start of round 2.

McDermott's hand speed troubled Fury, leaving him looking disorganised. McDermott appeared to sweep the opening three rounds, and there was concern in Fury's corner. But Fury showed real determination and his stamina held up – he'd never previously gone past four rounds. McDermott tested Fury's chin with his left hook as well as with his right hand a number of times that night. However, McDermott was no great puncher, Fury passed the test.

Both men were visibly tiring by round 7, and there was more holding. But when they traded blows, the crowd roared its approval. At one point, Fury's legs looked a little shaky though. Two big rights to the head landed flush for McDermott in the eighth, but Fury found the strength to fire back. Then he backed off, dropping his hands to his sides.

With a lump developing above his left eye, Fury worked hard in the last two rounds, sucking up punishment but still going for broke. Much of the fight had taken place at close quarters, giving McDermott a strategic victory and he felt he had done enough. As the final round approached, even Fury's corner could be heard telling him he was behind on points. However, at the bell, referee Terry O'Connor held Fury's arms aloft. He had scored the match 98–92 to the contender and there were howls of protest from McDermott's home crowd.

Puzzled by O'Connor's decision, *Sky Sports* commentator and former world lightweight champion Jim Watt asked, 'Has he got the names mixed up?' At the ringside, a tearful McDermott said, 'What do I have to do? He's a brave kid, a nice boxer, but I won the fight clearly. It was not even close – even his fans know that I won the fight.'

He later added, 'Going into the last round my corner told me, "John, you're at least four rounds in front." I thought the last round was level . . . I thought I nicked it. What have I got to do to win it? I'm a nice gentle guy, he's the one with the big mouth and I've been penalised for it. I'll have a rematch.'

Frank Maloney was left fuming at the result. 'I believe it is one of the worst decisions I have witnessed since I started promoting more than twenty-five years ago . . . I'm sure I will be called up before the board for my behaviour, but Terry O'Connor is a disgrace to British boxing for what he's done here. Why do I want to be in the business when you're getting robbed? At least Dick Turpin has a mask on when he robs you.' He said it was 'the most controversial decision since Henry Cooper was outpointed by Joe Bugner in 1971'. Maloney also suggested O'Connor looked at his fighter's corner and had flashbacks to 1977 and the night when John's father, Stanley McDermott, battled O'Connor at the Royal Albert Hall.

While admitting his performance was poor, Fury insisted he had done enough to take the belt, even saying that the video was biased towards McDermott. 'I deserved it,' he said. 'I worked very hard for that. John was a lot harder than I thought he'd be, all credit to him. But I thought I worked the harder throughout the fight and I deserved to win. If he wants a rematch, let's get it on. I will stop him next time.'

It was generally judged that Fury had been lucky with what was a very controversial decision. He had not been on top form and was visibly carrying a spare tyre. Even some Fury fans found fault with the decision. The *Guardian* reported, 'O'Connor's scoring of 98–92 was not just wrong; it was out of kilter with all good judges, without exception, who saw the fight exactly the other way. To put Fury six points clear of McDermott in a ten-round contest in which the "winner" shipped roundhouse right hands all night long was, to put it kindly, an aberration.' The paper's boxing correspondent, Kevin Mitchell, went on: 'Most of our referees are former fighters, which is what qualifies them to do the job. I can't believe O'Connor was getting square with John's dad for a loss so long ago. No, he just cocked it up. He read the fight poorly throughout, failing to see the steady if dull work McDermott was doing, and crediting Fury with points for eye-catching flurries. The 1–6 favourite couldn't get going, and should have paid the price. He boxed in spurts against an unfashionable opponent who trained his backside off for a contest that meant everything to him. This wasn't just a fight for the English heavyweight title; it was for bragging rights between two proud members of the travelling community.'

The Times boxing correspondent Ron Lewis said, 'Controversy seems to follow O'Connor around. There was his rather dubious handling of the first Danny Williams–Matt Skelton fight [25 February 2006, Williams won on a split decision], the Joe Calzaghe–Peter Manfredo stoppage [7 April 2007, Calzaghe defended his title]. It must be tough to referee two big guys like that and score, but I have no idea how he came up with his scorecard. Like most people I know, I thought Fury would win, and, like most, I thought McDermott did, although by not as big a margin as most people I spoke to. McDermott was just the cleaner puncher throughout, he was the smarter, landed the better shots and generally outworked Fury, who cuffed a bit much for me. Around the middle rounds, I thought he could stop Fury, but the big Mancunian came back well near the end – I gave him the last two rounds.'

The BBBC ordered an immediate rematch and stipulated that, in future, there should be three judges at all English titles. But Fury would fight as the holder of the belt after the board stood by O'Connor's controversial decision.

In the meantime, Fury took on other challengers. He faced twenty-seven-year-old Tomas Mrazek at the O2 in Dublin on 26 September on the under card of the WBA world super bantamweight title clash between Bernard Dunne and Poonsawat Kratingdaenggym. Mrazek already had twenty-two losses to his name, with only four wins out of thirty-one bouts. The Czech looked bemused as Fury entered the ring to traditional Irish music, donning green shorts with the words Clan Fury emblazoned above the tricolour. Playing on his Tipperary and Galway roots, Fury had the crowd right behind him. Rallying to the flag, the RTÉ commentator said, 'This man here is twenty-one years old – everything to look forward to. He can punch, he looks well, he's big, he's strong, he's white – very important for the American and the big markets there and that's not racist, believe me.'

Southpaw Mrazek was in reasonable shape at 222.5 lbs and fearless, but ultimately too small to take on Fury at 261 lbs. Fury took advantage of their size difference by prodding the jab in round 1, then hammering the body and reddening Mrazek's left eye in round 2. But facing no real resistance, he showed no great levels of urgency. Fury hurt his hand in that round and was reduced to going through the motions for the remainder of the fight. Nevertheless, he continued to hunt Mrazek's body, although he looked slightly uncomfortable when the wildly swinging Czech came backed at him. By round 5, the fight ran out of steam. Fury pushed his man repeatedly to the ropes with no admonishment from referee Emile Tiedt – but he couldn't find the finisher. Fury did cut the wilting Mrazek and drop him in the final round with a body shot. Tiedt scored the match 60–57, but everyone judged it to be a lacklustre performance. Fury was still upbeat though.

'I love fighting here, it's like nowhere I've fought before,' Fury said in his post-fight interview. 'I damaged my right knuckle in the second round, which was very sore, but I enjoyed the fight and this is a great crowd. When I win my world title I'll make the first defence in Croke Park.'

The damaged knuckle turned out to be a broken hand, which meant Fury couldn't fulfil the BBBC order to take on an immediate rematch with McDermott. Fury was then forced to vacate his English title without making a single defence. 'I'm sick about it, but they wouldn't give me any more time,' he said. 'My hand is still only around eighty per cent. Two specialists have recommended I have an operation and it looks like I'll have to. The board said they will match McDermott and Chisora for the vacant title and I'll get the winner in a final eliminator for the British. I won't lose my position and it gives my hand more time.'

Fury changed trainer again, joining Brian Hughes' gym in Collyhurst, Manchester after a brief spell with Robert McCracken who, in turn, had taken over from his long-term trainer Steve Egan. McCracken had turned Carl Froch into a world champion and Fury hoped that his Midas touch could work for him, too. But Fury said it was too far to travel to McCracken's Sheffield gym on a regular basis. He believed that Pat Barrett, at Hughes' gym in Manchester, was the man to take his career to the next step.

'We have been working on my speed and technique, just working on snapping the punches and not hitting them hard,' he said. Having racked up a nine-fight undefeated career over just twelve months, he said he would be more patient in 2010. 'I was rushing,' he said. 'But now I've sat down with my people and I'm not going to do that any more. Heavyweights don't mature until they are around twenty-five.'

On 5 March 2010, a slimmed-down Fury faced thirty-six-year-old German Hans-Joerg Blasko in front of a sell-out crowd in the Huddersfield Sports Centre. For Fury, having not fought for six months, it was an important match. 'I need to make a point this weekend,' he said in the run-up to the bout. 'I've been away and it's time to return back to my slot as the number one domestic heavyweight.' At six-foot-five and 245 lbs to Fury's 252.75 lbs, Blasko was big enough to take on Fury and had won nine of his twelve fights, scoring four knockouts in his last four contests.

Blasko landed a good early right counter to Fury's jab and caught Fury with one or two surprise punches. But those were the only blows he successfully landed as Fury's swift two-handed shots rocked him to the soles of his feet. A left hook to the body quickly dropped Blasko. He beat the count a second time, but did not want to go on and, after 2 min 14 sec, the referee was waving his hands over Blasko's head.

Among the cheering crowd was former world lightweight champion Barry McGuigan. 'Tyson looked much more controlled,' he said. 'He used a speedy left jab, and his right cross and left hooks were accurate and packed power.'

Brian Hughes said, 'Tyson had not fought for six months and this was a good start back from the lad. He has brilliant boxing skills besides knockout power. Britain has a future world champion in this young man if he continues to improve. His defence is much better than what he showed in this fight and we will get this right before his next bout. The world is his oyster.'

On 25 June, it was time to meet John McDermott again and it was back at the Brentwood Centre Arena to silence the critics once and for all. Fury had split from Brian Hughes a fortnight before the fight and was now with Uncle Hughie, who had overseen he first six fights. The preparation was not ideal and Fury, at 254 lbs, had put on 23 lbs since he had last faced McDermott. But for his part, Big Bad John was now thirty. The rematch was dubbed 'Conspiracy Fury' after the previous controversial points decision.

Fury's long jab largely kept McDermott at bay for the first five rounds; he landed two telling right crosses in round 1 alone. But Fury took a heavy right hook in the second and as the fight progressed through the fourth McDermott began to produce the better work behind his jab. In round 6, McDermott teed off against Fury, who was flagging. In the seventh, he landed a heavy right hook and, although Fury responded in kind, he looked exhausted and held on. He was warned by referee Dave Parris for doing so and had a point deducted. Fury ended the round with blood seeping from a cut in the corner of his right eye. But McDermott was soon to run out of steam himself. In the eighth, a decisive barrage dropped him close to the end of the round.

It was the first time McDermott had been knocked down in his thirty-two-fight career. Fury dug deep and McDermott was soon back on the canvas in the ninth after a short chopping right and in the next exchange went down again before staggering to his feet on the count of ten. All three judges had the contest 77–73 going into round 9, when the fight was stopped after 1 min 8 sec, giving Fury the vacant English heavyweight title.

'I'm not like any other boxer who wants to manufacture his record by fighting bums,' he said. 'Big John was my eighth fight. Normally guys don't go near him until they have twenty pro fights under their belt. But the difference between me, Big John and the British fighters like David Price, Audley Harrison, Sam Sexton and Dereck Chisora, is that we're men. We'd fight anyone. I don't see how someone like Price can call himself a man when he only takes on bums. Why doesn't he fight McDermott or me? The answer is because he knows we'd beat him up.'

Fury was now unbeaten in eleven professional fights and was once more finding it hard to find anyone willing to take him on. After three opponents dropped out on him, he took on Rich Power, an unbeaten thirty-year-old from Michigan Mixed Martial Arts who had won all twelve of his professional heavyweight fights, nine by knockouts. He was a replacement for Donnell Holmes, an American who had had two heavyweight title fights and had won thirty-three out of his thirty-seven bouts, twenty-nine by knockouts. Power took the fight at a week's notice.

The eight-round match was held in the York Hall, Bethnal Green, on 10 September. Fury, the bigger man, concentrated on landing the right early in the fight and, finding success, stayed with it. Though they were heavy punches and on target, Power soaked them up. As they grappled in a messy round 3, Fury's superior weight seem to sap Power's energy. They clashed heads in the fourth and Power dabbed his brow as if checking whether a cut sustained in sparring had opened up. Even so, Power stood in front of Fury, letting him hit him, as if to say, 'Come on, hit me – I can take it.' In the fifth, Power went down on one knee, but referee Jeff Hinds did not count it. The American seemed tired by the end of the round, but managed to stay on his feet for the rest of the bout, which was scored 80–72 to Fury.

On 19 December, in Quebec, Fury met another American, thirty-eight-year-old Zack Page, who weighed in at 268.25 lbs. Fury had recently spent three weeks in the training camp of

Wladimir Klitschko whose IBF, WBO and IBO world title defence against Dereck Chisora had been postponed due to an injury sustained by the Ukranian. Fury said of his training time, 'It was a great experience and opened my eyes to what being at a world title level is all about. He is a very nice fellow, helpful and a great boxer. I've had some great sparring in recent weeks, both in Austria and Detroit, so there will be no excuses in Quebec.' That said, there was already a rivalry building between Klitschko and Fury.

'When I first got there, I was asking questions and he was looking me straight in the eye as if he wanted me to look away,' Fury said later. 'When he saw I wouldn't be intimidated he came round and he was all right after that. It was friendly, but I'll only be his friend until I take his titles off him. Going to the camp I was expecting him to be superhuman or something. But I could see he was just a man like me with a pair of boxing gloves on. He did just the same stuff as I do, but he was a lot smaller than I thought. After seeing him, I am a hundred per cent confident I can be world champion. Seeing him sparring, I reckon with more experience I could take him.' Overall, he said, 'I wasn't impressed. I see the Klitschkos as robots. Wladimir sparred with an American who'd had only one fight – and he wasn't getting the best of it.'

He guessed that Klitschko still had a way to go in recovering from his injury and that was why he had to pull out of his bout with Chisora. 'I didn't think Chisora stood a chance against Klitschko,' said Fury. 'He is a limited fighter. He's British class and I don't think he will go any further. I'm his mandatory challenger and I'm going to take his title off him.'

In Fury's corner in Quebec was the legendary Emanuel 'Manny' Steward, who specialised in coaching big men. He had trained Thomas Hearns and Lennox Lewis, as well as the Klitschko brothers. When he met Fury at training camp, Steward tipped him to be the unified world champion within five years. 'The way that he's progressing now I believe he can be maybe the complete package for the heavyweight division,' said Steward. 'Because of his talent – he's a good-looking guy and a very colourful personality – I think he can be a tremendous shot in the arm for the heavyweight division in the future.'

Fury said, 'Manny has worked with all the greats and he has been giving me lots of advice and technical help in the build-up to this fight. I would love to work with him again and, hopefully, we can sort something out for the future, as I would like to make it permanent. When Manny talks, you listen. He is inspirational. He is just brilliant at his job and his list of world champions is never-ending. If we can, I would like to hook up with Manny for training before every fight and come back to England ten days prior to a bout. Hopefully, it can be sorted out in the new year.'

Fury and Page fought in the Colisée Pepsi in Quebec on the undercard of the Jean Pascal-Bernard Hopkins bill with the fight night being screened by Primetime TV and Sky. Page was a late replacement for American Galen 'Bad Boy' Brown, who Fury had been eager to take on. 'Brown has been in with some good fighters and even some world-class fighters,' he said. 'He will be bringing a lot of experience and know-how into the ring and I will have to work around that.

I will knock him out early, but I will take my time about it – at least for a round. He will fight like an American but I'm used to a European style so this will be good for my education.' Fury was aware of the pitfalls though. 'I would never take any opponent anything less than seriously because we have seen so often – especially in the heavyweight division – just how easy it is to come unstuck. I have never been lacking in confidence because I believe in myself. But I am a nice bloke who also knows the meaning of the word "humility". I don't have all the answers at my age, yet I'm a very willing learner and I'll continue to dedicate my life to my aim – to be the best heavyweight in the world one day.'

But the Brown bout was not to be and Zack Page was a less formidable opponent. He had won twenty-one and lost thirty-two of his fifty-five bouts, with two drawn, but Fury was keen to fight with the exposure it would bring him on the other side of the Atlantic. The match was a predictably dull affair. Page was slippery, but Fury stalked him, using his long-reaching jab to keep the smaller man at a distance and outboxing him for most of the fight.

Just six foot in height, Page had a lot of trouble landing a punch on Fury due to the difference in their size. Fury used his larger frame to corral Page and push him against the ropes to unleash combinations. Page covered up for the most part but wasn't able to put up much of a fight. Nevertheless, Fury failed to land clean on Page and get him into trouble. Fury fought with his hands held low and at times left himself open, but Page never looked like taking advantage and was content to last the distance, having only been stopped three times. As it was Fury never looked like producing a stoppage. The three judges scored the bout 80–72 unanimously, giving all eight rounds to Fury, who then threw down a challenge to all comers.

'I'm the best young heavyweight in the world and if you want to prove me wrong, just contact my promoter, Mick Hennessy,' he told the crowd. 'Let's get it on. I will fight anyone in boxing, in a winner-takes-all fight, in any country.'

Fury now had his eye on the British title held by Dereck Chisora, who had been disappointed when his world title challenge was cancelled against Klitschko earlier that month. If Chisora wanted to hang on to his Lonsdale belt he had to face Fury next. Otherwise he would have to vacate the British title to continue chasing his world title, rearranging the Klitschko fight. This would have left Fury to contest the belt with another Top 10 British heavyweight contender – possibly Martin Rogan, Michael Sprott, Sam Sexton or even Audley Harrison, who announced he was going to continue fighting, despite his defeat by David Haye in November.

'Next year will be the year of the Tyson,' Fury said. 'I want to fight Dereck Chisora next and beat him, then take on the best in Europe and beat them, too. There will be no mince pies or chocolate cake over Christmas. In fact, I am much fitter and trimmer than I have ever been. I am fed up with people watching me in the ring and seeing a fat pig, so all the excess stuff they have seen before has come off and will stay off. The McDermott wins were good for me. I would rather fight a tough kid like John and beat him twice than take on ten bums and not learn anything. He gave me problems and that's what I need.' As for the heavyweight division, Fury was determined to break through into the global ranks. 'I believe it's only a matter of time and dedication. I have got the dedication. Now all I need is careful guidance and I will get there.'

Fury also wanted Haye to postpone his retirement, scheduled for the following October. 'I need a few more fights but I am on Haye's tail,' said Fury. 'He is the one I am thinking of because he is the weakest of the heavyweight champions. I'm big, I've got the heart of a champion, I'm fast and I've got good power – so much power that Haye wouldn't stand a chance against me. His recent fight with Audley Harrison' – where Haye won in round 3 – 'was a terrible affair. But Haye was as scared as Harrison to throw a punch. He is terrified of a big man. Any big man who isn't scared of Haye will give him problems. But Haye had him beat before they went in. That was Harrison's last chance to gain respect, but he's done himself in. He will always be remembered for that fight. If it was me, I'd have been right into Haye. I've got a cousin who weighs ten stone and he'd have put up a better fight. Any boxer would.' Haye would be another stepping stone in Fury's quest to his unified world title. 'I want to knock out David Haye to prove to Wladimir that I'm the real deal. You have to respect what Wladimir Klitschko did. But fighting me he would be fighting a true heavyweight and not a blown-up cruiserweight. Wladimir has proved that he is the real deal but now it's my time to show the world that I'm the next big thing.'

But his taunts at Haye fell on deaf ears as the WBA world

heavyweight champion planned to hang up his gloves before his thirty-first birthday the following October. He was lambasted by Fury. 'When you're world champion you don't keep saying you're going to retire,' he said. 'I'm a fighting man. If I'm world champion, I'm going to defend my title until I can't walk, never mind quitting. When does a champion say he's going to retire? He's only just won the title.' Fury could not understand it. 'When I realise my dream and become unified heavyweight champion of the world, I will avoid no one. I am sure I will be the dominant heavyweight champion, just like Lennox Lewis. I am really looking forward to my next fight as this is a really big year for me. I am going to give boxing the shot in the arm it needs.'

Fury was building up to his next fight and as part of that preparation he sparred with Wladimir Klitschko. Fury said the experience of facing the IBF and WBO world champion was an invaluable one. 'It has given me a great deal of confidence training alongside such a champion,' said Fury. 'He is at the top of his game. There has been all sorts of speculation flying around about why David Haye is not fighting one of the Klitschko brothers but, in my honest opinion, it is because David is not big enough to deal with the likes of Wladimir or Vitali. I am going to change all that in the future.' He repeated, 'I'm not going to duck anyone when I become champion.'

The next battle in Fury's campaign for domination was against an unbeaten Brazilian, thirty-year-old Marcelo Luiz Nascimento – 'The Hammer' – in what was billed as a ten-round 'international special attraction fight' at London's Wembley Arena on 19 February 2011. He trained with Eddie

Chambers, who had himself fought Wladimir Klitschko for the world heavyweight title in May 2010. The match, sponsored by Hennessy Sports and airing on Premier Sport TV and Sky, was a replacement for the scheduled bout with Francois Botha, which had been knocked back by the British Boxing Board of Control. Fury had not hesitated to accept a challenge from 'The Hammer' Nascimento, whose record was thirteen wins out of thirteen, with eleven knockouts. He had knocked out his previous opponent, Gonzalo Basile, on enemy territory in Argentina in just 34 sec. Fury reckoned he would knock Nascimento out within three rounds.

'He can certainly dig. His nickname is "The Hammer" and you can see why – but I am ready for him,' said Fury. 'I believe I have it in me to become a world champion.'

Fury had first to deal with the jailing of his father, John, for eleven years for wounding with intent. Fury Sr had collapsed into tears when he heard how long he was to spend in prison. Tyson said, 'I just can't believe the length of the sentence, but I have to use what has happened to my dad as a spur. I cannot use it as an excuse for a poor performance. I have to be professional and show just why Emanuel Steward made those flattering comments. This has been a really hard time for my family, but when I beat Nascimento we can put what has happened to my dad to one side, if only for a little while.' Fury was worried that the sentence would mean that his father would never see him in the ring again. 'I was in court to give my support but you can't let it mentally break you down. You can't cry over spilt milk. He's probably never going to see me fight live again. It's terrible but we are appealing against the sentence.'

His father had always been his greatest fan. 'My dad's been all over with me from day one and now it's just finished. He's such a big fan that he drove to Siberia and Poland to see me fight as an amateur – as he doesn't like flying. I was upset, but you can't let it break you down, it's happened. I've got to concentrate on this fight . . . it hasn't interfered with my training,' he continued. 'I've just got to focus on what's coming Saturday, not what's happening outside boxing.'

When it came to his own upcoming battle in the ring, Fury did not think that Nascimento was going to be a pushover; he was clear that his opponent had shown only a fraction of what he believed he was capable of. 'I'm taking on a massive puncher and that shows I won't duck any challenge that comes my way. But it angers me when you see so-called heavyweight prospects keep having bums put in front of them every time. I don't want to go through my career like that. I want to show them how it's done, so I'm taking on this guy who has an unbeaten record and is a massive puncher. This is what you have to do to be a star – you have to take on the likes of Nascimento, who is such a powerful puncher.'

He wanted to be put to the test. 'Up until this point in my career I've been in with some very good fighters, but the hardest I've been punched in the face is by myself when I missed Lee Swaby with a right uppercut and hit myself between the eyes. This guy I'm fighting is dangerous. He's tough but I wanted a tough test. I would like to get the British title by the end of the year, but I'm struggling to get fights against British guys because they are avoiding me.'

But Fury was not one to duck a challenge and had a new

role model. 'I am never going to avoid fighting anyone, even when I fulfil my dream of becoming undisputed heavyweight champion of the world,' he said. 'I can be just like Lennox Lewis. I am athletic and talented and I aim to give boxing the shot in the arm that it deserves.'

Nascimento, who was from Sao Paulo, was being hailed by some as the Brazilian version of Colombia's Breidis Prescott, the man who KO'd Amir Khan in 54 sec. 'He [Nascimento] will be the most dangerous and hardest puncher I've ever been in the ring with,' said Fury. 'He's in great shape and with his height it's not hard to see where his punching power comes from. He is a really tough opponent. Although he is by far my most dangerous test to date, I'm going to show Amir Khan how to deal with a huge puncher from South America. This fight, with me being six-foot-nine and him being six-foot-five, and both being big punchers, has the recipe to be an edge-of-your seat, explosive encounter.'

When the fight started, the hard-hitting Brazilian did indeed come out swinging and Fury took a couple of licks before dropping him with a right cross in round 1. He knocked Nascimento out cold with another right to the temple in round 5. 'As soon as I hit him, I knew I had got him because I felt the shiver go right up my arm,' said Fury afterwards. 'But I want to pay credit to this guy because no one else had the nuts to fight me. Dereck Chisora, the British champion, is fighting Wladimir Klitschko because he doesn't want to fight me. I'm the only man willing to fight anyone in the world.'

He vowed to make Dereck Chisora pay for hanging on to

the British heavyweight title belt while challenging world champion Wladimir Klitschko. 'I'm being messed around,' he said. 'He's fighting Klitschko, he'll have a few months off, then he'll have to get fit again so it could take it right into next year. But I'll be ready whenever it happens. He'll get knocked out by Klitschko and then he can come back and get knocked out by me.'

Promoter Mick Hennessy had called on the BBBC to strip Chisora so mandatory challenger Fury can fight for the title. 'It's ridiculous what's going on,' said Hennessy. 'Tyson will have been waiting more than a year for his chance. Chisora won the title against Sam Sexton in October so his six months' grace is up next month but he's got the Klitschko fight on 30 April. We've talked non-stop to the board but we're not getting any answers that make any sense.'

Chisora was in the crowd for the Nascimento fight at Wembley and Fury taunted him in a post-fight interview. 'Chisora has been avoiding me,' he said. 'I know he's in the arena, so why don't you get him over and let's have a face-off right now. Then you can ask him why he's not giving his title up and why he won't fight me. "Del Boy No Good" Chisora – I would flatten him, just like I flattened that Brazilian.'

He was also eyeing Audley Harrison, believing that a match between an up-and-coming unbeaten young fighter and a man needing to win back some credibility made sense for both of them.

'I'd love to fight Harrison,' Fury said. 'He's just fought in a world title fight and is an Olympic gold medallist, I'm a brash youngster with a big mouth who's been accused of not being able to back it up. So we'd see if he's made of anything, and we'd also see whether or not I'm a phoney.'

And he was looking further down the road. 'I don't want to bunk in on any world title chance, I want to be mandatory. I don't want to be fighting for a world title for a hundred thousand pounds when I should be getting a million. We're not rushing. I'm twenty-two, I'm in the WBC rankings and I'm taking it fight by fight.'

Meanwhile, Fury was still loudly demanding that the board make the British title vacant so he could fight for it after defeating Nascimento so easily. 'I might be white as a ghost and fat but I can fight a bit,' said Fury. 'It was a good performance and he was a strong fighter who hits three times harder than Chisora. I've been mandatory challenger for six or seven months and I just want to fight for the British title because this is holding my career up . . . Chisora is fighting Klitschko for the world title but he's not even the best fighter in this country. He's just a little boy in a big man's trousers. He will have to relinquish the title or the board should strip him of the title. There's a meeting about it, I'm told, and I hope the board take the title off him and make me fight someone else for it. If I do get to fight for the vacant British I think it should be against John McDermott. He had a good first-round win and I don't rate any of the others. David Price has won an Olympic bronze medal but who has he fought as a pro? He's not on my level. I'm not ready for Klitschko at the moment and neither is Chisora, who isn't ready for it by a mile.' In any match, Chisora would start favourite, Fury acknowledged. 'If he doesn't finally get stripped of his title by

the Southern Area board for his run-in with the law last year
it won't matter,' Fury said, referring to Chisora's suspended
sentence the previous November for assaulting his girlfriend.
'I'm going to strip the title away from him along with the zero
on his record. Can't wait for this fight, it's been a long time in
the making, but one thing is for sure, it's not going to take me
as long to finish him off. Expect another brutal knockout to
be delivered by me.'

Chisora denied that he was ducking Fury in order to
fight Klitschko, though he was training hard for world
championship fight schedule for 30 April. 'I was at Wembley
on Saturday night to see Fury knock over some unknown
Brazilian in front of a handful of people and it told me
nothing other that I will never waste my time going to watch
Fury again and when we meet it would be a very easy night's
work for me,' he said. 'He came out with a stupid statement
afterwards saying that I'm only fighting Klitschko because
I'm scared of him! How can he say that I'm only fighting for
the world title to get a big pay day rather than face him in
a defence of the British and Commonwealth titles that are
mine. Listening to some of the nonsense he speaks I wonder
if he really believes all the hype surrounding him. For the
record, I fought the British champion Danny Williams in
May [2010], being a late replacement for Sam Sexton. When
I beat Williams, I inherited a mandatory defence against
Commonwealth Champion Sam Sexton, which I duly obliged
on 18 September by beating Sexton for the second time.

'That fight was my mandatory defence of both the British
championship and his of the Commonwealth championship

and I am not due to make another until, at the very earliest, March 2011. Fury is the mandatory contender for the British title, I know that. If he wants to win the title that's what he will have to do, win it against me. I have a world title fight coming up and that should have taken place in December but through no fault of my own Klitschko got injured and now I have had to wait until April. I want to enter the ring as British and Commonwealth champion because I am proud of holding the belts and the British Boxing Board of Control should be proud of a British champion challenging for the world heavyweight championship as their champion.

'Tyson can continue knocking over unknown Brazilians, or make embarrassing attempts to bring the likes of old men like Frans Botha over here to pad out his record, but the fact remains if Fury wants to be a real champion then he'll have to wait for me to either become world champion or, if I'm beaten as he says I will be, for me to defend my titles against him.'

Chisora also had a swipe at Fury's promoter Mick Hennessy, for trying to 'buy' the Commonwealth title from Chisora rather than let Fury fight him for it. 'Titles should be won and lost in the ring and not bought and sold like a second-hand Capri Ghia. His [Fury's] promoter got his matchmaker to try and do a deal with my promoter for me to vacate the Commonwealth title so he could fight another non-entity Canadian to pick up a vacant title rather than beat a champion. Apparently, Fury was not ready to face me yet and it would be a bigger fight between me and him down the line. I said, "No way," this Del Boy is not doing the deal. If he wants my belts he can win them like I had to by beating the champion. He is slagging off the British Boxing Board of Control for not stripping me, but how can they strip me? If Fury thinks he is the real deal then he should show me some respect and wait for his chance like I've had to wait for Klitschko. If he needs a fight in the interim he should fight the likes of Sam Sexton, Richard Towers, or the man who beat him in the amateurs, David Price, all young and fresh heavyweights with ambition. No one is fooled by wins over people like Nascimento or having the desire to fight the likes of Botha, such fights show a lack of respect for the sport and for a former world champion.

'Fury is full of hot air and he shouldn't allow his promoter to make stupid statements on his behalf. Let's face it, if he didn't have that name no one would have taken any notice of him based on his achievements. He reminds me of Jess Harding, another six-foot-plus who traded on being a traveller. Like Harding, Fury is all boots-and-braces but has no substance and what happened to him against Gary Mason [Harding was knocked out in Mason's defence of his heavyweight title in 1989] will happen to Fury as well when we do meet. My message to Tyson Fury is loud and clear, stop whining, talking rubbish and getting your promoter to do your dirty work, wait your chance like a man. Championships are won and lost, so stop trying to steal it underhandedly. I might be Del Boy, but Fury is just a fool with a horse – a total plonker!'

However, Fury's victory over Nascimento was key in the eyes of Mick Hennessy. 'That told me he is ready for anyone,' Hennessy said. 'I mean we weren't talking about Tyson meeting a shot fighter. Nascimento is the Latino heavyweight champion, had a higher ranking than Tyson, yet was blown away in five rounds. That comes down to Tyson's power and ability. This kid has it all and now we're working on his strength and conditioning, he'll only get better. He's a tough boy.' Hennessy had already guided two fighters, Junior Witter and Carl Froch, to WBC titles and said he aimed to push Fury down a similar route. 'I'm a traditionalist and the WBC belt is traditionally the most highly regarded championship. As Tyson's manager, I want him fighting the best around. I don't want him ducking anyone. And in any case, he wouldn't let me do that. Some boxers worry about who they meet. Tyson's the opposite. He isn't afraid of defeat. He doesn't care about building an unbeaten record. He wants to learn.'

The next important lesson was nutritional – Fury had to dispense with bags of crisps and Mars bars. In substitution came an elaborate strength and conditioning programme.

BRITISH AND COMMONWEALTH CHAMP

Following the victory over Nascimento, Chisora could not deny Fury a fight. When Klitschko signed to fight David Haye in July 2011, Chisora's status as British heavyweight champ became number one priority again and the British Boxing Board of Control set up a purse bid for Fury, the mandatory challenger.

Both Fury and Chisora were undefeated at 14–0. Chisora had won the British heavyweight title from Danny Williams in May 2010, stopping him in round 2. Then he knocked out Sam Sexton in round 9 in September, adding the Commonwealth title. He had been due to fight the WHO, IBF, IBO, lineal and *Ring* magazine heavyweight champion Wladimir Klitschko the previous December. The fight was rescheduled for April 2011 after Klitschko's injury, but he was still not recovered. Instead, Klitschko took on British WBA champion David Haye to unify the title. Back in 2009, at a pre-fight press conference in Germany, Haye had worn a T-shirt showing him holding the severed heads of the two Klitschko brothers and standing on their decapitated bodies. In 2011, reminded of the incident, he put the image on a poster. 'I have declared war on the Klitschko family, first on Wladimir and then Vitali,' he said. 'I am in my prime, my resume speaks for itself, I am not coming here to pick up a pay cheque like the rest of his opponents. I will be here to show The Hayemaker is the best in the world.'

Ahead of his Chisora bout, Tyson Fury was getting down to training and becoming more serious about being in shape. 'I know I looked like a fat pig before and could get away with it because I was big enough to keep winning,' he said. 'But now it's getting serious and I realise I have to get rid of the junk food.' He was not about to give up curry though. 'After every fight I go to my local Indian restaurant in Lancaster – it's my little routine. I have a special grilled chicken tikka on a bed of salad – healthy, but delicious.'

Fury also wanted to put the Klitschkos on notice that he was coming for the world title. 'I'm a young, up-and-coming fighter, while Wladimir is thirty-five and Vitali is forty,' he said. 'I'm taller than them with a longer jab. I'd like to see what would happen if they fought someone who is bigger than them.'

Hennessy beat Frank Warren in the purse bid to stage the Chisora–Fury contest, putting up £300,000.

'Del Boy has got no excuses now and my promoter has just handed him by far the biggest purse of his career,' said Fury. 'If he pulls out of this fight now he will prove himself a right plonker. It's time for Chisora to grow a set or shut up and walk away from the title. I have praised Chisora before because of his warrior attitude – now I just hope that he doesn't have any second thoughts about fighting me. This will be an enormous fight for the British boxing business and it will be a fight that the fans will love.'

Chisora did not rise to the bait. 'I like Tyson, but he is not yet ready for me,' he said. 'He's a boy with a big mouth and big ambitions – and I'm a man, a full-grown heavyweight man.'

But Fury's motormouth did him no harm in the media. The *Manchester Evening News*'s boxing correspondent James Robson said, 'Tyson Fury is a journalist's dream. Outspoken, controversial and extremely personable. The first time I interviewed him, I was taken aback at just how candid he was. But there was also the lingering doubt as to how much of what I was seeing was the real Tyson Fury, and how much was the character he was trying to project. There was a bit of Ali, a touch of Prince Naz, Chris Eubank, Floyd Mayweather, Apollo Creed and just about every pantomime villain you care to mention. Fury seemed to be an affectation of every boxer he had seen when growing up. While that's great for filling column inches, there is also the danger that it will come back to haunt him.'

Further fuelling the publicity machine, Fury took time out from training when a team from Comic Relief visited his gym for a humorous tanning session. 'I feel honoured to do what I can to help support a worthwhile cause such as Comic Relief,' he said. 'Even boxers have a heart and are not afraid to strip off and have a spraytan. In this sport and particularly when you're my size you can feel quite secure in your masculinity! It's for a good cause and that's all that matters.' The following year, he did his bit for Sport Relief by trying his hand at stand-up comedy under the guidance of comic Daniel Sloss. Otherwise, he relaxed by going clay pigeon shooting and off-road driving in his souped-up Mercedes G-Class. To relieve stress, he also went shoe-shopping, owning around 500 pairs. And he listened to music – in the gym, driving, everywhere. Then there were relaxing days out with the family.

His old trainer Steve Egan rated Fury's chances against Chisora as evens. 'I'd like to say Tyson will beat Dereck Chisora, but it is a 50/50 fight,' he said. 'Chisora's got a boxing brain and he's getting better. But why shouldn't Tyson win? He's six-foot eight-inches [*sic*] with a boxing brain. He's just got to develop more. I would love to see him do it. I trained him from day one and if he does go on to win a world title, I know I'll have had a massive hand in it.'

Hennessy was brimming with confidence though, both with Fury as a fighter and a a business investment. 'He's a dream for a promoter,' he said. 'Unlike most fighters who hide behind promoters, who say they will fight anybody, but in reality won't, he's the complete opposite. I have to reel him in. He would fight anybody. He would fight David Haye or Vitali Klitschko tomorrow, but I have to hold him back. From the day he turned professional I've had to manage his expectations, but he keeps taking on good fighters, kids with unbeaten records. He fought a seasoned pro like John McDermott after only eight professional fights. These are the minimum opponents he would take on. He wanted bigger fighters from day one. He's done it the hard way, but if it was down to him he would've taken on even bigger-named fighters.

'It's such a refreshing thing to see in this sport. He can wind up opponents and that happened with McDermott. McDermott trained like a Trojan for that fight and Tyson still won. There is no question he will be world champion in the future. I've believed that from day one, when I watched him as an amateur before I signed him. I have a solid belief he will be world champion, but not only that, he will unify the heavyweight division. He's a marketing dream, but there have been a lot of non-believers. We've had to get over that hurdle and now people are starting to believe in him.'

Coach Joe Gallagher, who trained European lightweight champion John Murray and British lightweight champion Anthony Crolla, rated Fury's chances, too. 'At the moment, Tyson Fury is most famous for punching himself in the face on YouTube. But I'd prefer he be known for hitting other people instead,' he said. 'I've no doubt he can do that and give Manchester its first heavyweight world champion. He's got all the physical attributes to do just that. He's got good size, good reach and as an amateur he always had very fast hands. He's been over to Germany to train with Wladimir Klitschko so it is unlikely that anything is going to intimidate him in the ring. This year he's got the chance to gatecrash the world rankings. He's been around for a while now and it's time to put up or shut up.'

The pre-match hype reached new heights with a ringside

clash between Fury and Chisora during a welterweight title fight between Frankie Gavin and Young Mutley at the O2 Arena in May. In the middle of round 8, Fury stripped to the waist, challenged Chisora to a fight, and the pair had to be pulled apart by ringside stewards. Fury was kicked out of the arena by officials while Chisora walked away from the melee. Chisora announced that he would defend his title against Fury two days later.

'Chisora's talked the talk and now he needs to walk the walk,' said Fury. 'I'm good to go, that's my game – walking the walk – so let's see if he is man enough to get in the ring with a dangerous, young, live opponent for the first time in his career.' There were no doubts in Fury's mind about who would come off best in this grudge match. 'When I win the title I will be dedicating my win to the memory of Sir Henry Cooper, the greatest boxer to ever come out of this country. He was a true inspiration to me and really was the people's champion. It would be an honour to follow in his footsteps and fight for the British, Commonwealth, European and world titles. It's a shame that he will never get to see his predictions for me come true. Cooper had died at the beginning of May.'

Fury then accused Chisora of disrespecting the title when Chisora said, 'It's all about his unbeaten record. The titles mean nothing to me.'

Fury responded that it was 'an honour to fight for the belt'. He then made a pledge to the fans. 'I'm promising boxing fans around the world that this is going to be a sensational performance from me and I'm going to show them why I'm the next big thing in world boxing. I was really pleased to receive the news that the Commonwealth title will also be on the line. I'm obviously going the traditional route by winning the English title first, then the British and Commonwealth next, then I will be going after European and genuine world honours.'

Sparks flew at a press conference in London where Fury arrived with two dwarfs. 'My little men could take you out. This fight will finally shut your mouth,' Fury taunted, pointing at his 'bodyguards'. 'I can outdo you at anything because I am the better man in all departments.'

Both fighters claimed they would win by a knockout. Chisora said a fight with Fury was a mismatch: 'Just because he's big and unbeaten doesn't mean he's ready for me – he's not. This fight will be easy.'

Fury said, 'Chisora doesn't want to fight me and he's crying about the money – I would fight for pride. This is personal between us and we will sort it out like proper men in the ring. I might have to send my little men to make sure he gets in the ring on the night.' He dedicated his next knockout to all the women who had ever been battered by men. Chisora had been convicted of assaulting his then girlfriend after finding messages from another man on her phone. Fury told the *Daily Star*, 'I'm going to serve justice with my fists for every woman in the UK, Ireland and the world, who has been beaten by a man. Dereck Chisora is a coward but when he steps into the ring with me he will be facing someone who will be hitting back. And I will teach him a lesson. My dad used to knock my mum about when I was really young and I hated it. It's such a cowardly thing to do. I'm going to take revenge for every woman by beating the shit out of him.' Fury also said he would give a percentage of his purse from the fight to domestic abuse charities.

Hennessy encouraged him, saying, 'Tyson is a great heavyweight, he is very marketable and a great talker.' His aim was to make Fury a household name, then his fight could move to the pay-per-view channel Primetime.

As the fight approached, Fury became more measured, but no less confident. 'This is a real grudge match,' he said. 'We are both undefeated, we have a similar KO record and the public want to see us in the same ring. I have the personality and the boxing style to be a major draw on TV. It's a massive fight, a big launchpad, and I want to make a positive statement. I am not only fighting for my own future, I am fighting for my family.' Paris and Tyson's daughter, Venezuela, was eighteen months old and another baby was due that October – a boy who would be named Prince John James.

Fury then revealed an unexpected aspect of his character. Although he appeared to be a hard-drinking, hard-fighting traveller, he claimed he was a practising Catholic. 'I'm very religious, I even take my Bible into the dressing room before fights, although I won't read it at that time,' he said. 'God has given me a talent. If you haven't got belief then you should never pull on a pair of gloves. From a very young age I have believed I will not only be world heavyweight champion but also the unified champion. Chisora is tough, he has power, quick hands and quick feet. I will not be underestimating him, he will have my respect. But it is my destiny to be heavyweight champion.'

Fury talked about his belief with the *Sun*: 'I'm very religious and go to church as often as I can. I am a big believer in God and I read the Bible regularly – although not as much as I should. My favourite verse has been called the Bible in a nutshell – John 3:16 – and it reads, "For God so loved the world, as to give his only begotten Son; that whosoever believeth in him, may not perish but may have life everlasting peace." I try to follow the words of God and spread the word. Everything I achieve in life, I achieve through God. Everywhere I go, I take my Bible . . . I feel when I am walking with God no one can beat me. My Uncle Ernest is a preacher in Congleton, near Manchester, and I've even given a testimony from the pulpit to the congregation.' Fury said he saw no conflict between the violence of boxing and his Catholic religion. He prayed every night and before and after each of his fights. 'If God's in my corner, no one can beat me,' he told the *Sun*.

Despite Fury's more emollient tone, Chisora said he was out to silence him. 'Tyson Fury's comments and attitude are quite funny,' he said. 'His wit is just not sharp enough to get under my skin but he keeps wasting his energy trying to. He is so desperate for fame it is taking him away from reality, it's laughable, and he would do anything or say anything to get a headline and when it matters most, in the ring, he just hasn't delivered. People ask what have I got that Fury hasn't. Well, the list is endless but most importantly, two championship belts. I really don't see anything in Fury that concerns me too greatly.'

After defeating David Haye on points on 2 July, Wladimir Klitschko pitched in to offer, if Haye did not want a rematch –

for which he was currently showing little interest – Klitschko would be keen to fight the winner of the Chisora–Fury match.

Fury was undaunted. 'The Haye–Klitschko fight was, not to put too fine a point on it, rubbish,' he said. 'Haye looked scared stiff all night and Klitschko wasn't prepared to take a risk to knock him out. In the end it was plain awful. I couldn't watch it. Haye built it up with talk of decapitations and then danced around the ring for twelve rounds trying not to get hurt. Then he blamed an injured little toe for his performance. That's not boxing. The way Haye conned the public is a disgrace. He and Klitschko stank the place out.

'As for my opponent, why would I want to talk him down? Chisora is a decent fighter. You have to be to be a British and Commonwealth champion. He is limited in some of the things he does and he is good at others. I like his head movement, he punches in bunches, is quick and gutsy, but I also think Dereck has little resistance to body shots, has never been truly tested and his chin is questionable. Under pressure from a serious fighter like me, he will collapse. If I am to achieve my ambition of becoming world heavyweight champion, I have to beat the likes of Chisora – and beat him easily. I am sure Klitschko would make short work of him and I have to do the same. But I am not making daft comments like the ones Haye made. I have too much respect for my opponent to do that. Chisora is a brave fighter, like me. I am just better at it than he is.'

Again he told the *Daily Express* that he was fighting for his family. 'We are about to be blessed with a little who we will call Emmanuel, as it means "God with us".' I am going to beat Chisora to feed my family. There can be no bigger incentive than that.' And he was a man in a hurry. 'I'm the sort of bloke who has no patience at all. If I see a watch and I want to buy it in a shop, I will buy it. If they then say they haven't got my size but the shopkeeper says he has another in Scotland, I would drive up to Scotland to get it straight away. That is just the sort of person I am. Rome wasn't built in a day – but if I had been in charge it would have been. I know people say the Chisora fight is too early for me and Klitschko would be too early, but I am a bloke who likes to grasp the nettle.'

Fury could not wait to earn his shot at Klitschko on free-to-air television. 'The fact this fight is on Channel 5 means millions will be able to watch me destroy Chisora and become the new heavyweight sensation. There will be a clamour for me to face Klitschko afterwards and I am more than happy to get in the ring with him before the end of the year. In fact, I cannot wait.' As always he was supremely confident. 'I know Klitschko can be beaten and I know I can beat him. Different day, different story though.'

He looked back to his biggest professional test to date where he overcame Big Bad John McDermott, winning the rematch with authority. 'I went in the first time with McDermott a boy and came out a man,' he said. 'It shows what I am all about. I am willing to learn, but I am also prepared to go through any brick wall out there to achieve my ultimate ambition – to be the world heavyweight champion.'

Meanwhile, Fury landed himself a part in a film – the gangster movie *St George's Day*. His scene was shot in Le Pont de la Tour restaurant near Tower Bridge in London. 'I met [actor] Craig Fairbrass in Marbella and he suggested I star in the movie,' he said. 'I jumped at the chance. It was a great experience.'

Back to the day job and after the disappointing Haye–Klitschko match, Fury said he was out to reclaim the honour of the art of boxing in his fight against Chisora in Wembley Arena. 'I saw the Haye–Klitschko fight and didn't think it was a great fight to be honest, a lot of people got conned for their money,' said Fury. 'I thought it was a put-up job. Haye didn't really get stuck in or try and win in my opinion, Klitschko did what he had to do and it was just a let-down for the British public. Hopefully, I'll redeem heavyweight boxing come 23 July. I'm going to go in there and will give fight fans a real fight, value for money and what they want to see.'

With just a week to go to the fight, Chisora broke off a conference call with Fury after Fury said he was going to kill him, then resorted to profanity. 'I've a wife and two kids to provide for and if it means killing you in the ring, that's what I will have to do,' said Fury. 'To beat me he will have to kill me because I'm prepared to die in the ring. I'm putting it all on the line. I'm going to snap your chin off your body. You are an arrogant little prick. I'll smash your face in. You are a shithouse as well. It will come down to one thing on the night: who's got the bigger heart? Who wants it more? I know I want it so badly, nothing will stop me.'

Chisora responded, 'You can say what you want to say to up your spirits. You can motivate yourself by saying you will kill me, but there is nothing you can do now that will make you a better fighter before this fight. And you aren't good enough to beat me.'

The grudge was not just between the fighters, but the promoters as well. Frank Warren, Chisora's man, and Hennessy had not spoken for twelve years. Warren complained to the BBBC, saying, 'It's totally unacceptable, unprofessional and unprovoked behaviour. It did nothing to enhance a British title fight. It doesn't enhance the sport as a whole, either. His vile insults and disgusting comments have no place in British boxing. Fury hasn't got much upstairs. In my view, empty vessels make the most noise. My man will not be at the head-to-head press conference on Monday listening to any more of that talk.'

Chisora echoed what Warren said about Fury. 'He comes across as someone trying hard to convince himself more than others. Empty vessels make the most noise,' he said. 'I will show everyone that I am the top domestic heavyweight and that Fury isn't what he thinks. I am the British and Commonwealth heavyweight champion and beating Fury will prove that and remove another pretender. I've fought on US TV before but the more exposure, the better. I'm adaptable, fast and exciting. I don't know any other way to fight. Providing Fury backs his words and comes to fight, fans won't be disappointed. It will be exciting with him fending me off as the reality of life at the top slowly kicks in.'

After the altercation, Chisora confirmed he intended to boycott the rest of his pre-fight publicity events. Meanwhile, Fury ate his words – with a pinch of salt. 'Don't be a plonker, I wasn't serious,' he said. 'Of course I apologise for saying that I would kill him. No fighter wants that to happen. I have a strong faith in God and it was just in the heat of the moment. It all sounds a bit hypocritical to me. Muhammad Ali said things to Joe Frazier he regretted and Mike Tyson said countless things. It happens when you have a real fight on your hands. What I won't apologise for is the beating I'm going to give him. We are in the hurt business. As Ricky Hatton said, it is not a tickling contest. The British Boxing Board of Control has not suspended me, so let's cut out the excuses and don't be a muppet, Del Boy. Chisora needs to grow up. The people around him know that he was able to bully other opponents but he can't do that with me. They know his reign as champion is coming to an end.'

When challenged further about his comments, Fury said, 'I didn't come on to this phone call to be aggressive, but when he comes out with stuff about me having no heart, what do you expect me to do? I'm doing this for my family and I'm going to smash his face in. But I do apologise to anyone listening if I have offended them. All this trash talk is rubbish. I'm sick of talking. I just want to get in the ring and I just can't wait for fight night to come along.'

He explained to another interviewer that he used the word 'murder' as a slang term and did not mean it to be a real threat. 'I don't use it as in "I'm going to murder you" literally. It's like a slang word for "You're going to get it if you don't behave",' he said.

He also accused Chisora of hiding behind Frank Warren. 'Chisora can't speak for himself. He's like a puppet,' Fury said. 'He needs a puppet-master to do the talking for him because he hasn't got the brains to talk for himself. It seems to me that the people around him know that Chisora was able to bully other opponents, but he can't do that with me. They know that his reign as champion is coming to an end. They know that his world title chance is out the window on Saturday night.'

Despite the apologies, the battle of words went on. Next, it was Chisora's turn: 'Everything is on the line against Fury. We are both unbeaten and the winner goes on to better things,' he said. 'But the one thing I have that he doesn't is skills – and that's going to be the big difference on the night, believe me. I punch harder and my all-round skills are better. I am the number one in Britain and I want to be at the top for another five years and nobody is going to push me off this throne. I can't wait to get in there with Tyson. It will be a good fight. Once I get through with him, then I want to meet the likes of David Price and John McDermott before I go on for the world title.'

Fury's confidence, of course, was undimmed. 'I can't wait because he is not going to be able to stand up to me,' he said. 'He hasn't got the bottle for a real fight. I have been calling him out for a long time and the only reason he is fighting me now is because I am the mandatory challenger. He doesn't have the power he says he has and I'm going to show that next week.' Nevertheless, Fury was praying for his opponent. 'Religion is everything to me,' he said. 'Without it I would have nothing. I'm a practising Catholic, not as much as I should do but I do go to church as often as possible. I try to do everything by the Bible. I've read Testaments in church and I pray a lot. It's the most important thing to me, more important than boxing. I would rather be knocked out ten times by DC than not go to heaven. I'm God-fearing. I pray for Dereck Chisora and everyone. I pray that I win and he is OK. This is the fight game, it's not ballet-dancing, so there's going to be fierce talk before the fight but I don't wish Chisora dead or anything like that. This is sport. I will hold no grudges after the fight. I pray that he comes to the fight first of all, that it's a good fight, and I win. I also pray that he is OK after it. I don't have a problem reconciling my religion with boxing. God gives me the strength and belief to win. I'm up for it more than any other fight. He has not been in the ring for a while so he will be a bit ring-rusty, but I have never felt so fired up for a fight.'

Fury was still drawing inspiration from the disappointing Klitschko–Haye fight. 'David Haye didn't do what he said he would do and he let everyone down,' he said. 'I'm hoping I can make Britain happy about heavyweight boxing again and stop people talking about David Haye's little toe. It's great for British boxing that this fight is back on terrestrial TV, free to watch, because everyone is sick of paying for fights that end up being shit. Millions of people bought Haye's fight with Klitschko but it was shit. People can watch this fight for free. You can get more well known for fighting on terrestrial television; Sky gets ninety thousand for its boxing, but we are looking at getting 2.5 million for this fight.'

He also drew on his heritage and upbringing. 'I was born a fighter. I was born premature and was just a few pounds when I came out. I was in an incubator and had to fight for life.

Fighting comes naturally to me. I don't think I'm ready for the big time – I know I'm ready. I've been appalled by some of the goings-on in recent heavyweight fights involving David Haye. First, we had the no-show against Audley Harrison last year when Harrison barely threw a punch and then we had Haye's performance against Klitschko. He talked a great game, then the bell went. At least I can guarantee this: Chisora is going to try to beat me and I'm going to knock him spark out. At least Chisora will come looking to fight. Haye never even did that. He should be ashamed. I learnt a lot from the McDermott fights and it will stand me in good stead against Chisora. You can build up Chisora's record because he has beaten Danny Williams. But you have to accept that Williams is a shot fighter these days so I don't take much, if anything, from that. Sam Sexton was a good win, but Sexton is a domestic-level boxer. I'm a world-level fighter.'

Likewise, Chisora dismissed Fury's credentials, insisting he would be far too ring-savvy for the youngster – Fury being five years his junior. Although giving away more than six inches in height, he rejected the idea that the fight would be a replay of the Haye–Klitschko match. 'That fight has nothing to do with me and Fury,' he said. 'Evander Holyfield was my height – six-foot two-inches – and it didn't stop him becoming the undisputed world heavyweight champion and beating great fighters like Mike Tyson. It's not about who is the bigger, but who is the braver and I want this more than he does. This is a passport for me to Klitschko.'

The hype continued relentlessly. Fury: 'I'm the future of heavyweight boxing in Britain and the world. When you looked at how Haye boxed against Klitschko, it's not how a true heavyweight with a true heart should fight. British fans shouldn't worry because I'm the coming force and I'll show that when I knock out Chisora. If I had boxed the way Haye did I don't think I could look at myself in the mirror ever again. Then I want to knock out David Haye to prove to Wladimir that I'm the real deal. Me and Dereck are both going to come and fight. We're not there to dance. Proper fighting men don't dance. The fans deserve a proper fight and they'll get one with us. I want to bring pride and honour back to the British heavyweight scene. There's going to be fireworks.'

Another source of inspiration for Fury was golfer Rory McIlroy, who had just won the US Open at the age of twenty-two. 'After the fall of Tiger Woods, Rory gave golf the lift it needed,' said Fury. 'Now I plan to do the same for British boxing after David Haye's defeat.' But despite his bluster, Fury admitted he was in no hurry to face the Klitschkos. 'I simply don't feel I'm ready for a fight with the Klitschko brothers yet,' he said, sounding a note of caution. 'I wouldn't want to agree to a fight where I'm just making up the numbers. I'm still learning and I want to get more fights in before I even think of jumping up to that level. I need more experience and the only way to get that is by having plenty of learning fights. I've said from the start that I want to get to the top the old-fashioned way – and that's by winning the British title, then the European and then I'll start looking at a world title.'

With just three days to go, Chisora upped the ante. 'After I whup Tyson Fury, I will fight the next most eligible opponent, like the winner of David Price or John McDermott,' he said.

'I also hear Audley Harrison has been calling me out but he had better stay in Las Vegas because no one would pay to see me eat him up. I'd also fuck up David Haye – blow his ass off. The guy disrespects the sport, talking about putting people in wheelchairs. Cut out all his talk and bullshit and I am far more vicious than him. I would walk through him. I am number one in Britain now and I have got all the belts.'

With two days to go, Fury said he would quit boxing if he lost to Chisora. 'My career would be over. If I can't beat Chisora I have no right being a professional boxer. If I can't beat Chisora I'm going nowhere. I see Chisora as a bum. If I lose to Chisora I'm an even bigger bum, so I'm definitely going to pack it in and try a different job. He's fought a washed-up Danny Williams, and Sam Sexton he had already beaten before. I just see him as an easy challenge. He doesn't possess massive power, he doesn't possess a great work rate, and he can't beat me.'

In a wide-ranging interview with Fury just one day before the fight, TV presenter Matthew Wright posited that boxing should be banned on medical grounds and for its sheer brutality. Fury replied, 'I don't agree with anything you just said. I think boxing is one of the greatest sports of all. You can name on your hand the amount of people who have died due to injury caused by boxing. There is more chance of me dying eating a lollipop than by being beaten up by Dereck Chisora.' His threat to kill Chisora was brought up again. 'I didn't mean I would kill him dead. I mean I will beat him up,' he explained. 'It's the heat of the battle. I got told off for it. I didn't mean what I said and I've apologised.'

Moving away from his sport, he was asked whether Rupert Murdoch should resign over the phone-hacking scandal. Murdoch's newspapers were being investigated for monitoring the calls of celebrities and figures in the news. The media magnate's flagship *News of the World* had just been shut down as a result of the ongoing crisis at News International. It was one of the biggest news stories of the year. Fury simply said, 'He's eighty. He's like my granddad. I doubt he can even work a phone.' And on plans to open the biggest McDonald's in the world at the heart of the London Olympic village for the 2012 Games, he said, 'Anything in moderation is OK now and again. I wouldn't have it during training because I've got a fat problem. My body stores lots of fat. Anything I eat stores on my sides and I look like a fat pig when I'm boxing. I don't like it when I look like that.'

Fury said he had left his wife and children in Cheshire while he trained in Austria and Canada, and had lived for the last few weeks at his uncle and trainer Hughie's caravan park in Lancaster. 'That just shows how determined I am. It is a lonely existence,' he said. 'Training, sleeping and eating is all I am doing.'

In the days before the fight Chirosa continued his verbal attack on his opponent. However, his trainer Don Charles was more circumspect. 'I actually like Tyson because he spices boxing up,' he said. 'He talks the talk and so far he's backed it up because he's beaten everyone put in front of him.'

Even Chirosa himself was prepared to make some concessions. 'Tyson Fury is a real talent,' he said. 'But I do believe in the saying, "The bigger they are the harder they fall" and I will prove that on Saturday. I am not one to say a fighter is useless just because I am trying to sell tickets. I don't see the point with this fight because everyone wants to see me in the ring with Fury. It is a natural fight. A fight I would love to watch. He is not experienced enough to handle someone like me, but that does not make him a rubbish boxer. It is just that I will go on to fight for the world title later this year against Klitschko and he will have to prove himself again at British level . . . he is a pretender. I am the British champion.'

Throughout it all, Fury kept his cool and on the eve of the fight he was already claiming victory. 'This fight is already won and lost,' he said. 'He's already lost it mentally. He's mentally scared of me, physically scared of me, and it will show on the night – just like Michael Spinks was of Mike Tyson [who knocked out Spinks in 1988 after 91 sec]. He's already lost his bottle.'

He also claimed that his height would give him the decisive advantage. 'The way Wladimir Klitschko toyed with David Haye tells you that you need those kind of attributes to be a successful world champion,' said Fury. 'I know people will point to Evander Holyfield and even Mike Tyson for evidence that the smaller heavyweights can beat the bigger ones, but generally bigger comes out on top – and they don't come much bigger than me. I will knock out Chisora in the early rounds. He isn't going to know what has hit him. I don't even think this is my hardest fight. John McDermott was a better boxer than Chisora and I stopped him in our second fight.'

For Chisora, these were just words. He insisted he had the experience. 'Fury talks a great game,' said Chisora. 'Fine, I have got no problem with that. He is entitled to his opinion – as long as he realises those opinions don't mean a damned thing once the bell goes. He is a decent prospect with some good qualities, but I have been in with better boxers and always come out on top. Tyson Fury knows he can dig, but once the tough rounds start rolling by he will come unstuck. I will have too much ring knowledge for him. I have learnt boxing is a mental game. He has yet to learn that lesson, but he is about to.'

Fury dismissed that notion. 'It doesn't matter what Chisora says or does. He is getting flattened. Then it is onwards and upwards to Klitschko.'

Chisora came back with, 'I'm ready to knock out this useless lump once and for all. He's a David Haye wannabe – all mouth and no action.'

Fury's response: 'There are no big threats in the UK for me and I don't think Chisora is any good, to be honest.'

Waiting in the wings was Wladimir Klitschko, who said he was ready to take on the victor before the end of the year. 'I was going to fight Chisora in December and then again in April but I had some business to do before that could go ahead,' Klitschko explained. 'That business was getting rid of David Haye. I have now done that and next up is either Chisora or Fury. I am now free to fight either of them and I want to get back into training.' He dismissed Haye as 'a pest that needed to be controlled'. He said, 'Now I am moving onwards. I have another fight to consider and I cannot wait to get back into the ring. I did not really extend myself fully by beating Haye. I won, but I wish I had knocked him out.

It should be a great fight whoever I face. The fans in Britain are very enthusiastic about their boxing and very experienced too. They know the fight game better than anyone.'

The Chisora–Fury fight was billed as 'The Big Brawl to Settle it All'. It took place at Wembley Arena on 23 July 2011 and was shown live on Channel 5 to some three million viewers. The fight was also televised live in the USA on pay-per-view. Given a build-up full of ill-temper and acrimony, the 20,000 sell-out crowd had every reason to expect an exciting encounter. However, the boxers did not enter the ring until past midnight and the venue was less than half-full by the end, with spectators needing to catch their last trains home.

Twenty-seven-year-old Chisora weighed in at a career-high of 261 lbs – 16 lbs higher than when he fought Sexton ten months earlier. Fury was still twenty-two and a respectable 255 lbs. Fury had a smile on his face as he jabbed his way through round 1. He tied up Chisora on the inside when he stepped in, otherwise peppering him with right crosses. But halfway through round 2, things seemed to take a serious turn when Chisora hurt him with a big left hook, followed by a flurry of overhand rights and hooks that sent Fury staggering. This would be the only time the champion looked like he might win the fight.

'Tyson! Keep your fucking head back!' yelled Uncle Hughie from the corner. At ringside, Hennessy was also looking concerned.

Chisora had simply changed gear, using more head movement and picking his shots with guile. But Fury kept his head and brought the uppercut into play. Eight inches taller than his opponent, Fury used his jab to keep his man off him, letting go the occasional right. That didn't stop Chisora pressing forward and landing a good right of his own just moments before the bell sounded for the end of the third.

Both men looked to be tiring in the fourth and continued to hold anytime they came within reach of each other. Chisora was still getting through with his single shots and landed a big left hand that shook Fury. Nevertheless, Fury took both the third and fourth rounds, and dominated from then on. Switching regularly to southpaw and back, he was able to box off the back foot, landing most of his big shots and blocking or slipping out of Chisora's attacks.

The pace dropped considerably at the start of the fifth. Fury then cleared his head and reignited the fight again midway through the round. He caught the champion with a stinging right uppercut just as he let his guard slip and he followed it up soon after with a stunning combination. It was another round for Fury as he clearly hurt Chisora for the first time and he was able to push his opponent back against the ropes. That gave Fury space to pick his shots and batter Chisora's head and body.

Fury continued to take the lead in the sixth as he put the Londoner against the ropes again and was able to calmly find gaps in Chisora's guard. At one point the end looked near as Fury pummelled him in the corner. But just as it looked like referee Victor Loughlin might step in, Chisora came out with a massive right hand.

Fury threw beautiful combinations but never looked like

ending the fight early. Nevertheless, he did the damage. Chisora cut a battered, bloodied and disheartened figure as the fight wore on. At one stage his corner threatened to pull him out of the fight in an attempt to spark him into life. It made no difference.

Fury also tired towards the end of the fight, but Chisora had been spent since the fourth. He went passive in the eighth, but Fury did not take the bait.

'He was conning me on,' he said later. 'He wanted me to unload so he could come back with about twenty-five shots, but it's just about brains isn't it?'

Chisora switched tactics and came back at Fury with a series of big, over-the-top, right hands, but by the end of the eighth he was back against the ropes. He gave it one last push in the tenth and looked to have Fury in big trouble for the first time as he managed to land a number of big shots in quick succession. It was not enough. Constantly worn down by Fury's physical dominance and relentless work rate, Chisora's thirty-second burst in the tenth didn't turn the fight around. He knew he needed a stoppage in the final round but he lacked energy and intensity as Fury managed to keep him at a distance. Fury's rapier-like jab controlled the twelve rounds and although Chisora had occasional success with haymaker shots, his work rate was never enough to win over the judges.

Fury won the fight by a unanimous decision and took the British and Commonwealth titles. Two of the three judges gave Fury the fight by 117–112, and the third by 118–111.

'I was in the best shape of my career tonight,' said Fury.

'I'm tired because I've boxed twelve rounds but to be honest I could have gone twenty. I might well have finished him and I'm not one to make excuses, but my hand is hurt and I don't tell any lies about that.' Still looking fresh, Fury added, 'This is a dream come true and it means the world to me . . . never mind all the trash-talking and bullshit, I am really a humble guy . . . I would have beaten anyone they put in front of me tonight.'

After so many harsh words had been exchanged, Fury paid tribute to Chisora but said he was now ready to take on the world. 'I've never been rocked in my life. He opened up in round 2 but it was my time,' he said. 'I don't care who's put in front of me now. I'm willing to take on anyone in the world.'

The first to offer his services was Audley Harrison, who wanted a fight to restore his dignity after being booed out the ring following his three-round defeat by David Haye the previous November. Then he had barely thrown a punch. 'I know boxing fans want to see the end of me and this is the perfect opportunity to wish me goodbye,' he said.

But that was not on Fury's agenda. 'I'm ready for Klitschko now, I don't need another warm-up fight,' he said. 'I would go in the ring with Klitschko any time. If he wants to take me on, that's fine by me, I'm ready for it.'

There were kind words for Chisora. 'I said to Dereck after the fight, "That was brilliant." I hit him with some good shots and he took everything I could throw at him and for that I give him the utmost respect,' he said. 'He's a proud warrior and deserved to be the British and Commonwealth champion. I said before I was the better fighter and I proved that. I'm just amazed he took some of my best shots. I said I would do a number on him and I did. Obviously I'm disappointed I couldn't stop him but it was a wide points margin and I think I proved I'm heading towards the world heavyweight title.'

Fury still faced disciplinary action by the BBBC for his threat to kill Chisora and his string of obscenities at a pre-match press conference. The board said that it wanted to curb the traditional pre-fight bad-mouthing, which, they said, had brought the sport into disrepute.

'We have had enough,' said general secretary Robert Smith. 'This sort of trash-talking has got to stop. In retrospect we may have treated this too softly, but now we will take a much stronger line.'

CLIMBING THE WORLD CHAMPIONSHIP LADDER

Six weeks after taking the British and Commonwealth titles, Tyson Fury was back in the ring, this time in the King's Hall, Belfast, in mid-September 2011, and again in front of millions of Channel 5 viewers. Beforehand, in an interview with the *Belfast Telegraph*, Fury got a chance to parade his religious credentials again.

'Boxing is sport, and you know going to heaven means more to me than beating Wladimir or Vitali Klitschko on the same night with one hand,' he said. 'The ultimate sacrifice has been made for me on the cross and I could never emulate what Jesus has done for me. Anyway, a man's good deeds are nothing but dirty rags. If you have faith in God you can achieve anything.'

His opponent was Nicolai Firtha, from Ohio, who had battled WBA champion Alexander Povetkin the previous December. He was a last-minute substitute for Belfast cabbie

Martin Rogan, who had narrowly beaten Audley Harrison over ten rounds. Firtha came in at short notice. But it would be no pushover. 'Anybody who knows anything about boxing can see that this is a risky fight because Firtha has gone the distance with the man who now holds the WBA belt,' said Fury. 'With two weeks to go I know this is a risk, a gamble, but I'm a true fighting man, a man of honour, and I'm prepared to fight any man on the planet.'

Firtha was pleased to be taking to the ring in Belfast as his mother was Irish and he had relatives there. He entered the ring in green and white shorts with a shamrock insignia. Fury took round 1, blooding Firtha's nose with clubbing right hands. He dished out similar punishment in round 2, jabbing in the style of Larry Holmes in his prime. He continued to dominate in round 3, until out of nowhere he was wobbled by an overhand right shot over his jab. Roared on by his corner, Firtha followed up with combinations as Fury desperately tried to clinch. Some began to wonder whether, taking this fight so soon after winning the British and Commonwealth titles, he had been reckless. But as always Fury came back strongly.

In round 4, he lifted the crowd off their seats when he knocked Firtha down at the end of the round. In round 5, Fury couldn't miss. Still stunned, Firtha lost his ability to slip Fury's punches. After a decent right hook, which Firtha took without flinching, referee John Keane stepped in to call a halt to the contest. It had been a big round for Fury and a humiliating end for the man who had gone twelve rounds with Povetkin.

Fury was then keen to get back and fight in front of his

home crowd again. He had not fought in Manchester since 2007, when he was still an amateur. 'So far all my publicity has been done away from Manchester,' he said. 'I've fought in London, Ireland, Canada, but I really wanted to fight in Manchester. I want to fill out the MEN Arena one day but I can't do that until I build up my following here.' He would get in the neighbourhood when defending his Commonwealth title against thirty-four-year-old Neven Pajkić – born in Sarajevo, Bosnia-Herzegovina, but a naturalised Canadian – at EventCity, Trafford Park, on 12 November. 'It's fantastic to be fighting at home and I promise to put on a great show for my fans,' said Fury. Again, the bout would be televised by Channel 5, allowing Fury to expand his British fanbase.

Both men boasted sixteen-fight undefeated records – though the Canadian heavyweight champion only had five KOs – and a lot was at stake. 'He knows that if he beats me he's on for a world title shot against Wladimir Klitschko,' said Fury. 'People want to fight me now because I'm one of the biggest names in boxing. This is going to be even more of a grudge match than Chisora. We've been calling each other out for a while. I went to one of his fights in Canada and we almost started at ringside.' Indeed, Pajkić called Fury 'a classless piece of shit' in the run-up to the fight. Asked about the feud, Pajkić told *Boxing Insider*, 'I didn't mind Fury at first, but I'm starting to wonder about him lately. I just read the other day his wife gave birth and he named his son Jesus.'

Fury's wife confirmed this had been Tyson's intention, but said she put her foot down and he was christened Prince John James instead. Paris also said there was no shortage of exotic names in the Fury household. 'With Tyson being named after Mike Tyson and me being named after the capital of France, we couldn't really have ordinary names for our children, could we?'

Her husband was still keen on his first choice. 'Jesus Fury – I like that name,' said Tyson. 'A lot of Mexicans are called Jesus.'

Others suggested that, by calling his son Jesus, Tyson would have himself as God. As for Pajkić, he said, 'I'm a religious kind of guy, I believe in Jesus and all, and I do my prayer. I'd like to have him on my side, but what if the other guy does the same thing and he's a good guy? Then the best man wins, you know. Naming your kid "Jesus", I don't know. He's just a dumb kid, what the fuck he knows? Maybe he was just overwhelmed by religion in the moment, five years from now he'll look back and say . . . ' In the event, Prince John James Fury remained the boy's name.

At six-foot-three, Pajkić was six inches shorter than Fury. 'Yeah, but I'm a real heavyweight man, you know?' he said. 'I really have to struggle to get down to 230. Other guys have to get juiced up to get to 220, 215, whatever. I walk around 245, 240. When fight time comes I'll be trimming the weight, I'll go under 240, between 235 and 240. I'm a true heavyweight.'

He also rated Firtha. 'Hey, man, Nicolai Firtha is a tough cookie, let me tell you, man,' he said. 'He's a tough fucking guy. He doesn't look like much, but he's a tough cookie, man.' He admitted that Fury was a big talker but, 'I can run my mouth, too, but I prefer to do my talking inside the ropes, you know, especially at the time of the fight.' So did Tyson.

On 12 November, Fury took round 1, with Pajkić marching forward into his jabs. But in the second, a surprise awaited. Fury squared up, stuck out a lazy left jab and was met by a big overhand right to the head that knocked him to the canvas. He had walked right into it. It was his first career knockdown and again an overhand right had been his undoing. He got to his feet in shock and survived another heavy blow before the bell.

Fury's new trainer Chris Johnson gave him a pep talk before sending him storming out for the third. First, the Canadian champion was sent stumbling into the ropes and on to his knee under a barrage of heavy blows. Moments later he was down again, having struggled to regain his composure. Fury went in for the knockout blow, but before he could administer it, referee Phil Edwards stepped in to stop the fight after 2 min 44 sec, to the dismay of both fighters. Clearly, Pajkić wanted to fight on and Fury had words with Edwards. He told a press conference after the fight what he'd communicated: 'I said, "You shouldn't have stopped it, I was about to knock him out." He said, "Exactly."'

Asked how it felt to be knocked down, Fury said, 'The greatest feeling you've ever felt in your life – what do you think it felt like! I was too relaxed I think. As soon as I got hit I woke up.' But he was as confident as ever that he would be world champion. 'Champions go down and get back up,' he said. 'It shows true grit to get back up and knock the other guy out. I get tagged and I'm half-asleep sometimes. In the first round, I had my eyes closed but I woke up and pulled it out of the bag. I was rocked in my last two fights, put down in the third one; who knows what's going to happen in the next one? That's what's so exciting about me. It's heavyweight boxing. It only takes one punch to get sparked out. I never doubted myself and even when I was on the floor I thought, I will get him now. Now's [the] time to get rid of him, and that's what I did. It's a long, slow process and you have to learn with hard fights. One day I will be world champion and it's not far off.'

At the post-fight press conference, Hennessy revealed his 2012 plans for Fury. He would fight again in Blackpool in January before making his US debut at New York's Madison Square Garden in March.

'Hopefully, I'm going to have a big year next year with plenty of fights, plenty of wins and plenty of excitement,' said his fighter. 'I wouldn't fear going in with any man in the world. I believe I can beat any man and I will fight anyone in the division.'

However, first Fury would return to Belfast to fight Martin Rogan, who had pulled out from the earlier fight. He had watched Fury fight his previous opponent in Manchester and had not been impressed. Rogan said, 'It was a terrible fight and Fury did not look good in there. They are talking about him fighting Wladimir and Vitali Klitschko. Are they serious? Why do they not come over here at the beginning of the year and fight me at the Odyssey. I am the best heavyweight in Ireland, so let us fight for the Irish, British and Commonwealth titles in Belfast. I am up for that and if he beats me I will retire and they can take all the praise. If they believe he can fight the Klitschko brothers, he should be able to walk through me. I want the fight and it is a contest the fans would love to see. So let's do it.'

Hennessy was confident that Fury would soon be ruler of his division. 'He's just got to stop getting drawn into a gunfight and start being smart,' he said. 'Once he does that he's the best heavyweight on the planet. I'd say we're probably about eighteen months away. He's got a lot of work to do, but by the time he gets there in eighteen months' time he'll be a different fighter. I honestly believe he could beat WBA champion Alexander Povetkin tomorrow. But he's looking bigger than that, he's better than that. He wants the Klitschkos. So eighteen months from now he'll beat the Klitschkos.'

David Price also issued a challenge. 'Fury is the British and Commonwealth champion and I respect him for that but after I get past McDermott I will be out to prove a point,' Price said. 'I beat Fury in the amateurs, and I will beat him in the professionals and I just hope that both promoters can get this fight on. But it is up to the Board of Control to sanction this fight. I give Tyson Fury credit. To get up off the canvas and go on to win the fight takes a lot of heart and courage and I hope he shows the same guts by taking me on. This is a fight that the British public want and deserve.'

Promoter Frank Maloney agreed: 'I once resurrected British boxing with Lennox Lewis and took him to the top and I believe I can do the same with David Price. And if Hennessy wants to sit down and negotiate a deal for this fight I am more than happy.'

But Hennessy wanted Rogan. Northern Ireland-based trainer John Breen was also taking an interest: 'I watched

Fury on Saturday night and he had a big belly and did not look fit,' Breen said. 'When he was over in Belfast recently I did four rounds on the pads with him in the Kennedy Centre. I did not work him hard and his promoter Mick Hennessy said to him about coming and doing some work with me. Tyson said, "John works you too hard." You have to be fit in this game and Tyson can get away with it at the minute, because of the guys he is fighting against.'

Breen was concerned about Fury facing Rogan. 'He has the size and talent to go a long way, but he has to use his ability,' he said. 'Pajkić knocked him down in the second round and he was not a big puncher. If Martin Rogan hit him a shot like that, would he get up again? I don't know, because Rogan is a big strong man. He has to use the ability he has, because if he doesn't do that, when he faces better fighters than Pajkić, he will get knocked out, even though he has a good chin.'

Breen, who had trained numerous World Champions, believed Fury has some growing up to do. 'He is only a kid of twenty-four years of age. He will not peak until he is thirty,' Breen said. 'Tyson has to stop talking to the crowd and showboating in the ring, or he will be punished. He has to focus on what he is doing in the ring and if I was in his corner he would not be getting away with that sort of thing. Boxing is a hard game and you have to concentrate on the job. And if I had him I would get the problem with his hands sorted out. He has not been able to spar or do the pads before fights because of it. He is a fighting man and wants to fight, but I would get that sorted and then bring him along slowly. He is still very young for a heavyweight.'

When the Fury–Rogan fight was confirmed in February 2012, Martin 'Iron Man' – 'Rogie' – Rogan said, 'Tyson is in the world Top 10. So this is a big opportunity for me. I'm a great heavyweight, I've proved that by beating Matt Skelton, the undefeated guy. I beat Audley Harrison, so I've got the pedigree to do the business.' He had beaten Harrison on points in December 2008, then took the Commonwealth heavyweight title from Matt Skelton in February 2009, but lost it on his first defence to Sam Sexton that May. He also lost a rematch that November after sustaining a cut above the right eye in a clash of heads midway through round 5.

On 14 April 2012, Fury and Rogan would fight in Belfast's Odyssey Arena for the vacant Irish title. This time no one questioned Fury's eligibility. Fury's cousin Andy Lee was, said Fury, proof of the Manchester-based fighter's Irish roots. Tyson: 'Andy's father went to the Boxing Union of Ireland and signed an affidavit that my grandmother was Irish so all the talk about me being Irish or not has been put to bed. Fighting Martin Rogan at the Odyssey Arena was always a fight I wanted and for it to be confirmed for the Irish title is fantastic. I will be in unbelievable shape and I think everyone will be shocked by just how good I look.'

He looked back to the time when he was denied the chance to compete for Ireland in the Olympics. 'When I knock out Rogan and get that Irish title it will be like me winning the gold medal at the Olympics. To win the title in the year of London 2012 will be very special,' said Fury. 'I always knew I was Irish and now everybody knows that those who prevented me from boxing for Ireland at the Olympics in Beijing denied

Ireland an Olympic heavyweight gold medallist. It hurt me deeply not being able to fight for Ireland at the Olympics and to win this Irish title will be just fantastic. I don't care about Wladimir or Vitali Klitschko. Those guys can wait because winning the Irish heavyweight championship in Belfast means everything to me.'

Indeed, Fury was even comparing himself to a first-century BC figure of Irish legend who was supposed to have been ten foot tall. 'The ultimate Irish warrior was Cuchulain, everybody knows that,' said Fury. 'Now Rogan and I will decide who is the rightful heir to his throne and I have no doubt it will be me. The legend goes that Cuchulain could stand single-handed against an army and that his sword inflicted wounds from which you could never recover and Martin Rogan is going to feel pain that he has never felt before when I land my big shots. Rogan thinks he is the king of the Irish but on 14 April he will realise that I am the true king.'

However, Frank Maloney was calling Tyson 'Chicken Fury' for electing to settle his differences with Rogan rather than defend his title against the mandatory challenger David Price, vacating his British and Commonwealth titles in order to pursue a future world title match even though a £100,000 was on offer.

Rogan: 'It is as simple as this. Tyson Fury doesn't know what he has let himself for. He has never been in with anyone with the grit and desire I have and he couldn't have found an opponent that wanted it more than me. I have a massive want. All I can think about is winning this fight. He could have fought Price and I know from talking to his team why that fight didn't happen. It's money, TV and boxing politics. I know he isn't a chicken and I know he has a fighter's heart. But Price could have been a wiser move because I know Price doesn't want it more than me.'

Rogan was forty. He had not fought in eighteen months and had not won a fight against a boxer with a winning record since Skelton in February 2009. He was not daunted. 'I am fit as ever,' said Rogan. 'I am working with former Ulster player Stephen Bell on my strength and conditioning. I have already noticed improvements. [Panamanian-born, Belfast-based coach] Bernardo Checa has added a bit of refinement to the brawler in me, too, and I know I can beat him. I can't change the year I was born and the inactivity wasn't because I didn't want to fight. I don't see either as an issue. Look at the great Muhammad Ali; he was three years out and came back better than ever. They say the only difference between me and Ali is our skin colour.'

Iron Man – so-called because of the titanium plate screwed into his neck after an injury in 2009 – also fancied a shot at the world title. 'The Klitschkos won't want to fight Haye or Chisora again,' he said. 'Tyson Fury has been linked with them more than once so if I beat him it's only natural I am an option.' In the meantime there would be no Chisora-style badmouthing. 'I wouldn't lower myself. I would never spit at or slap anyone. I will fight Tyson in the ring and shake his hand after, no matter what the result.' He did not like others badmouthing his opponent either. 'Some of the phrases that were used against Tyson calling him a chicken and stuff like that I find very disrespectful. Any man who steps in the ring is far from a chicken and I respect the chance that I've been given to step in the ring.'

Fury was also respectful of his opponent. 'I know Martin Rogan, I've grown up my full career watching him so I've nothing but respect for the man,' he said. 'I was watching the fights when he beat Matt Skelton and Audley Harrison and I know he is coming firing with both hands to take away what I've got. But I'm No. 6 in the world and I'm working my way to a world title shot and I'm hoping I'm going to get there.'

At a pre-match press conference, Rogan said, 'I've fought everyone that's been put in front of me, never ducked anyone and I'm not starting now. I'm wiser as I get older and I'll use my education in the ring to put together some destruction. Fury's world No. 6 and this is a great opportunity for me – a lifeline. He'll get it into the ring and get beaten by a good, hard Irishman. All my focus is on 14 April, I'm not underestimating him at all. I've been working so hard in training and it's only right that the Klitschkos have mentioned Fury's name because he's world-rated. I should've got a crack at a world title after I beat Matt Skelton, but I'll not cry over spilt milk. I'll move on to the next episode of my career.'

He also called for home support to cheer him to victory. 'The fans are going to be out in their numbers, as Belfast's a fight city and the kids will like Fury and be inspired by a big guy like him, they'll know him from Channel 5,' he said. 'Everybody saw what happened between Dereck Chisora and David Haye.' The two had a brawl at the press conference following Chisora's match against Vitali Klitschko in February

2012. 'And there will be nothing like that here. We'll do our fighting in the ring.'

Fury wasn't about to bandy words about either. 'Martin has a lot to say about his destruction and devastation, but what can you say? All will be revealed on 14 April, and I hope his fight is as good as his words, because I've been sitting here listening to him ramble on,' he said. 'I just hope he's prepared, because I've never put myself through this much training ever in my life. This, for me, may as well be for the unified heavyweight championship of the world. This is where it is; Martin Rogan in Belfast, nothing else – no other fighter in the world matters more to me right now, not even the Klitschkos. I've put myself to hell and back for this one and I never, ever want to go there again. I am going to go come here in perfect shape, perform to the best of my ability and climb up the world championship ladder. To be honest, I've often in the past gone into fights not being in one hundred per cent condition and not one hundred per cent mentally right as well. What can I say? I had a few problems going on at the time that I'm not going to go into, but now I am one hundred per cent focused on my aim, my goal – and that's to be the heavyweight champion of the world. I see Rogan as being in my way, he's holding the key for me; he's stopping my family from eating, so any man who's going to get in with a six-foot-nine man who weighs eighteen stone and has been training like a demon – away from the celebrity lifestyle and away from my family for fifteen weeks by fight time – is in trouble.'

But he could not resist having a pop at the forty-year-old Rogan. 'An army won't stop me on 14 April, so Martin Rogan hasn't got a chance. He's getting on a bit, too, to be honest. To be honest, at forty years of age he can't beat me . . . he's one of those fighters who always gives it his all. There's no nancy business with him, it was always get stuck in with him. He's got his chance now to fight a Top 10-rated fighter but, to be honest, I think it'll be one of [those] things where the young man is going to prevail over the old one. The young warrior always overtakes the old one.'

Rogan dismissed the idea that he was over the hill at forty. 'That should concern Tyson more – it makes me hungry,' he said. 'It doesn't matter if I'm out of the ring twenty years, I'm still going to get in a fight. I'm going to do so much damage in there it's going to be unreal.'

But there was genuine affection between the two fighters when they got to Northern Ireland. 'You might call him "Big Rogie" over here but to me he is "wee cuddly Rogie",' said Fury. And if he lost, Fury would retire. 'If I can't beat Martin Rogan I have no chance of winning a world title. If he beat me I would be going nowhere anyway. What would Klitschko do to me then? Put his fist through me. If a twenty-three-year-old man can't beat a forty-year-old fighter he would have to retire. If he beats me I will go to his house and shine his shoes for a living.'

Hennessy said that it was going to be the best fight Ireland had seen since Muhammad Ali beat Al Lewis in Croke Park in 1972. 'This fight's been a long time coming, everybody's been talking about it, everybody wants it and here it is, at last we've delivered it,' Hennessy said. 'It's a sensational fight between two proven warriors. Martin Rogan's got great wins over the likes of Audley Harrison. Tyson has beaten Dereck Chisora and we've just seen what Chisora did with Klitschko in Germany recently.' He'd gone the distance, although Klitschko won on points in Munich in February to emerge victorious from the 'Showdown In München' and retain his WBC title. 'We've got a great fight here, it's something that will put bums on seats and get people to tune in, which is what we need for boxing.'

A crowd of 9,000 were expected at the Odyssey to watch Fury and Rogan, and Hennessy was keen to see his boy win a fresh accolade. 'Tyson has already won the English, British and Commonwealth titles. He now wants to add the Irish and European belts to his collection en route to winning a genuine world title. In doing this, he will become the first ever boxer to do so.'

But for Fury it was more about proving his credentials as an Irishman. 'Wee Rogie is going to give it everything and I hope he has been training hard because I am going to be in the shape of my life. It's going to be a painful night for wee Rogie. I have locked myself away like never before to make sure I am ready to show the Irish people how good I am and how much it means to be Irish champion,' he said. He had been paying special attention to fighting the flab. 'I am embarrassed every time I look at myself in my last couple of fights. Now that fat kid is gone and everyone will see the huge difference that has taken place under my new coach and with the expertise of the Body Fuel team in Liverpool [nutrition and supplement specialists]. I feel like a new fighter. My diet has been totally overhauled and I'll be tipping the scales at about 17 st 10 lbs. I can't wait to take off my dressing gown as you will all be able to see the new me.'

Fury admitted he had piled on the pounds after his young son, Prince, was hospitalised with breathing difficulties. The boy spent almost two months in intensive care after a virus hit his immune system, and every night Fury slept in a chair at the hospital. Both depressed and stressed, he developed an eating disorder. He told the *Daily Telegraph* that he had even contemplated quitting the fight game. 'In January, I looked in the mirror and I saw an obese, fat pig. And I didn't like what I saw. So I said to myself I either get in shape and be a proper athlete, or hang up my gloves, undefeated,' he said, knowing that he had no alternative but to go on. 'I don't have any other education, I don't have any qualifications, so I have to be boxer. I thought to myself I'd better get myself in shape because if I want to be a world champion, I'm not going to be one looking like this and performing like it. So I got my mind into gear, sat down with my Uncle Peter and we worked out a training programme. We've stuck to it like Trojans for the past year.'

His infant son's illness had been an ordeal. 'After the problems with Prince, I wasn't training because my head wasn't right and I put on five stone. I was in hospital all the time with him while he was poorly, and there was only a vending machine and a café so I was just eating junk food. I also went through bouts of depression, but I'm positive and focused on what I need to do now. I trained over Christmas to get it all off and it has killed me. But it's been worth it. I'm in better shape now than in all of my previous fights. I want to prove my critics wrong and reveal a new side of Tyson Fury.'

His child's suffering had proved to be an epiphany for Fury. Before that he was out drinking until 5 a.m. – 'which a married man shouldn't do' – and had lost interest in his boxing and felt out of shape. 'Didn't think there was anything worth living for. Didn't care about money, fighting.' He often thought of death. 'I was thinking like a crazy man. I wasn't reading the Bible, had murderous thoughts about my wife, even. It was terrible. The devil is very strong and can pull you into thinking terrible things.' But when Prince became gravely ill and they feared they might lose him, he said a voice spoke to him in a way that several trainers, including the legendary Emanuel Steward, had been unable to.

'I got down on my knees and asked God to help me. And every night of my life since I was a child I prayed for forgiveness and health and safety for my family and friends and for world peace. That has always been my prayer. And now . . . I just feel I am on the right road and am doing something for a purpose. You don't have to be educated to be sensible. There are plenty of educated fools out there who can't earn a living, can't do nothing. Without boxing, I'm fucked. And God forgive me for swearing.'

After that, he occasionally permitted himself a night out, but always in a group. That way, if any hothead decided to try a crack at Britain's biggest and more recognisable boxer, Fury always had backup. Tyson explained that he would just tell any wannabe brawlers that he couldn't fight them but that any of his team would be happy to oblige. 'These boys aren't professional or worried about an assault charge of a fight outside. So then they step up and – *smash!* – it's goodnight, Vienna. But that's my excuse, that I fight like a lady.'

He had lost five stone since his son's illness and was confident that he was only one bout away from a shot at the world championship. 'I am ready now for the Klitschkos. I have not been beaten and when I stop Rogan that will be the time to face either Wladimir or Vitali next,' he said. 'Rogan is a tough old bruiser and nothing will be easy against him – but it will be explosive and just like my last two bouts. Don't blink.'

Keeping up his bluster, Rogan responded by calling the Klitschko brothers out as well as Fury. 'Why can't I call the Klitschkos out if I win it?' he asked. 'When I down Tyson, why can't I? He is world No. 6 and they are talking about fighting him. So when I beat him I can call them out and say, "I beat the man you want to fight. Now I want to beat you." I don't care which one of them it is. I would even take two in the ring together to get a world title shot.' In the meantime, he relished being the underdog.

'This is a great opportunity for me and one I am grateful for,' he said. 'I have been off the map for a while with the injury and then finding it hard to get fights. Tyson Fury is world-ranked and I am coming in a world number nought because they took me off the rankings, but that suits me. I absolutely love being the underdog. I revel in it. I think he is underestimating me and to be honest I hope he is because he will get the shock of his life.'

But with two weeks to go to the fight, John Breen said he was backing Fury: 'If Fury is in shape and uses his boxing skills, he will win the fight. He is also about twenty years younger than Rogie and he has the hunger and the drive to become the best in the world. He is the bigger and stronger man, but if he comes to fight and prove he is a fighting man, then Rogan will have a great chance of winning the fight. Fury has to be in great shape for this fight and stick to the plan his corner have for him. If he diverts from that plan and gets involved in a brawl with Martin, then there will be trouble. Fury has to keep moving and use that jab of his.' He also said that he might be in Fury's corner for the fight.

'I could be asked to do that but I would have to see what shape he is in for the fight. He may not be fit enough for the fight and if that is the case I will not do it. If he is not fit enough to carry out my instructions, I won't do it. He was supposed to come over and train with me at the start of the year, but he hasn't turned up. I would like to train him and he would not be waving at his friends during the rounds. That would not be on.' The veteran trainer also had words of wisdom for Rogan's trainer, Bernardo Checa. 'You have to train Martin's head. He has to go into that ring believing he can get the job done. I remember in Prizefighter [the Barry Hearn tournament], he was tiring and I said to him, "Look, Martin, your man called you a so-and-so." And Martin got up and put him over. There was also the fight against Skelton. We had to pep him up and he knocked Skelton over. Martin is a very strong and determined man. I have never fallen out with him and he has always been very respectful towards me, but I just think Fury will win this one.'

However, Checa, who had been head coach for Irish

promoter Barney Eastwood when he was churning out champions in the 1980s and 1990s, was confident. 'I have watched Fury quite a few times and he has been hurt in many fights,' said the trainer, who had also worked with Roberto Duran. 'He has been put down and there is a pattern, there is a reason and I plan to exploit those weaknesses. The key for Rogie is to be super-fit and I will have him super-fit. He has quick hands for a big man. This is a massive opportunity . . . beating Fury would be one of my biggest achievements. You know with heavyweights, you just have to hit the right spot and the opponent will go down. We know that Fury has a good jab and we have to neutralise that to have a chance of winning, but he is also slow and that is in Rogie's favour.'

Rogan himself then upped the battle of words, saying, 'Tyson Fury is a bullshitter. Every fight he goes into he's saying, "This is the hardest I've ever trained," or "I've been to hell to prepare." Well, guess what, Tyson Fury, welcome back to hell because that's where you're going. I'm going to meet him there. He always comes into the ring looking like a pudding anyway. He keeps going on about the Klitschkos but what is he trying to do? Jump on the bandwagon with the Irish people, with the Belfast people. My training has been going very well with Bernardo Checa. And I know there is the height, weight, age difference to deal with. There's no doubt about it. He's world No. 6, he's got a great jab and he's a big lad. I've put in so much training and the question mark doesn't lie with me. The question is – why did he choose to fight Martin Rogan? Why?' Again he dismissed the age difference as an issue, pointing out that he did not even box at

Fury's age, only taking up the sport at the age of twenty-eight and turning professional at thirty-three.

'I started off in boxing in 1999 at an age where people are packing it in,' he said. 'A year later, Audley Harrison won a gold medal at the Olympics but I beat him when we met. I'm going to have an answer for everything that he does. If he wants to box, if he wants to fight, I'll have an answer on the night. He is judging me on one fight that I should have won three years ago against Sam Sexton. He's gonna be shocked in there. Shocked.'

Fury said that Rogan could not even depend on his home crowd. 'The support that I have been getting is unbelievable. When I boxed in Belfast last year, I got a fantastic reception wherever I went and on the night the atmosphere was amazing. Now the Irish fans are getting right behind me, they want to see me knock out Rogan. They know how good I am and they know a real Irish warrior when they see one. You'll never see me sit on my stool and quit or complain about a bad toe – I'm the real deal. Rogan probably thought that he would have all the support in the arena on 14 April, but he's in for a shock because I'm going to feed off the great support that is coming my way. I'm very proud of my Irish roots. My uncle lives just outside Belfast, so there's going to be great support for me and I will do them proud by knocking out wee Rogie. He's a proud guy and I'm sure he'll give it his best but when you look at the two of us there's a big difference in class and that will be the difference on the night.'

Indeed, the battle between the two Irish titans would ensure a good turnout and the fight would also be broadcast live on

Channel 5. 'The Irish fans are just fantastic, I really feel at home there,' said Fury. 'The Odyssey Arena is going to be packed out, the tickets are flying and after I beat Rogan I know the fans will want to come back again and again because they will have a world-class heavyweight to support. Bringing a world heavyweight title fight to Irish soil would be very special and there's nobody else [who] can do that except me.'

Former WBC world bantamweight champion Wayne 'Pocket Rocket' McCullough was backing Rogan. 'I hope he knocks him out and wins the Irish title in Belfast,' said McCullough. 'They say Fury is the better boxer – but Rogan has guts and heart – and that can win fights. Martin has guts and heart by the bucket-load and he will have to show those when he takes on Fury. I think that if he is in shape, and he looks as if he is, he is in with a shout. I also rate his coach Bernardo Checa and he will have him in good shape for the fight and he will have a plan as well. I have been telling him a few things that he should do against a taller man – but that is between the two of us. But he has to go in there and get the job done. He has to go in there and knock Fury out. And I hope he does.'

Barry McGuigan was another who fancied Rogan. 'Rogan reminds me of the Desperate Dan character [from *The Dandy* children's comic] and I mean that in a good way,' he said. 'He is a big, immensely strong man and he comes to fight. Rogan is always in good shape because of the physique he has and he is a very determined man. He has that inner strength that you need in the ring and in a time of a crisis it is people like Martin who come to the fore. He came to professional boxing late and he will never be a technically gifted boxer – but he has other positives. He has strength, he has determination, he has guts and he has heart. He is also a grafter and has worked hard to get where he is because he is not a great boxer. But I admire him greatly because of the graft and the hard work he has put in. He will need all of that if he is to beat Fury at the Odyssey. But I know one thing – if Fury comes into this fight and he is not in shape – there could be trouble ahead.' Though Fury was the fresher of the two, Rogan hit harder than his previous opponents – 'so if Rogan hits him it could all be over'.

But Sky pundit and former cruiserweight champ Johnny Nelson said, 'I like Rogan. Tough nut, but I think Fury will be too fresh for him.'

Emanuel Steward warned Rogan that it would take a special fighter to beat Fury, though he did not think that Fury was ready for the world title that year. 'Tyson has decided to go the European route so I don't think he is an option at present but he is a big star and can have a big career in heavyweight boxing,' said Steward. 'He does seem to have some issues with training, organisation and issues in his career but he is the biggest contender of all the heavyweights. Tyson may look sloppy at times but he always manages to win. He has the size to cause any fighter problems.'

Fury himself also said that he was in no hurry. 'We have lots of fights planned and I want to keep busy. I'm not in a rush to fight for the world title. What's the rush? I'm only twenty-three. All the world champions are old. I am the new blood in this division and I will do it in my own time.'

Klitschko had said he would relish a fight with Fury or

Price and Fury said, 'I have respect for both of them. They are both bigger than me.'

Despite being dubbed a coward by Price after vacating the British and Commonwealth titles, torpedoing a fight between the two of them, Fury pointed out that it was actually a contractual problem that prevented him taking on Price. 'Yeah, I'll fight him – no problem,' he said, 'but people forget there is a business side to boxing. I have a contract with Channel 5 and I cannot fight on another channel. It's not a case of me not wanting to fight him, or him not wanting to fight me. At the moment, I don't think that fight can be agreed. It won't happen.'

At the beginning of what Hennessy was calling 'fight week', Fury and Rogan were brought together for a final press conference in the shipbuilders Harland and Wolff's drawing office – where the *Titanic* had been designed. The company was located in the docks, near the arena that was to host the fight and close to the new *Titanic* museum.

'The singing, the dancing, the stand-up comedy, the entertainment is finished and we've got one hell of a heavyweight battle here for the Irish title,' said Hennessy. 'I don't think that there has ever been such a high-profile fight for an Irish title that has more meaning on the world stage than this one and it's a heavyweight fight to boot.'

'This is my world title fight, the Irish heavyweight championship of the world,' said Fury. 'It couldn't be any better. This is what it's all about.'

While Rogan had admitted he was the underdog, he was not prepared to be disregarded. 'Fury is overlooking me once again,' he said. 'He thinks it will be an easy ride but he will find out the hard way. It's looks very much like he's already looked past me. I haven't looked past Saturday night. My eyes are firmly on taking him out and that's what I'm going to do. I'm prepared to die in the ring.'

He went on to compare Fury to the *Titanic* itself. 'It was such a massive ship, "The Unsinkable". It reminds me so much of Tyson Fury, "The Unbeatable", who on the same night is going to get hit by me and they'll call me the iceberg because when I hit him, he's going down, too. He's six-foot-nine, but I've thrown bigger guys out of the way just getting to the ring. It doesn't matter how hard he trains because the end result will still be the same and I know that I've trained hard. There will only be one true Irishman lifting that belt above on Saturday night – and that's me.'

Fury sighed and shook his head. 'You can check the paperwork if you want,' he said. 'I've answered this a million times. But with a name like Fury, I'm not Chinese. I'm not from Afghanistan. My grandparents are Irish, end of story.'

Rogan was asked if he was irritated by Fury's claim to Irish heritage. 'It doesn't irritate me, but come on, get real,' he boomed. 'If you're born in America, you're not Polish. Tyson Fury doesn't know where he's from. One day he's from Manchester, the next he's from Nutts Corner, then it's Galway. He doesn't know. If he wants to be Irish, fair play. If his grandparents are Irish, happy days. But come Saturday night at the Odyssey, he'll need to let someone know where he's from. Because after I hit him, he'll not know where he is. He won't know where he's from.'

Fury was convinced that having been born and bred in Ireland was not going to help Rogan. 'I've been doing a few trips around Belfast and I'm struggling to find anyone that likes Rogan,' he said. 'Everyone is asking me to knock him out and I'll happily do that. Rogan might be a great fighter but I'm supreme and there's a difference between world class and domestic level. You're talking and listening to a world-class athlete and Martin Rogan is coming for a war but he's a British-level fighter. I'll hit Rogan with so many left jabs that he'll be begging for the right hand to come over and knock him out. It's going to be crazy.'

Fury also spoke candidly about the general opinion that his punch resistance was not up to scratch as he had been dropped and rocked in his last two bouts. 'It's obvious that I've been hurt in my last two fights and Rogan is a bigger puncher than Pajkić and Firtha,' he said, 'so on paper it looks like he's going to smash me to bits, but I've never trained like this before. My chin won't be a problem on the night. Martin, you've never been any good and I'm going to expose you on Saturday night.'

Tyson then took the opportunity to move to the floor and remove his tracksuit top and T-shirt, allowing Rogan to quip, 'The only six-pack he has is sitting in the fridge at home.'

'Take a look for yourself,' Fury replied, before singing, 'I'm sexy and I know it.'

'Aye, that's magic,' said Rogan. 'He'll be thinking Martin's over-the-hill, he's been round the block, all this pantomime crap, but realistically come Saturday night at 10 p.m., there will be a pantomime, and it will be Tyson Fury running around the ring on his tiptoes away from me.'

'No, the crowd will be shouting, "Where's Martin, where's Martin?"' retorted Fury. 'I'll point to the canvas and say, "There he is . . . " I don't care if he's in the best shape of his life. It doesn't matter if he's run five hundred miles, if he's trained with fourteen armies, if he's had a million sparring partners, it doesn't matter if he's got sixteen hands. He can't beat me. He doesn't have the attributes to beat me – that's how confident I am. It's as simple as that.'

But the last word went to Rogan. 'I'm fed up listening to this child,' he said. 'We'll find out on Saturday night, but I tell you now – he is not beating me. Mark my words. He is *not* beating me.'

As the fight approached, the British Boxing Board of Control and the Boxing Union of Ireland fell out over the latter's choice of referees and Fury ratcheted up his goading. 'Joe Louis once went on a "bum of the month" campaign and Tyson Fury is starting his very own, beginning with Martin Rogan,' he said.

With three days to go Rogan complained that, what he was assured was going to be a ten-round fight, was going to twelve. 'The Irish title has always been fought over ten rounds and that was my understanding. How can they change the rules three days before the fight?' he asked. 'I have been made to feel like an after-thought. I feel as if I've been treated like dirt. It's the principle and a matter of respect. It's not the number of rounds I'm worried about. I'll knock Fury out long before it goes ten or twelve rounds. I'm standing up for other boxers. We are the ones who go through the physical and mental strain . . . changes of rules and regulations at this late stage is wrong.'

But Fury had no complaints. He continued to act as if the fight was already won. 'I'm ready to step up to the Klitschkos right now,' he said. 'There are no more warm-ups or European-level fights left in me any more. That's not to say I don't rate Martin Rogan very highly. I do – and his record shows he is a decent boxer.' He claimed that, once they had seen him fight Rogan, the Klitschkos would be 'quaking in their boots'. Instead of hurling insults at them, Fury hailed the brothers as role models and hoped that, at forty, Vitali would retire soon to avoid getting beaten.

'They are very honourable men and have shown you don't have be a great aggressor in boxing to be a world champion. They have shown [that] a bit of brains and boxing can win,' Fury said. 'These guys are military people from their backgrounds in the old Soviet days, they have degrees, doctorates, speak different languages and are superb athletes. They are totally different to how it was before for world heavyweight champions, who came from the ghettos and poor backgrounds. They have reigned for a long time and it has been hard to see how anyone could change that, but that's where I come into play. There's always some young challenger who comes along and beats the champion. I think the Klitschkos should move on before they get beat, especially Vitali.'

Fury also dismissed the disruption in his camp during the handover from Uncle Hughie to Uncle Peter as his trainer. Fury insisted he had benefited. 'The fans in Belfast will see the difference in my body shape when I take off my dressing gown,' he said. 'They will notice straight away that I now look like a fighter. Rogan's going to pay the price of my new regime.'

Top Manchester coach Joe Gallagher was looking forward to the entertainment Fury provided. 'He might not be the finished article, but he is pure theatre,' he said. He also looked forward to a fight against David Price. 'Fury–Price is bigger than just a British title fight,' he said. 'Down the road, I can see the pair challenging for world titles and massive pay days.'

In the Rogan fight, the odds were on Fury and the man himself wasted no time in pointing it out: 'The bookies are rarely wrong – they aren't daft,' Fury said the day before the fight. 'I can't see it going the distance. To be honest, I can't see it going past six rounds. I fancy winning it in six. Martin Rogan is forty now, he is older and he is perfect for my style. I am looking to inflict some damage on his face. It will maybe improve his looks, but what can you do? I anticipate a master-class performance on Saturday night.'

Rogan said he was going to 'clean out the bookies' and dismissed Fury as a 'fake' and 'full of crap'. 'I'm not interested in all that,' Rogan said. 'People talk a lot of nonsense. And let's remember, there won't be words or insults being thrown on Saturday night. It will be punches.' He said he was in peak condition. 'People are going to see a different Martin Rogan to the one they saw against Sam Sexton.'

This was grist to Fury's mill. 'Sam Sexton's busted you twice and Tyson Fury is a million times better than Sexton ever dreams of being. You talk a good fight but your bark is worse than your bite. You've already lost twice, as your record shows, and I'm undefeated.'

Fury weighed in at 17 st 7 lbs, the lightest he had ever been, while Rogan was 16 st 4 lbs – a stone lighter than when he had lost to Sexton. Rogan complained that, on the night before the fight, he was still signing more paperwork. 'People in the background have tried to humiliate me,' he said. 'What has gone on in the background is a disgrace to boxing.'

It was still unclear whether the Irish belt was still in contention, but Rogan was determined to go through with the fight. 'Throw the ring up now and I'll fight him,' he said. 'I'm ready to derail the Fury bandwagon.'

Fury admitted that 'bad blood' had seeped into the fight and said it would be 'me against a punchbag because that's what Martin's gonna be.' He added that Rogan was old enough to be his dad. Once he had the Irish title, he wanted to move on to the European. 'That's my next target after I'm finished with Rogan . . . The only way someone will beat me is to nail me to the floor.'

It was soon time to stop talking and start fighting. In round 1, Fury came out as a southpaw. Although Rogan was out of condition and six inches shorter than his opponent, he managed to outwork Fury in the first two rounds with a series of right-hand blows. His best moment came at the end of round 2, when he landed a powerful right uppercut.

Fury finally came to life in round 3. A flurry of right jabs were followed by a vicious left hook to the body which put Rogan on the canvas. Rogan was in trouble from then on. Fury dominated round 4, with Rogan visibly wincing as Fury continued to deliver body blows. In round 5, Rogan gave a long look to his corner when he found himself on the end of another brutal shot. Fury dropped him again with another blow to the body. Rogan got to his feet but, with just 7 sec to go, Bernardo Checa jumped into the ring to call a halt and save his fighter further punishment.

'I didn't see it coming, he hit me on the turn,' Rogan said later. He had no complaint about Checa's decision to stop the fight so close to the bell and give the fight to Fury. Rogan: 'Whoever says he can't punch, my face will tell you different. He caught me on the front of the rib. I was OK for about a tenth of a second, then I was just on the deck. I'm a fighter, I'm going to come back out, but you have to trust your cornermen, if they made the wrong decision they made the wrong one. I stick by my team.'

Fury agreed. 'You've got two fighters here, gloves on, who are gonna smash each other's face in,' he said. 'We're not in there to get brain damage. This is a job and we've got families to provide for. We've got wives to go home to. Martin would have carried on. I would carry on until we're dead. That's what we do, we're fighting men. But the cornerman and the ref are there to do a job and that's to make sure we don't get lumps knocked off us.'

The two fighters embraced warmly afterwards and Fury was quick to pay tribute to his opponent. The bad blood was now over. 'I just want to say that Martin Rogan is an absolute Irish warrior,' Fury said. 'He couldn't land a glove on me but he kept coming at me for five rounds. He's not a loser just because he has lost this fight. He has had some great fights here and in England but he is a boxer on his way out and I am on my way to a world title . . . in the past I've done a lot of talking. I've called out a lot of people, but now my boxing is doing that.'

Asked about his decision to switch to a southpaw stance, he said, 'I was practising a few things. I found it comfortable to go left-handed so I did. I'm a world-class heavyweight and I'm going to try different things. I'm ambidextrous. I can box with both hands. I can hit as hard with the right as I can with the left. We've been trying different things. We worked out a game plan for Martin Rogan and he looked like the type of person we could try it on.'

Rogan admitted being caught out by Fury's plan. 'I thought it was just to confuse me for two minutes or something but then it went another round,' he said. 'I was, like, "What's going on here?"'

Fury said, 'You can't have the same game plan for every fight, so I showed I can adapt. I deal with my opponent. I hit him with some solid shots. It's the ones you don't see coming and I wasn't loading up in my shots, I was just letting them go.' He also paid tribute to Belfast. 'I feel like it is my home town. I had a great welcome out here and I hope to bring big title fights to Ireland . . . I'm very honoured to fight for this belt. It's the Irish heavyweight championship of the world for me. I think people should be proud to have a new Irish heavyweight champion of world-class ability to go and win a world title.'

Hennessy said his boy was the 'most exciting thing in heavyweight boxing after the Klitschkos. He looks so relaxed, he looked awesome, he never looked out of third gear, and wasn't troubled. He can go all the way and be world champion as quick as he wants. We're going to keep him busy. He's been British and Commonwealth and now Irish champion. European would be nice then world honours.'

Fury said he was up for any challenge. 'I am ready to fight anyone in the world right now,' he said. 'If Mick Hennessy told me I had to fight Klitschko in the morning I'd say. "OK, no problem." Then again if he said we have got someone else, I'd say no problem. I have watched Wladimir and he is a man – if you hit him he will get hurt. He is not super-human.'

Fury already felt he had won a moral victory over the Ukrainian champion after a battle of wills in a training camp sauna room. 'I know how to beat him. I have already got one over on him from the mental side of things,' he said. 'We had a sauna competition at his training camp in Austria last year and I mentally broke him. You are only supposed to be in for five minutes but we got to ten. I was going to leave but Wladimir insisted we stay. We got to fifteen minutes – I was having to count the seconds in my head. He's looking at me and I'm looking at him. I was prepared to pass out. I wasn't for moving, I rubbed oil over myself and in the end he got up in a huff and walked out without speaking to anyone. He was definitely upset – so I have one over on him already.'

After Rogan, Fury was brimming with pride over his unique achievement. 'I have made history tonight – I am the first person to win the Commonwealth, the British and the Irish titles all within the same time frame,' he said. 'I'm not gaining anything from saying I am Irish. You are what you are. I'm not changing for anyone. If people want to get behind me and support me then I am willing to fight for them. It meant a hell of a lot to me to win it . . .

'I am only twenty-three-years old, I am the youngest heavyweight prospect in the world,' he went on. 'All the rest are in their thirties. I have been fighting tough opponents since my second fight. I have been brought along very well. When I get to be world champion I won't be a one-hit wonder. I could have fought for the world title already. I don't want to go there just to make up the numbers, I want to go there and smash up one of the brothers. I want people to think I have more than just a puncher's chance and until I'm ready to do that I'm not going to rush things. Good things come to those who wait.'

THE ULTIMATE FIGHTING MACHINE

On the day Tyson Fury beat Martin Rogan in Belfast in April 2012, Mick Hennessy said he was convinced his fighter was ready to challenge for world titles, but would instead aim for the European belt before seeking a bout with WBA heavyweight champion Alexander Povetkin.

'He would beat Povetkin tomorrow,' said Hennessy. 'Let's be real. He would wipe the floor with Povetkin. That fight's not going to happen any time soon because Povetkin's the champion and it would end up being in Germany. Tyson is the star. He's the biggest star in heavyweight boxing behind the Klitschkos. We're going to manoeuvre him into a position where we bring the top fighters over here. He's the only heavyweight that can do it. How many heavyweights can do what he did tonight in world boxing and turn to left-handed? He looked so relaxed, he was awesome. His jab was sensational and he never really got out of third gear.

'There is so much more to come from him. He's in incredible shape. He can go all the way. He can be world champion whenever he wants. He's looking at fighting on 30 June to keep him busy. He wanted the Irish belt. The European would be nice and then genuine world title honours.'

In fact, Fury's next fight was on 7 July 2012 in the Hand Arena in Clevedon, near Bristol, against thirty-eight-year-old American Vinny Maddalone. It was for the vacant WBO intercontinental heavyweight title. A New York brawler, Maddalone was a regular on ESPN mid-week cards and had twenty-six knockouts in his thirty-five wins. It was a fight to take seriously. Maddalone was a danger with his signature overhand right that had caused Fury so much trouble in the past. Fury, who was at a training camp in Essen, Germany, when the fight was announced, said, 'He's a good opponent, a real tough guy, who leaves nothing in the changing room; he certainly comes to fight. Training has gone well and I'm in the best shape of my life and I'm looking forward to some good rounds and after I beat him maybe we can go out and get something to eat.'

Maddalone said, 'I respect Tyson Fury, hats off because he shows lots of balls. I'm really happy for this opportunity. Two guys with balls will make for a great fight.'

Martin Rogan didn't think much of the match though. 'To be honest, I don't know much about the guy he is fighting,' he said, 'but no doubt the guy is smaller and can't punch.' Maddalone was six-foot-two and Rogan had something more to say about David Price, who was six-foot-eight. 'Fury doesn't like to fight anyone tall. People will eventually realise he is fighting nobodies and get bored. What he needs to do is to fight David Price. Price is up-and-coming and people want to see him in the ring with Fury. Tyson won't take that fight though. He is wary of Price because he is tall, too, and can punch. If he is to call himself a real fighter he has to fight Price.'

But Maddalone's manager Mike Boroa described him as being 'like the fictional Rocky [with] the heart of a lion. I congratulate Hennessy Sports and Channel 5 for giving the fans in Britain a fight that promises to be a war.'

The match was almost immediately a sell-out. Fury had been ready for it long before the name of his opponent was announced. 'I've done nothing but train, eat, sleep and drink water since January,' he said. 'We now have a spartan training camp in Belgium, in the middle of a forest, away from anyone else. We live at the training camp all year round. We train six days a week, three times a day. We've had a lot of fighters who come over and try to train with us but they leave after a couple of weeks or even a week because they can't hack it. It's just too hard. We do nothing apart from eat chicken, rice and vegetables. We train, and we sleep. Nothing else.'

Almost nothing else – Fury and his team left the training camp and drove across the border into Holland where they were mistaken for a gang of armed robbers and arrested. The police surrounded his car. Eight officers ordered Fury and his crew out of the vehicle and forced them to kneel at gunpoint.

'It was the scariest moment of my life,' Fury said. 'I couldn't believe it. They were pointing guns at us and shouting, "Get down, get down." There had been a robbery in which someone was murdered and some guys in a bar had given the police a description of the robbers and apparently it matched us in our BMW X5. I was shocked but I kept calm because I knew we had done nothing wrong. It was the strangest thing that has ever happened to me.'

They were held in handcuffs for thirty minutes while officers searched the BMW, and a police helicopter circled overhead. Then they were taken to a police station where they were strip-searched and questioned about the robbery and murder.

'I kept telling them I was a boxer,' said Fury. 'It was a mistake but what can you do? Strange things do happen.'

Dutch police confirmed the men matched the description of a gang of raiders who had shot a victim dead. They were held for eleven hours before detectives accepted it was a case of mistaken identity.

'The ironical thing is I came to Belgium and Holland to get away from distractions at home,' Fury said. 'What a choice. Boxing Vinny Maddalone should be easy compared with this. I'll be a relieved man when I finally arrive in Bristol.'

Getting in shape had been difficult. Fury's weight had spiralled out of control after his last fight, hitting 23 stone. He was also suffering from a form of bulimia. 'I was in a patch when I didn't care about anything – boxing, marriage, life,' he said. 'I've knuckled down and got my diet right at last. If I kept on eating rubbish, I'd have been a diabetic or have heart problems.

'I'd pull into a garage and buy a carrier bag full of sweets, eat them, throw up and start again . . . I have not been back there since I sorted myself out. I've knuckled down and got my diet right at last . . . I used to eat and drink what I liked and thought I could just turn up and knock opponents out. But then I realised that this is what I did for a living and I realised I had to start taking things seriously. Now I eat well, train well, sleep well and, hopefully, fight well. If I want to get to the very top, then I know I have to do things the right way.'

Battling his demons, he had considered killing himself by smashing his car into a wall because he felt so down. Suicidal thoughts would plague him for years to come. Nevertheless he picked himself up and slimmed down to 17 st 7.5 lbs for the weigh-in. Maddalone weighed in at 16 st 8.5 lbs.

Fury promised the pre-fight press conference he would make short work of Maddalone: 'I know I am within touching distance of taking on and beating either of the Klitschkos. So it's important I keep on my steep learning curve and that means a quick and decisive victory over Maddalone, who I respect as an opponent who has gone in with the best.'

Fury also admitted to having problems with depression and alcohol. 'The hardest part is when you've got unplanned days and you're not training, or if I think about stupid things and start to think rubbish. Like if the Klitschkos get into my head, then I could eat half of Lancaster. It's not them as people, rather where I'm standing with my career. Everything takes so long. At one stage I was turning into an alcoholic, I'd go out and get smashed. I'd get depressed, get legless and then feel OK. Then I'd get up in the morning and think, what have I done?' Controlling his weight had been a recurring problem. 'I am disgusted about the way I used to look, with big rolls of fat hanging off me. I suffered a really bad spell at the end of last year and the start of this, as my newborn son was not well, and I was getting down about everything. Thankfully I have snapped out of it now and I am a different person, much happier in myself and a different fighter. Look at my body. It bears no resemblance to what I used to look like. There's no fat on me.'

It was Uncle Peter, taking over as his trainer after Pajkić floored him, who turned him around. Peter said, 'He had a scare when he fought in Belfast and I rang him and told him to come and see me.' Peter had himself had a short-lived professional career. 'I didn't want to step in, but what I said to him every time he fought was that he was doing a lot of things wrong. I said, "You're my nephew and I want to see you do it correctly."

'He went with Chris Johnson, who was saying, "You'll be world champion."

'But I said, "Look at your feet, your balance. All of that's wrong." I said, "You've reached a level where you are not going to get away with it." He promised me he'd take a rest and then a week later he took another fight. He went down when he walked on to a punch and I think that was the straw that broke the camel's back.'

He recommended that Tyson go to the Ingle Gym in Sheffield and Tyson asked Peter, who also trained his own son, ABA junior champion Hughie, to come with him. Peter agreed. 'I told him that I wanted him to do it and that I would do my best, but he had to do what I told him. Now he's on the up and up and he's learning all the time. He's not the polished article yet. He's not fighting for world titles.

We want to take four or five fights before that – perhaps the back end of next July.'

Before then, Peter said, there was work to be done. 'When I saw him box I said, "Obviously you are talented, but you're a rough diamond. You need polishing up. Everyone is in your ear. Let's get back to basics. You're still learning." I've only been with him since Rogan and I'm over the moon with how it's going. I train him hard but if you want to be world-class, you can't train like a normal person.'

Peter believed it was the trust between the two men that would get results. Uncle and nephew were close. 'I'm very proud of him and look at him like he's my son,' said Peter. 'I'm close to his dad. We are a close family. I always find time to talk to him. We get on like a house on fire. The trust is there. And it's not a financial thing. I'm doing it with passion because I want him to be the best. I believe he can do it because he is a special talent.'

For all his innate strength and skill, Fury admitted that was never blessed with a chiselled physique. He saw the Klitschkos as his benchmark. 'I don't think it's possible for me to look like David Haye,' he said. 'Our body types are totally different. But the Klitschkos have good bodies and they have different body types to David Haye. They are proof that with fantastic living, it can be done. I'm naturally fat inside and it is screaming to get out. It wasn't that I couldn't run or train. There was never a problem with that. It was my dedication when it came to food because being a heavyweight, you don't have to make weight. I was getting so fat that none of my clothes fit and I used to walk around with buttons undone. Now I'm working on my condition to look the part like Haye and the Klitschkos. I'm not there yet, but I will be.'

He drew some inspiration from reviewing his old fights. 'I was watching one of my fights recently and I just thought, what a mess. I don't know how I got to a record of eighteen and none,' he said. 'My condition was bordering on obesity for an athlete. I watched the fight with Rich Power from 2010 and I remember thinking at the time that I was in good shape. But I was slow and ponderous. Now it's coming together. I'm living evidence of what you can achieve if you work hard enough. I've got my head on and I don't want to eat junk. It's easy to comfort eat, but when you put the hard work in you don't want to get out of shape again.' Recent months of training had done the trick. 'I feel fantastic, my life is all sorted out. I'm fitter than I've ever been. My body fat is down to 9.4 per cent. I've really been knuckling down.'

The day before the Maddalone fight, Fury told the *Birmingham Evening Post* that he saw it as just another stepping stone. Nevertheless, he was determined to entertain the crowd. 'I want people to enjoy the fight and say what a great fight it was when they talk about it afterwards,' he said. 'It is not my place to talk about other boxers and the things they do, but I know we all have a responsibility to do the right things. When people switch on their TV sets on Saturday night, they will see that I'm a nice guy who does not do these bad things.'

Hennessy was also bigging him up. 'I honestly believe we have the best heavyweight prospect in world boxing by a long shot,' he said. 'People have to remember that, at this moment in time, Tyson is still only twenty-three. His achievements to date have been incredible. His trainer, Peter Fury, has done a tremendous job and Tyson is in the shape of his life. He is coming on in leaps and bounds and is improving in every aspect – footwork, speed, power and stamina. Tyson is a work in progress and there are still things he needs to learn. But he is heading in the right direction and is definitely capable of getting to the very top.'

By the end of the year, Fury aimed to get a shot at Vitali Klitschko's WBC crown. 'It's not hard to get a title shot, it's about getting a mandatory title shot,' Fury said. 'If it's a mandatory, then you're talking millions – it's life-changing money, not month-changing money. By December, I should be the mandatory for the WBC title. Now that would be something to go for, but I'm not rushing. I won't sell myself down the river for a couple of hundred grand. I don't want to just put up a fight and wobble one of the Klitschkos. I want to come home with a "W" by my name and the world title.'

Fury compared himself to Rocky Marciano, but with eighteen wins and thirteen knockouts he had a long way to go to match Marciano's forty-nine wins and forty-three KOs. Fury said, 'Like Rocky, I want to finish with that zero on my record. My career is progressing nicely. I'm ranked six in the world by the WBC so there is no point taking any foolish fights. I aim to get into a mandatory position to fight for the world title and then take out the big boys.' In the meantime, there was more work to be done. 'The things I can change are the way I train and prepare – and getting up the rankings by winning fights.' Then there was Maddalone to overcome and Fury knew it was not going to be an easy fight. 'You can't go

into a swimming pool without getting wet and you can't step
into a ring without getting hurt. It is how you react to it that
matters.' He was conscious of being put on the seat of his
pants in two of his last three outings. 'Against those fighters
I bounced back and stopped both of them in double-quick
time. I am a completely changed fighter from the one that
fought Pajkić and Firtha. I will destroy Maddalone.

'I then think I will need another fight in about October,
another maybe just before Christmas and 2013 is the year I'll
become heavyweight world champion. I'll be ready for the
Klitschkos by then and I will beat them.' He was taking one
thing at a time though. 'My focus is all on Maddalone right
now. You can't buy experience and that's what I need.'

As the fight began it was clear that it was Maddalone's bad
luck that he faced Fury on the top of his form. He was all
movement from the start, using his long reach advantage
to jab at Maddalone's head to set up his heavy power shots.
Reverting to the traditional right-handed stance, he delivered a
couple of heavy punches in round 1 that stunned an opponent
who was outclassed from the beginning. Working behind
his left jab, Fury threw some impressive combinations as his
movement and speed proved too much for the thirty-eight-
year-old. There were few wasted punches as he punished
the body as well as the head. Whenever Maddalone came
in, he was met by an uppercut, or Fury got him in a clinch.
Vinny got a battering. In round 4, Fury opened a cut under
his left eye. Then, 1 min 35 sec into round 5, referee Ian John
Lewis stepped in as blood streamed from the cut. No one was
complaining about this stoppage.

'I knew it was a matter of time. I actually called the referee over, he was taking some big shots,' Fury said. 'I'm still undefeated. I would like to say I'm ready for anyone in the world. Klitschkos: bring them on. Americans: bring them on.'

After the fight, Fury named who he thought should be brought on as his next opponent. 'Bring on Tomasz Adamek. He's too small for me and I see an early win for me,' he said. The Polish former cruiserweight champion was six-foot-two, with a reach of seventy-five inches, against Fury's eighty-five inches. He was also eight years older than Fury, but had gone ten rounds with Vitali Klitschko the previous September. Nevertheless, Fury said, 'I would eat him up. But I would also like to fight either of the Klitschkos and I am ready for them now. If my promoter Mick Hennessy puts me in there with anyone in the world I would beat them – and that includes the Klitschkos. They have had their time. I am twenty-three years old and I am only going to get better. This is just a small sign of things to come.'

He also thanked the people of Bristol for their support. 'Fighting in Bristol has been fantastic,' he said. 'This is the first time I've been here and the people have been brilliant to me. I told them I will be back one day with a world championship belt to show them.'

Meanwhile, Mick Hennessy was fielding questions on when a Klitschko fight was on the cards. 'Two, maybe three fights away,' he said. 'We'll go into that fight when he's ready to do a number on them . . . it's getting closer. We're still one fight at a time. He's twenty-three. To pull off a result like that tonight was unbelievable. It was a masterclass in heavyweight boxing. Did you see that jab? It was like a Larry Holmes jab. I'm liking Adamek next, either here or in the US.'

There were other contenders. On 13 October, Fury was at the Echo Arena in Liverpool when David Price knocked out Audley Harrison 82 sec into round 1. Fury told Channel 5, 'To be honest, Harrison's the biggest bum inside boxing. And my reaction to David Price and Frank Maloney calling me out [Maloney had said that he wanted Fury to take on Price], that midget – yeah? I'll fight David Price any day of the week. See you, you plumber from Liverpool, it's personal between me and you and I'm gonna do you some serious damage you big stiff idiot!' He also averred that he would fight Liverpool light heavyweight Tony Bellew, who he alleged was Price's 'gay lover', between rounds.

Price was taken aback at Fury's vitriol. 'He's round the bend,' he said. 'I don't know what to make of that. He cannot handle other people getting praise and credit and that's why he spat his dummy out on TV and made an absolute fool of himself by the sound of it.'

Fury doubled down a few days later with a tweet aimed directly at Price, saying, 'I'm gonna smash your face in u shithouse scouse prick I look in your eyes and c fear! Ill take your sole and give it the devil.'

Fury was called in front of the board for this rant and fined £3,000. But he was not entirely repentant. 'People like outspoken people and I am outspoken,' he said. 'But when you are getting hit for three grand, it's time to maybe quieten down a bit. The board has been more than lenient with me and it was a hefty fine that I will take on the chin.'

A week after the Fury–Maddalone fight, Haye faced Chisora at Upton Park. Fury was backing Haye. 'I see Haye winning on points,' he said. 'Chisora has a decent chance but it depends if Haye comes for a fight or not. That is not the strategy he needs to take into the ring. As long as Haye comes to box and not go toe-to-toe, he will beat Chisora comfortably.' Though Fury respected Chisora, he had no fear of a rematch. 'Chisora has to hit you with five, six, seven shots in a row before he hurts you, before the ref is forced to jump in and stop the fight. Chisora is good when fighting at close range and I expect it to be another cagey fight like the one against Klitschko.'

Refering to the brawl at the press conference between Haye and Chisora in February, Fury said he believed that controversy helped fighters to get noticed and he did not mind his rivals stealing the headlines. 'Good luck to them,' said Fury. 'To achieve anything in boxing you have to work very hard. I hope they make as much money as they can, they deserve every penny. Sometimes you need to do something outrageous to make everyone take notice, but it is not like they were nobodies before that brawl in Munich. Since he lost to me, Dereck has done very well. He lost to Robert Helenius for the European title, which I felt he won, then gave Vitali Klitschko his toughest fight in years.'

Nevertheless, Fury said that he did a better job on Chisora that Vitali had. 'I think that I could get a Klitschko brother now, but that is not part of the plan and when I get my chance I want to win. I'm not in the boxing business to make up the numbers and just be another loser on the Klitschkos' record – when I get my chance I will win it and keep it.'

Fury said he had no intention of facing the winner of the Upton Park fight. He had his sights set on higher things. 'Haye blew it, then complained about his toe against Wladimir, while Chisora was a competitive loser against Vitali. They have had their chance. They are losers and it's my time to shine now. I'm the leading heavyweight in Britain by a mile. I've fought the best opponents compared to the other British heavyweights. Their fight might get a lot of interest but it could be a stinker because if Haye doesn't come to fight, it will be awful. But I'm not interested in fighting them. I fought Chisora and beat him a year ago anyway. If Haye wins he will try to get a Klitschko fight but it will be me who fights one of them next. Vitali is probably going to retire anyway after September and his brother says he won't fight again.'

Wladimir was running out of people to beat up after stopping American Tony Thompson with a knockout in round 11 on the same day Fury fought Maddalone. 'I'm not interested in taking a payday against Klitschko and I've got a year until that. I'll take the fight when it's right. I'm on my time, not his. I won't be rushed and I've got a long time left. I've got a lot of learning to do and I want big fights, but they take time to happen so it's going to take a while to set up. Wladimir needs new challengers badly, but when it's my time and not before. He can carry on having easy fights until then.' Fury was not fussy about who he faced next. 'I would take on anyone in the Top 10. It doesn't matter who they are. This is my time now. I am ready for any challenge Mick Hennessy can throw at me. The Klitschkos are the ultimate aim, and winning the world title, but if it has to be someone else to get me a shot at them beforehand, then I would take that.'

It would not be David Price though. Fury thought it would be too big a clash for the Lonsdale belt. 'I can see it happening, but it is another fight that I've got nothing to gain from. What will I gain from beating him? Nothing. If one of us won the world title, then it would be a good defence. I don't think it should be wasted on the British title. It deserves to be a big title fight. Let him build up his record and one day it will happen.'

In the end, Haye did 'come to fight' at Upton Park. The fight was stopped in round 5 after Chisora had hit the canvas twice. The bout had been billed as 'Licensed To Thrill'. Fury clearly thought the title was misplaced and he knew who was the man to fulfil it. 'I keep hearing people claim that the heavyweight division is dead and I just want to let the world know that it is not,' he said. 'I'm here and I will bring it back to life.'

With his Uncle Peter as his trainer, Fury felt he was primed to be the dominant force in the heavyweight division. 'Whatever happens, I will have a new era of my own. I will rule the division. Price, Haye, Chisora – there is no outstanding British heavyweight. They are all beatable.'

When he became, as he believed he would, the mandatory challenger for their world titles, he wanted to take on the Klitschkos. Until then, he was satisfied with his progress. 'When I sit down and think of the things I've achieved, I've done everything I wanted to do. I won the English title, became the youngest ever British champion, won the

Commonwealth title and did the clean sweep with the Irish title. 'I've not done badly for a fat slob who can't fight.'

Wladimir Klitschko said he was ready to take on Fury. 'I think we could end up fighting very soon, probably next year,' he told Channel 5. 'I doubt it's going to happen this year but probably next year. I think he will make a lot of problems for a lot of guys and from fight to fight he's just going to get better.'

And Fury was convinced he could beat the thirty-six-year-old Ukrainian. 'I think I can win because Wladimir Klitschko hasn't fought anyone like me in his whole career,' he said. 'He hasn't fought anybody the size of me, the way I fight, the ambition I bring, the youth, the power and the determination. There's never been anybody like me before. I'm unique. The only thing he's got on me is experience and having lots of big-time fights. When I get the experience, and with another few fights I should be ready to take on anybody, I think it will be another matter completely.'

On 1 December 2012, Fury returned to Belfast for a WBC heavyweight title eliminator against the thirty-three-year-old American Kevin 'Kingpin' Johnson. It was Fury's third fight of the year. Johnson was a veteran of forty-six fights – with thirty-three wins, seventeen by knockout. He had gone the distance with Vitali Klitschko in 2009. 'Johnson is just the kind of opponent that I want at this stage of my career. We needed a world-class fighter and we have got one and when I take him apart the world will sit up and take notice,' Fury explained.

'I'm not going around getting opponents out of graveyards, fighting guys well past their best like some other heavyweights in Britain. I'm taking on Kevin Johnson, who has fought for a major world title and been the distance with Vitali Klitschko. I am getting closer to a shot at Klitschko myself and I'm going to show Vitali why he has to fight me because when I do a number on Johnson and get him out of there, I'll have done a better job than Vitali did on him. I'm really looking forward to fighting again in Belfast; the support I get there is great and to bring such a big fight there is terrific for the fans. Johnson is going to be tough, he's a hard man, but I'll be in the best shape of my life. The fans can expect fireworks, that's for sure.'

Johnson said that Fury could put the gags away as the joke was going to be on him. 'Tyson is a hell of a fighter but he's never seen anything like the Kingpin up close,' he said. 'I'm on a mission to claim the heavyweight title and Tyson Fury is in my way. It's going to be a short night.' He was confident that beating Fury would cause him no problems. 'I'll beat Fury so bad he'll want to retire, everyone will see that on 1 December in Belfast. Fury's just not in my class.'

He would win thanks to former world heavyweight champion Larry Holmes: 'I learnt from the best working with Holmes at the start of my career. He's a boxing legend and he taught me everything I know – he taught me all the things that Fury wishes he knew. It was a real boxing education working with Larry. He did it all in the ring. So I know that I have the tools to beat Fury, no doubt.'

Peter Fury had every confidence in his nephew – though the fight would be another step up. 'Johnson is a world-class fighter. This is no longer domestic-level fighters. He's a couple of steps up from anyone Tyson has ever fought before,' he said. 'He's a strong guy with his own world title aspirations so Tyson has to be ready for a hard night. And we're looking forward to going to Belfast, the fans there have always given Tyson a great reception. And they are going to see a great fight between two world-class heavyweights with Tyson coming out on top.

'Tyson couldn't be in better shape. He has had great sparring and I think a lot of people are going to be shocked by just how good he looks and the performance he gives. It's going to be a world-class performance and every other fighter in the heavyweight division will see that. I have been very pleased with the way Tyson has dedicated himself and after beating Johnson he will be ready for Vitali or Wladimir Klitschko or anyone else for that matter. Next year is going to be a huge year for Tyson. He's the best heavyweight in the world right now.'

Tyson was so confident that he looked past the Johnson fight. 'After Johnson we are going to Wladimir straight away,' he said. 'We're not messing around with anyone else – there's no one else in the division to challenge me. I don't want to fight showcases or any other idiots in the division – it's Wladimir or nobody. We've made contact and Wladimir has said we can do the fight whenever. I read he might be fighting Alexander Povetkin in early 2013, so we'll be looking to take him after that, maybe April, May or June. I want it as soon as possible because I'm in tremendous shape and mark these words now – I will beat Wladimir Klitschko for sure.

'I will go to Germany to do it – Hamburg or Berlin,

wherever he wants it, he can have it. I want to be a total underdog, I don't want anything on my side. I'm going to go over there and I'm going to wreck him. And I'm not David Haye speaking, who goes in and doesn't try – I'm going to give it everything. I've no interest in fighting his brother, Vitali. He's an old man, he's finished. I'll leave that to the likes of Haye. I want to fight the No. 1 in the heavyweight division and that's Wladimir. Why fight for one belt when I can fight for all of them? I'm not going to get in any better shape. I'm the fittest I've ever been or am ever going to be. Wladimir's in trouble once I get through with Johnson.' Fury said he would win because he was unique. 'There has never been a fighter like me. There hasn't been a six-foot-nine heavyweight who can move with the speed I've got and angles I give off. If they're six-foot-nine they're slow as hell. It's my time. I'm going to deal with Johnson and I'm going to deal with Wladimir, no problem.'

With five days to go, Fury was seen to be chilled out, relaxing in his Belfast hotel, and said he was going to give Johnson a masterclass in fighting that Saturday night. 'He's slick and a tough customer but we have a game plan and we are going to put it all together on Saturday night,' he said. 'And I will tell you one thing. Johnson is in deep water. He can talk a lot, he thinks he can talk a good fight but I am going to rip him apart on Saturday night. I am well up for this one. I am not going to let myself down. I am not going to let my family down. I am not going to let my team down. And there is no way I am going to let some Yank fly in and beat me in a big fight. He will be destroyed on Saturday night. He is flying in to upset the applecart, but this applecart will take some turning over. There is no way an American like Johnson could turn me over. I hope he has trained hard because if he hasn't he is going to be in trouble. I hope he has an army with him because he will need that to stop me on Saturday night.'

Fury then said he was not thinking of anyone else apart from Johnson. 'I am not interested in sending out any messages. I just want to win this fight and then I am going to take Christmas off and enjoy it. I am not interested in calling anyone out. I want Wladimir – he has to fight me. I am the WBC's No. 1 ranked challenger, so he has to fight me. He is the one I want, but I am totally focused on Johnson. That is all I am thinking about.'

Fury's training had been particularly rigorous. Previously his weight and fitness had been hit-and-miss. Now he had got his weight and conditioning under control, with his body fat now down to 8.2 per cent. For the past few months, he had knuckled down. He told his fans, 'You will see a good-looking and sexy Tyson Fury. The camp has been absolutely brilliant and I am doing things I have never done before. I have been training non-stop since January, so I have been doing this nearly a year. I have put my heart and soul into it and I have trained right, my diet is right, my weights programme is right. I have done everything right and I have been sparring for a long time as well. I am in the best shape of my life.'

Fury admitted he may not have focused on training as much as he should have in the past. 'To be honest, I never did weights or things like that,' he said, 'but I have really been concentrating on my conditioning and my strength work.

I am lifting 250 kilos from the floor and I am doing things that I thought I would never be able to do. My maximum bench press in the past was 110 kilos but I am now doing 140. Everything has improved loads and I am strong, I am fit and I am ready to go on Saturday. And if Johnson hasn't trained the way he should have, he is going to be in some serious trouble.'

And he had a Christmas present for his fans: 'Everybody is starting to get ready for their Christmas parties and in Belfast at the Odyssey Arena my fans are going to have the ultimate party – they'll see a great fight and then go out and party knowing they've just seen the future heavyweight champion of the world. This is a huge fight for me, it's going to be a fight to the finish. I think Johnson and I are going to take each other to the limits because we're both world-class. There's going to be no quarter asked, we're both going to be landing big bombs.'

Although Fury said he was concentrating on the Johnson fight, he had already been putting out feelers for future contests. The matter was complicated by the fact that Vitali Klitschko was standing for election to the Ukrainian parliament. Promoter Mick Hennessy said, 'I've spoken to [Klitschko manager] Bernd Boente a few times now about fighting Wladimir. We were waiting for the Vitali situation to be resolved with the elections and he's going to make a decision about carrying on in December. There's also the option to do a fight with Wladimir and it depends on what Vitali is going to do. The fight with Wladimir will be a stadium fight and we would be looking to do it in May,

June or July. Germany would be the favourite place for it to happen, but I've spoken to them about Old Trafford or Croke Park. They are businessmen and we know that it would sell out. They would prefer to work with us rather than any other candidates.'

Hennessy also insisted Fury was willing to face British champion David Price – if the money was right. 'We asked David Price to step forward,' he said, 'but because Tyson is ahead of him in terms of world ranking and profile, it wouldn't be a 50/50 deal. If he was prepared to be sensible, we could do a sensible deal and that fight would happen.'

The Hennessy Sports boss also said, 'Tyson is the future of the heavyweight division and the fans watching live on Channel 5 and those in the Odyssey Arena in Belfast are going to see that on Saturday night. The WBC have confirmed that the fight is an official world-title eliminator, which is great news for Tyson. David Haye is messing around in the jungle. David Price is fighting the elderly while Tyson is getting on with being the real deal in the heavyweight division. He's already shown that he's the best in Britain and when he beats Johnson he'll prove that he's ready to go on and rule the heavyweight division in 2013. If Tyson does what I believe he's going to do on Saturday night, Tyson will be ready for the world title. Tyson has come a long way over the past twelve months. His coach Peter Fury has transformed him into the ultimate fighting machine and come next year nobody will stand in his way.'

Johnson could not be dismissed though. 'Johnson is a very awkward, tough fighter who proved his worth when he went the distance with Vitali Klitschko. For Tyson this is by far the biggest test of his career,' said Hennessy.

Johnson, then being trained by Floyd Mayweather's uncle Jeff Mayweather, insisted that he was not just there to make up the numbers. 'I'll beat Fury so bad he'll want to retire. Fury's just not in my class,' he said. 'I have learnt a lot from the Klitschko fight. There were mistakes I made in that fight but I am the better man for it and I will get another world title fight. When I beat Fury that should put me back in the frame for another world title shot. I've been like a lot of American fighters recently who have been on the outside of the world heavyweight scene, but when I beat Fury that will change. Fury's a good fighter, he's done well, but I'll take him to school in Belfast. I am the professor and he is the student and I will win on Saturday night at the Odyssey in front of the Belfast fans.'

Fury and Johnson traded insults at the pre-fight press conference on 27 November. First, Tyson picked on the American's colourful attire. 'I can see he's a very classy guy by the way he's dressed for the press conference. You can see he's oozing in class,' said Fury. 'And I've trained very hard for this fight but everyone knows what Kevin Johnson is going to do. He's gonna come here, put up a good fight, go home a happy loser with a big pay cheque.' Fury dismissed Johnson as 'a bum' and was determined to put the contender in his place. 'Listen, this is The Tyson Fury Show. This mug is part of the game. I'm going to take over this fool, take whatever he's got to bring to the table, and move on to the next level. I am going to be the first Irish heavyweight champion of the world. I'm the greatest heavyweight since Lennox Lewis. This mug is not going to take me anywhere. This mug is in serious trouble because I have been to hell and back in my training camp. His trainer, Jeff Mayweather, had a lot to say in the newspaper – that I'm slow, methodical, predictable – that I'm not going to be a super world champion. He's going to have to eat his words on Saturday because I want an official apology after his man is smashed to bits. What more can I say?'

Later Mayweather himself was more conciliatory, saying, 'I met Tyson and he's an OK guy. He's not the asshole that I thought after listening to him on the radio. But he's beyond realistic if he thinks he can challenge a Klitschko. He has no chance at all. This guy is big and clumsy – those are athletes. He just happens to be a big guy that's involved in boxing. I don't fear him at all. He's a big guy and that's always something you gotta worry about. Kevin's the guy for it because he's the best defensive heavyweight there is. He has one of the best jabs in the heavyweight division.'

Kingpin Johnson was a man not lost for words and began by having a pop at Fury's promoter Mick Hennessy. 'Just like Hennessy said – I like to call him by his last name Hennessy because it'll be a beautiful celebration with a glass of that – there's a lot of guys who wouldn't take this fight,' he said. 'But that's not because they say Fury is something dangerous. It's just a lot of heavyweights don't want to fight up to the level of their opposition. I've never once run from anybody and this is all I asked for – give me my level of opposition. Let me face off with a report card that's gonna come out to be an A. I applaud that man – a lot of people wouldn't take a fight with me. Not one Top 10 heavyweight would ever fight me over the last few years. Why? Because I'm one of the most feared heavyweights out there – not an easy walk in the park. I've been working on a closed casket. I don't know what he's been working on but I bet he's got the same funeral plans for me. So let's see who ends up in the casket. Because one of us is going to be laid the hell out. But it damn sure ain't gonna be me, 'cos Jeff didn't bring no flowers. Ain't nobody gonna be singing for me. So, Hennessy – hope you got the champagne and I hope you got the 1738 VSOP Hennessy, baby, 'cos we gonna celebrate.'

Mayweather added, 'We're here to win the fight. Kevin likes to talk – Tyson likes to talk. To be honest, that's how I first heard of Tyson Fury. He was on some radio interview, bragging, talking about what he was going to do to this person. Then I got the chance to watch him for myself. I wasn't impressed at all.'

Tyson upped the insults, too. 'I'm the best heavyweight in the world. I'll prove that against anybody. This fool's an idiot, he's gonna get smashed to bits,' he said. 'Kevin Johnson is a fat pudding and is a slow fighter who throws a few punches a round and tries to old-man his opponents. I will cut him in half with one of the body shots I have been working on. If he comes for a fight, it's Christmas come early for me. I'm not here to dance or play possum on the ropes. I'm here to fight. I'm going to give it to him proper and he's going to go home sick as a pig. He's got a great big head so how am I going to miss that? He looks like Chubby Checker and after this I want Wladimir Klitschko next. He's going to go home a happy loser with a pay cheque whereas I'm going to move on to the next level. I'm the greatest heavyweight since Lennox Lewis and I'm just happy someone has finally grown a pair and agreed to fight me. He's going to have to eat his words on Saturday after he is smashed to bits and I want an official apology after what he has been saying about me.'

Fury made it clear he intended to step over Johnson. 'Whatever Vitali decides to do I will fight for the vacant title against the winner of Chris Arreola and Bermane Stiverne, or I will go and fight Wladimir next summer.'

Johnson had gone the distance with Vitali Klitschko in his world title shot three years earlier, he had lost every round against the six-foot-seven-inch champion. He suffered a second career defeat on points to Tor Hamer in the Prizefighter tournament final in June. But he shrugged off the six-inch height difference with Fury and the three-inch difference in reach. 'How is Tyson Fury going to dominate me? He's only got a few inches' reach on me, but I use my reach better than him. He could have fought after this but after getting his ass whipped by what I'm going to do, he will never be heard of again. He will be a nobody.'

This was water off a duck's back for Fury. 'I have never needed any motivation to step on to the canvas anyway and I certainly don't need it now,' he said. 'Johnson is a top-level fighter and will bring out the best in me. I cannot wait to knock him out and show that I am the future of the heavyweight division.'

But Johnson was eager to continue the war of words. 'I am going to send Fury into retirement. He is going to find out what it is like to be hit by a proper heavyweight contender and someone who can take whatever he throws at me. Fury has knocked over some deadbeats but he took the fight with me and now he is going to pay. He will be knocked out.'

Still undefeated, Fury refused to be drawn. 'I've no doubt Johnson is my hardest opponent to date, but my dream has always been to become world heavyweight champion and eventually you have to face the best in order to achieve that,' he said. 'I feel like I have been ready to fight for the world title for years now but boxing is about education and learning and I now believe I am ready. I have battled my way through some decent tests so far and always come out the other side, so now everything is geared towards fighting for the world title and winning it. Being world champion is not a question of if, but when.'

He also heaped praise on Uncle Peter. 'I look at the shape I used to be and I'm embarrassed about it now,' said Fury. 'I now look every inch a proper fighter and the work I have done in the gym with Peter has been the reason for that. I look after myself in and out of the ring and I know I am now ready for anything.' The rigorous training had helped him get over the depression that he said had afflicted him and his brothers. 'I'm all over that now. The depression I was going through was because I was not training enough. I didn't know how to make it better. It has gone now, I've got a better camp. I don't think I have anything like that any more. I don't know anyone in life that doesn't have days where they go, "This is shit." I'm no different.'

However, for the last three fights, he had taken his training seriously. 'I consider myself a three-fight novice now. I say that as those are the only fights I prepared properly for. I've been in camp for most of the last eighteen months. I've totally given up my life for this. Before, I was fat and unfit. There were times in those fights I could have given in but the only way someone will find me giving up is if I'm nailed to the canvas.'

He missed his old mentor, Emanuel Steward, who had died in October, but his faith helped keep the demons away. 'I'm not the best Christian but I believe that if you've done wrong, you can ask for forgiveness,' he admitted. Fury said he found salvation staying in a small log cabin in Essen, Germany, away from his wife and two children. He was at peace, surrounded by greenery and tall pines, three miles away from anything that might distract him. 'There's nothing out there, it's perfect. You just sleep, eat or train, that's it. It'd be a lovely relaxing spot if I wasn't preparing for a big fight.'

It was a rare thing for Tyson to be away from his family. Paris and the children usually accompanied him to the training camp. 'Tyson always wants me to go with him, but this time I have stayed home so he can concentrate and I can sort out all the jobs that need doing.' They were apart for six weeks. 'This is one of the longest periods I have gone without seeing Tyson but he needs to prepare for the fight.'

Otherwise Paris loved to be on her husband's arm when he was invited to parties and premieres, but did not deliberately seek out the limelight and was not a wannabe WAG. 'My friends joke and say I could be a BAG instead of a WAG!' she said. 'When Tyson is being interviewed and photographed and getting all the adulation, I just stand back and don't push myself into the limelight. It is Tyson's place. He has earned the right to have that profile.'

She also wanted more children. 'I would love a big family. 'My granny had eight kids and I would absolutely love to have that many and Tyson is a great dad.'

With two days to go to the fight, Fury complained in the *Manchester Evening News* that he was not getting the support of people from his own hometown. 'I'm a Manchester person but Manchester fans have not got behind me,' he said. 'Why not? I'm boxing in Belfast and they come out to watch me. I can't fight in Manchester. I sell about twelve hundred tickets there, whereas I can sell five thousand in Belfast.' He said his brother had asked him why he always kept fighting abroad. 'I explained that when I fought at EventCity [Trafford Park], we had a big press conference, a public workout and it didn't work. There is no one else in Manchester at my level. I'm No. 3 in the world, unbeaten. I can talk the talk and I can fight but they are not interested. Maybe they want someone who is a good loser, who puts up a decent show. But if they want a good fighter, then I'm that person. I'd love to sell out twenty thousand at the Manchester Arena but I don't see it happening. People don't seem to be showing an interest. I've got to fight in other locations – places like Somerset, where the place was buzzing. My fights are always exciting. I've stopped fourteen out of nineteen opponents.'

He pointed out that David Price got the support of the people of Liverpool. Merseyside fans were always on Fury's back on Twitter. 'You look at David Price and people are getting behind him,' he said. 'I get all of this abuse from

Liverpool because they are behind him. I don't know what more I've got to do to get Manchester behind me. I don't mind being the villain. It's a big fight down the line and someone has got to be the outlaw.'

Fury complained that he had not had the praise he deserved for winning the English, Irish, British and Commonwealth titles in a career that had yet to reach twenty fights. Even his comprehensive points win over Dereck Chisora the previous year had gone largely unnoticed in his hometown. 'It doesn't matter what I do or who I beat,' he said. 'I could beat a guy who has won fifty fights but afterwards everyone would say he's rubbish. People say Chisora was out of shape and didn't take it seriously. My achievement doesn't mean anything. If Tyson Fury beats him then he's obviously no good. That Chisora win doesn't mean anything to me.'

Price said he would not be watching the Fury–Johnson fight, having accepted an invitation to attend a local amateur show. This was his response to Fury's outburst on Channel 5 when Price knocked out Audley Harrison. Fury had been so vitriolic it had to be cut short by the producers. Price claimed he was saving his repost for the ring. 'It's always fun to watch someone make a fool of themselves,' Price said. 'It's a fight that will happen some day, but not too soon, so the more he shouts his mouth off the better. It's great to have a big domestic rival. He's great for me and I'm great for him.'

Fury, meanwhile, was still hyping the Johnson fight as the biggest of his career. 'It's a big step up for me but there's no way he'll win,' said Fury. 'He won't have seen combinations like mine or had anyone work the body like I do. He has had his time at thirty-three.' Having seen Wladimir beat Mariusz Wach on points earlier that month, Fury said he believed Johnson was the tougher obstacle. 'Look at his face after that fight – he'd hardly got hit and he looked like he'd taken a beating. So just wait until someone hits him properly.'

Uncle Peter also thought Johnson was a difficult opponent. 'He's an awkward customer,' Peter Fury said. 'He's hard to hit and goes into a kind of survival mode in most of his fights. It makes it very hard to get him out of there, which is what Vitali Klitschko found. Johnson's a world-class fighter but we're looking to make an example out of him, which no one else has done.'

However, Johnson hadn't been Hennessy's first choice of opponent. A host of names turned down the fight, including the undefeated Russian Denis Boytsov who had looked set for a clash at one point. Peter Fury: 'Tyson's got all the ability. He's got great speed and ability for a heavyweight and people don't want to get in the ring with him because they know they're taking a big risk. People in the fight trade know how good Tyson is. Denis Boytsov said he needed more time to prepare and Ruslan Chagaev said Tyson was one of the best fighters in the world and didn't want to take it with six to eight weeks' notice. Tomasz Adamek priced himself out of the fight deliberately, Alexander Dimitrenko turned us down, Michael Grant turned us down and Tor Hamer, the first person we went to, turned it down as well. No one can say Tyson is avoiding anyone. Tyson is ready for anyone in the world, which is maybe why we've had problems trying to make this fight.'

In the past, Fury had been criticised for his lack of preparation for his fights, but Uncle Peter said people had to remember that he was still a comparative novice. The WBO intercontinental champion was still only twenty-four. 'He's only fought twice this year but we've been working on developing him into a man,' he said. 'He's had learning fights and was getting hurt but he was only twenty-two and twenty-three and also has experience of going ten or twelve rounds when not being in the best shape. But that's all in the past now. He's grown up properly and is a proper athlete. I'm very excited about the future.'

Controlling Fury's weight was key. 'I think he is the whole package now, as he has got himself into fantastic shape,' said Peter Fury. 'We got his weight down for the Martin Rogan fight and then the Vinny Maddalone fight and he is now 17 st 10 lbs for this fight. He is very powerful at this weight. He is ready and he can do twelve rounds at any kind of pace. He is ready and you have to remember Tyson is a mover, he uses his jab, he's on his toes, his foot speed is very good and to be that kind of fighter you have to be really fit. Before, when he was not in the shape he is now, he was flat-footed, he was a static fighter and that is not what he is good at. He is now in tremendous shape to perform the way we know he can.'

But Johnson's trainer Jeff Mayweather was also confident. 'As long as there is no home-cooking, if it goes to points, hopefully, we get a fair decision,' he said. 'But as far as skill sets go, they are two different levels – and Johnson is way ahead. Wladimir and Vitali Klitschko are the No. 1 and 2 in the world – it's not this guy. And Kevin has faced the best so all he has to do is to turn up and perform.'

By the eve of the fight, Johnson was confident: 'My thoughts on the fight were over ten days ago. Thinking was done ten days ago, preparation was done ten days ago,' he said. 'Heavyweight world champion Larry Holmes said if you don't have it ten days before a fight – it's over, done, finished. I'm not ready, I'm more than ready to face Fury. On your marks, get set, let's go, give them a show. I am going to annihilate, assassinate and take out any opponent who stands in front of me now. People in Belfast can expect to see the big tree fall down – the end.'

Fury had also given up the war of words by then. 'It's going to be an exciting fight, Kevin Johnson is an exciting man and an entertainer,' he said. 'I had the best fun ever at the press conference on Wednesday and I am looking forward to the fight now. Everything has gone well in preparation and I am up for Saturday night. I am in the best shape of my life and I am up for this one, one hundred per cent.'

To get to Klitschko, he knew he had to get Johnson out of the way first. Echoing his uncle, Peter Fury, he said, 'He is an awkward customer. I may have to kick him in the leg or something to win the fight – but I will win this fight.' He admitted his failings in previous bouts. 'In the past I haven't always been in great shape. Actually, I've been in terrible shape, I'll say that myself. All boxers need to do weights, diet, it's all conditioning work. But to be a great athlete you need to be physically superb – and I am in superb shape now. I'm 8.2 per cent body fat, muscle mass is 109 kilos, body weight is 112 kilos. I couldn't be in any better shape than I'm in.'

Under Uncle Peter, Fury had shed nearly 6 stone since January, when he had been grossly overweight. Peter claimed Fury's lack of self-esteem, depression and weight problems were all linked to not training properly. 'When I started working with him, he was over 23.5 stone,' he said. 'The problem was he had no confidence because he knew he was doing the wrong things in training, but didn't know what the right things were. He was feeling tired in fights, so that's where the depression came from – and on it went. We went back to basics and we have seen a total transformation in Tyson. He can box for every minute of every round, he feels good, the mental side is better and we are looking at a hundred per cent improvement.'

Fury was reconciled to the forthcoming fight being savage. He told *Seconds Out*, 'I don't think boxing is a sport. How is going in there and getting your face smashed in a sport? That's not a sport. Boxing is a brutal thing. You're going in there to smash somebody to pieces. It's taking bread out of your family's mouth. I'm going in there to do damage. I'm going in there to fight, not to go, "Oh, I'm a good sportsman." If this is a sport, this is a bad, bad, bad sport. Fighting isn't a sport – fighting is what you do when you don't like somebody. It's nothing to do with a sport.

'If it's a sport it's got to be the hardest, most horrible sport in the world because I don't know any other sportsmen who have to do things where you're going to get set about to get forward in life. That ain't sport to me. Sport to me is going out for a game of golf. You're not going to get done in.'

Boxing was a serious business. 'My job isn't nine to five – it's fucking eight in the morning until the next day, every day – twenty-four seven, 365 days a year. That's a funny old sport. People who want to say this is a sport must be stupid. This is a shrewd business. I'm fighting out there. I ain't fighting for a cup or a belt. I'm fighting to make my family have a better future, and to make my name go down in history – nothing to do with my sport. People can say what they want – I'm there to destroy.'

As for Johnson, Fury said, 'I'm not going in there to make a statement by looking to knock him out. He's never been stopped, Vitali Klitschko couldn't stop him. I've watched his performances on Prizefighter and I thought he lost his second fight, let alone the final. But I'm not reading anything into that. I just want to get in the ring and box well behind my jab and whatever happens, happens.'

But Fury could not help himself. 'I'm not interested in making any statement against Johnson – Tyson Fury is already a statement in himself. I'm not going in there to try and take him out with big shots from the first bell. I'm going to box to my usual best and I'm not looking to knock anyone out. I'm not going in there to try and take him out with big shots from the first bell. I'm going to box to my usual best and I'm not looking to knock anyone out. I'm looking to box sensible, and set traps against a clever, awkward, defensively minded, world-class opponent. This is my world title fight on the line. If I slip up, I lose everything. I'm not here to dance or play possum on the ropes, I'm here to fight. I'm going to give it to him proper and he's going to go home as sick as a pig.'

Fury also dismissed his own assessment of Johnson's performance in Prizefighter. He said, 'He's not a Prizefighter three-round fighter. He doesn't start for three or four rounds, so his performances in Prizefighter mean nothing.'

Meanwhile, Johnson was still saying of Fury, 'I'm going to crack his ass.' But then he began to show a little more respect towards his opponent. 'One thing I like about Irish fighters is they got a lot of heart and they got a lot of mouth,' he said. 'With American fighters – and there are only about two of us left in the game – we're very artistic and we're very hard to dominate. That's the hardest thing for Fury in this fight. How in the hell is he going to dominate me in any way possible? The stuff I'm gonna do? It ain't even been heard of.'

In the run-up to the fight, Fury said there had been nothing to compare with his arrest for armed robbery before the Maddalone bout. 'There has been nothing anywhere nearly as exciting this time,' said Fury. 'Well, there was the naked jogging, er, first thing in the morning.' In order to lighten up his training, Tyson and his uncle took their clothes off one morning and went for a run. 'Imagine what the neighbours would have thought of that,' said Fury. 'Fortunately, where we train is in the middle of a dense forest so I don't think we were spotted. It was just done as a joke. It was very funny.'

Then there was a snowball fight. 'It was actually fake snow,' said Fury's promoter Mick Hennessy. 'Tyson and Kevin Johnson did a photo session at the Kennedy shopping centre in Belfast where they had to go into Santa's grotto. It all got a bit out of hand when they both started throwing presents and snow at each other. It got a touch heated towards the end, but I think Tyson won that one.'

While in the pre-fight banter fans had seen the old Fury that they knew and loved, in the ring they saw a new Tyson. He began by dominating the first rounds with combinations set up by his jab, as usual. But this time his game plan was different. Usually he would keep up the pace until he knocked his man out, or was rocked himself. This time he was in no hurry to go in for the kill.

Despite his pre-fight bluster Johnson had taken the fight at three weeks' notice and was not in the best of shape. He abandoned the offence and seemed to have his eyes set on survival, rather then threatening his opponent. Fury moved for the entire fight, refusing to be drawn in and caught in exchanges. He dropped the pace in the middle rounds, turning in a conservative, ultra-disciplined performance dictated by Uncle Peter from his corner. Fury circled the ring, picking Johnson off with jabs and occasional combinations. But Johnson was never in trouble and soaked up everything Fury threw at him.

Fury had a point deducted by referee Howard Foster in round 7, after hitting the cagey Johnson with a left hook after being told to break. He had been warned twice previously. The crowd were far from happy. They made their frustrations clear as early as round 4. They wanted the old Tyson the hellraiser, and by round 8 the booing started. The referee called the two fighters together at the start of the tenth and told them to step up the action, but still Johnson took no chances.

Fury didn't seem flustered by the negative crowd reaction

and continued to go about his work in a mature fashion, while Johnson took everything that was thrown at him, offering very little himself. Fury landed a stinging right hand towards the end of round 12, but it was not enough to stop Johnson and the fight went the full twelve rounds. Fury won with unanimous points decisions – 108–119, 108–199, 110–119.

'Credit to Kevin Johnson, he's a slippery guy,' said Fury. 'I never went in to knock him out, I boxed to a game plan. He's not a guy to go and smash up. I knew he was a world-class fighter who makes you miss and I vowed not to let my heart get to me; I knew that would be a war and I outboxed him.'

Fury said he was unconcerned with the boos they got from the crowd in the eighth and ninth rounds. 'Sometimes when you get two boxers, it is not an exciting fight but we had a job to do. We are here to win, end of story. We had a strategy and it worked. And credit to my uncle and trainer, Peter. He has turned me into a machine. I was a twenty-stone fighter and he has made me into an athlete. Look at my fitness tonight and the way I moved. I am really fit and that is down to Peter.'

Uncle Peter said, 'I think Tyson made a big statement tonight. I gave Kevin Johnson respect and if you stand in front of him he will give you problems. I knew we would not knock him out. We had a look at him and, after round 5, I told Tyson this guy is going nowhere. We wanted to soften him up and then take him out later – but we decided to box this guy because he was going nowhere.

'Tyson is going in the right direction – but there are things to work on. Nobody wants to fight Johnson because he is awkward and we totally boxed him. We are doing things properly and Tyson has all the tools. We all believe Tyson has the tools to go the whole way. This was another stepping stone and Tyson did what he had to do with some class.'

Johnson commented, 'Him and his team stuck to a smart game plan. He didn't come out and fight with anger, which I had planned to exploit. He kept boxing. This kid is long, very long – longer than what you think. Anyone who can beat me is close to a world title fight.' A good loser, Johnson exhibited renewed respect for Fury. 'He boxed and he did well and there were a couple of things that I could have done differently but it's no good complaining about that now. I was trying to lead him into a killer shot, but it was difficult to get him to walk into them. But he did something completely different in there, that I did not expect from him. His performance tonight I did not expect at all. I had to press the action – which is something I have never done before.

'He let his hands go and he landed some clean shots. But I expected that and I have one of the best chins in boxing, so I was not worried about him hurting me. I pressed him all night, but you can press and still lose as I did tonight. He brought in a new strategy to the ring tonight and stuck to that. If this fight had been a few months ago and he fought the way he did a few months ago, he would have fallen for a couple of booby traps that I had set for him. He created a couple of chances for himself, but it was only a couple of times. Will he become a world champion? He has a great chance.'

After the fight, Fury paid tribute to his old mentor, dedicating his win to Emanuel Steward 'because he said to me that I would be WBC champion within eighteen months. That was nearly eighteen months ago, so I'm one step away now.'

Fury said that Johnson had been a tricky fighter and explained his tactics. 'I am here to win and that is what I did tonight. I had a game plan tonight, I executed it perfectly and I am not a one-trick pony. And if you look at my last four fights I have had a different game plan every time. I fought southpaw, I switched, I stood and fought. I can box, I can fight, I can slip and slide and for this fight we looked at how he boxed and this guy is the most awkward guy in heavyweight boxing. No one can land shots on this guy and his best weapons are his eyes, he sees everything. When you load up on him, you can't get him and we looked at his defence and the way he fights and we thought, yes, we'll have a bit of that. The shoulder rolls, the right hand protecting the chin, and it was a beautiful game against a shorter fighter. But you can't do that against a bigger fighter. For someone like Vitali Klitschko you will see a completely different game plan – but you will have to wait and see what happens next.'

Although Fury believed the time was right to face the WBC champion, he ruled out that fight. 'Vitali is an old man. He is forty-two or forty-three years of age. He is not the same Vitali of five years ago,' said Fury. 'Anyone with a pair of eyes can see he is on the slide. Dereck Chisora pushed him hard. Manuel Childs landed shots on him. I bet you any money he will not fight me. He will hang his gloves up before he faces me in the ring. And here is a challenge to Vitali and his brother Wladimir – let's get it on.'

He issued the challenge from the ring.

'Vitali won't fight me, he's on the slide and he will not want to fight a twenty-four-year-old, six-foot-nine heavyweight who is on the way up. He isn't going to fight me and if he doesn't want to fight me, let his brother step-up and fight me.'

Viewers of Channel 5's coverage of the Fury–Johnson fight were then treated to the bizarre spectacle at the post-fight press conference – Johnson playing the piano while Fury serenaded him with Bette Midler's Grammy-award-winning 'Wind Beneath My Wings'. Despite all the bad words, the two fighters ended in harmony.

MADISON SQUARE GARDEN

With the scalp of another American under his belt, the canny move, business-wise was for Fury to increase his exposure on the other side of the Atlantic, where there was serious money to be made. But the twenty-four-year-old Tyson was eager to get on with his career in the ring.

'I want Vitali or Wladimir Klitschko,' said Fury. 'Forget about David Haye and David Price, they're not in my league. There's also no American left who could take on the Klitschkos so that just leaves me. I can fight, I can box, I do anything in the ring. Nobody can live with me and that includes the Klitschkos.'

But speculation about a match for Fury with Price continued after his second-round knockout of Matt Skelton on 30 November 2012, the night before Fury's defeat of Johnson, making him undefeated in fifteen bouts. Fury was not impressed. 'He beat a fifty-year-old fighter,' said Fury.

Skelton was forty-five. 'There is no comparison between my fight and David Price versus Matt Skelton. Johnson would beat Price, I have no doubts about that. This was a 50/50. Price versus Skelton was not a 50/50 fight. I did not see the fight but Price has not changed since the amateurs. He is a typical European fighter. They march forward, throw a one-two and a left hook. They push weights and bulk up. They come forward and throw big shots – that is all they do.

'Look there is a difference between a domestic-level fight and a world-class fighter. You can blow away some fat domestic-level fighter or one that is on steroids. But you cannot do that to a world-class fighter like Johnson. You have to set him up if he is a world-class fighter. There are miles of difference between a world-class fighter and a domestic-level fighter and you saw that here tonight.'

Nevertheless, Price wanted a shot. 'I was expecting more of Tyson Fury,' he said. 'I thought he was a fighting man, but he's proved me wrong again. He is a coward, no two ways about it.'

But Hennessy put the blame on Price. He told the *Daily Telegraph*, 'We asked David Price to step forward if he wants this fight because Tyson's in the driving seat. He was quite vocal after two of Tyson's fights. But when we've asked him to step forward now – lo and behold: nothing. What Tyson has said – and his entire team agrees – is that we would put a world title fight on hold for David Price if he stepped up to the table. We view Price as still a novice who hasn't really been tested yet. If he's prepared to be sensible, we'll do a proper deal and this fight would happen.'

Fury also dismissed David Haye as 'just a part-time boxer and full-time game show contestant desperate for publicity'. Meanwhile, he was having a Twitter battle with American Tony Thompson, who accused Fury of ducking a fight with him before the Johnson bout. Fury tweeted, 'He's shit, Hennessy offered him to us and we don't want grandads ESP with no chin tell the gutless twat that!!'

Thompson had been stopped after six rounds with Wladimir Klitschko in July 2012. Then, Thompson faced Price on 23 February 2013, knocking him to the canvas with a right behind the ear. Price beat the count, but was unsteady on his feet and the bout was waved off. Fury was uncharacteristically sympathetic. 'Price can get a world title chance,' he said. 'He has been badly knocked out, so he has got to dig deep into his soul and learn properly.' Thompson would stop Price again after five rounds in a rematch on 6 July, but already, for Fury, Price was no longer a contender. So he set sail for America.

On 20 April 2013, Fury was to make his US debut in the Madison Square Garden Theater, which has a capacity of 5,600 compared with the main auditorium and mecca of boxing, which holds over 20,000. Fury's opponent was to be two-time IBF cruiserweight title holder and former sailor Steve 'USS' Cunningham, who had eight world title fights behind him. However, the previous December he had lost to Tomasz Adamek in a split decision. Fury said, 'If I don't impress against this man, I will retire. I'm just too big for him.'

He tweeted, 'Coming to America to smash up some bitches New York New York!'

His fight had just one aim. 'It's to show the American people I'm the real deal and not just a joke,' Fury said. Cunningham certainly wasn't the opponent he would have picked. But the fight would be televised by NBC in the US and Channel 5 in the UK and the TV bosses were calling the shots. 'I only get the opponents nobody else wants to fight,' said Fury, who was then ranked No. 4 by the WBC and No. 6 by the WBO. 'They turned down Deontay Wilder, they turned down Bryant Jennings – TV turned them all down. They said the only ones you can fight are Tomasz Adamek or Cunningham, and Adamek wasn't willing.'

Nevertheless, the fight gave him the platform he needed. 'I'm looking to put on a devastating performance – the best of my career to date. I'm absolutely ecstatic to be fighting at Madison Square Garden. It goes back in history and I can't wait to put my name with a long list of champions who have fought there – I'm a historian of boxing myself so this is definitely the pinnacle of my career so far.'

Peter Fury said, 'Tyson wants to conquer the States. We know that is a place where he can do very good things – and to have Cunningham first is brilliant.' He was confident Tyson could do it. 'He gives his heart and soul in every fight. He has got the willpower and determination to succeed and that is an immense quality.'

Cunningham responded that Fury was a giant while he was a street fighter from the ghettos of Philadelphia. 'I'm looking forward to getting back in the ring on 20 April to face Fury. For the first time in my career I have a guy coming to my country to face me. I am certain he's never faced a fighter like me.'

Fury was not intimidated. At an acrimonious press conference in New York in March, Fury told Cunningham, 'This is going to be a three-hit fight. I hit you, you hit the floor, I hit New York.' He lamented the paucity of challengers. 'There's not another heavyweight on the planet who wants to step in the ring with me and that's why I'm giving Steve respect. Wladimir Klitschko doesn't want to fight me and I'm not even going to talk about Vitali because he's a pensioner. I don't want to fight him.' Pointing at Cunningham, he said, 'This guy has got no chance at all. Let's talk about talent, size, whatever you want. I'm the best fighter on the planet. There's not a man born from his mother who can beat Tyson Fury. I don't care if he is seven foot or three foot tall. Steve Cunningham's in big trouble. Come 20 April, this guy is getting knocked spark out. Guaranteed, a hundred per cent. Steve Cunningham, with the whole of Philadelphia behind him, couldn't beat me together. There have been a lot of fighters in the world that didn't want to fight Tyson Fury. You've got to give credit where credit is due. I haven't come here to play games and talk nonsense. I'm here to fight and I hope you're here to fight, too.'

Cunningham dismissed both Fury's banter and his ability. 'The guys who talk a lot are chumps,' he said. 'That's why I'm not going to talk. He can talk all he wants but that's not going to help him on 20 April. The only reason that this dude is winning fights is because he's big. Shrink him down to six-foot-two and six-foot-three or six-foot-four and he's garbage. One thing I can say about the Klitschko brothers, and I've been in camp with Wladimir, is they're big, they work hard, they're talented and they're skilful. If they were a normal size they would still be champions.'

Nevertheless, Cunningham was rattled by Fury's jibes. 'I'm from Philly, a great boxing city and I grew up street fighting – that was my introduction to boxing. This guy talks too much,' he said.

Fury was dismissive: 'I have heard it all before from you lot [Americans] about how you all grew up surrounded by drugs and shootings. Well, fighting is in my blood, I don't have to invent a story about fighting – it's what we do in our community.' He was, he said, 'a fighting man, a fighting man with generations of fighting men before me in my family. That's all we do, we fight.'

Cunningham later admitted that Fury's pre-fight talk did annoy him. 'It was disrespectful,' he said. 'Tyson did get a little under my skin. He talked and he woke up a little anger in me that probably wasn't there before. He sparked a little fire in me that's helping my drive. It's helping me get up and run and do what I'm supposed to do. He woke up another dragon that's in me . . . we know he's not a chump. We know he's not scared, but something's up. There were four guys on his list to fight, solid heavyweights almost his own size, but he chooses me, the smallest guy on the list, and the one who's supposedly not a heavyweight.'

Hennessy paid due respect to Cunningham, simply for consenting to fight. 'Steve Cunningham is a tremendous athlete, he's a former two-time champion, he's a brilliant boxer and tremendous-looking athlete. But this is a new era of boxing – a new era of heavyweight boxing. We have a six-foot-nine modern heavyweight, who's not cumbersome, not overweight, is athletic, in the best shape of his life and to top it off, he can box. He can punch, he can fight, he can talk. He's got a great character. He's going to give the heavyweight division the shot in the arm that it's needed for many years now. He's a real special talent and a real special person and everyone in the US is going to realise that come 20 April. I want to thank Steve for stepping up. He is a man of steel because there are a lot of people that turned this twenty-four-year-old down. He's got many years to come in this sport and he's already being avoided. I see the sacrifice and hard work all paying off.'

Tyson Fury had to prepare in Canada because his trainer Peter Fury had served a prison sentence in the UK and needed a special visa to enter the States. They had run out of time to obtain the necessary documents. 'It is an inconvenience,' said Peter, 'but rest assured Tyson is ready and knows his game plan very well.' Tyson was fully prepared.

'We've not done much different with preparation because for the last three fights we left no stone unturned,' said Tyson. 'We've been working on different game plans for a lighter fighter, such as Steve Cunningham, a speed guy, and we just hope it all goes to plan on the night.' Here was a thoughtful, considered Tyson, rather that the big gypsy traveller who simply knocked out opponents.

He also presented two faces to the public. On the front page of his Twitter account, he sent a gentle message to his 86,000-plus followers: 'God loves us all so much trust in him! Family is the way forward dont trust strangers. Never let anyone no your buisness. Love your woman & enjoy life. Bless u.' But elsewhere, there was a war cry for his hardcore fans: 'Live life to the max hold nothing back fuck yesterday& tomorrow live for now! Be free & fly!... Born to fight & am happy always up for a laugh & ready to rumble!... go fuck ya selfs all the haters!'

Fury offered to advertise his Twitter page on the bottom of Cunningham's boots – because he thought plenty of people would see the soles. 'There's only one star here and it's not Steve Cunningham,' said Fury. 'This is the Tyson Fury Roadshow and Steve Cunningham is the opponent, a stepping stone.'

The next fifteen years were going to make up his era, he said, and he kept on winding up his opponent. 'I'll run you through the fight – Fury comes out jabbing, Cunningham's running around the ring and boom – spark out. Game over. That's all I have to say. It's a cat-and-mouse job – the cat always wins. I'm expecting him to come and have a fight and go home with his pay cheque, just like the rest of them do.'

'He sure does talk a lot,' said Cunningham. 'I just hope I get some respect when I whup him.'

When they got into the ring, Fury outweighed Cunningham by 44 lbs and was 6 inches taller. But at thirty-six Cunningham was still in superb condition. He was able to find Fury's body with sharp jabs in round 1 and cut down on punishment by some nifty lateral movement.

'Come on! That ain't nothing!' Fury shouted at him after taking a couple of shots. But Cunningham remained unperturbed, even when Fury walked up to him and shoved him after the bell.

Round 2 had barely started before Cunningham launched

a huge overhand right that dropped Fury. It was a rougher knockdown than the one Pajkić had meted out. This time Fury appeared genuinely hurt, but he rallied to land a few decent shots of his own. Relying on aggression, Fury edged a scrappy round 3, but Cunningham took round 4 with his movement and accuracy. There were complaints that referee Eddie Cotton broke up the action in Cunningham's favour and the ref went on to deduct a point from Fury in the fifth for the use of his head. Nevertheless, Fury took that round and the following one with solid connections that started to wear Cunningham down and he began to struggle, with Fury taking the opportunity to lean on him with his elbows.

The end came in the seventh, when Fury backed Cunningham on to the ropes. A body shot and an uppercut clearly had Cunningham in trouble before a right hook landed plumb on his chin and left the American with no chance of beating the count with just 10 seconds remaining. He was knocked spark out and needed medical attention. It was the first time the American had been stopped inside the distance. From the ring, Fury treated the crowd to a rendition of 'Keep it Between the Lines' by American country music star Ricky Van Shelton. Fury claimed, 'I was in control for the whole fight and showed just what Tyson Fury is all about.'

On Channel 5 he said, 'What a fight it was. Cunningham put up a good fight, but he lost to the better fighter on the night.' Asked about being knocked down in round 2, he said, 'It's one of those things, you come over here and you can't go swimming without getting wet. I got caught with a big swinging right hand and when you don't see them coming you go down, but you've got to get back up. This is a learning experience but many are picked and few are chosen. The Lord Jesus Christ has given me the ability that if I get knocked down, I can come back and win the fight. I am the ultimate fighting man. A good big one will always beat a good little one. That was a good hook to the side of the jaw. I felt I was in control all the way through and it was a matter of time before I got hold of him. As Lennox Lewis said, "You can run but you can't hide" – and he was running after he got hit with a few shots. When I caught him in the seventh, it was curtains.'

Cunningham admitted the size difference was too much for him. 'He kept leaning on me and leaning on me. It was like I was fighting two people. He's a giant. I was dazed, couldn't make count.'

Fury's confidence was at an all-time high. 'I have arrived,' he said. 'I can guarantee one thing and that is excitement. When Wladimir Klitschko fights me I will knock him out just like I knocked Steve Cunningham out. If I have to go through [Kubrat] Pulev first then fine – I'll knock him out, too. I couldn't give a shit what they think about me, I just hope they sign a contract and fight. That's what I do – Tyson Fury is the name, fighting's the game.' Fury shrugged off criticism for the use of dirty tricks after being penalised for headbutting in the fifth. 'What was I supposed to do? Let him hit me? I was in a dogfight and he couldn't hack it.'

A week after Fury beat Cunningham, Deontay Wilder – a.k.a. the 'Bronze Bomber' – disposed of Audley Harrison in Sheffield in just 70 seconds. He stepped up to the plate as a potential challenger. Taunting Fury, he said, 'I'm a beast with

God-given talent. I will come back to England whenever he wants to fight.'

Fury responded on Twitter, saying, 'Long way to go boy windmilling and KOing [an] old man, great job! Join the queue.'

Team Fury were aiming to set up a final International Boxing Federation eliminator with unbeaten Bulgarian Kubrat Pulev. The winner of the fight would be the mandatory challenger for Wladimir Klitschko's IBF heavyweight crown. But Fury first wanted to dispose of David Haye. The former WBA champion had twenty-five knockouts in his twenty-six wins and would be his toughest opponent yet.

'I was going to get paid five million pounds to fight in a huge, packed arena on pay-per-view in my home country as opposed to collecting a measly one hundred grand to fight Pulev over in Germany,' said Fury of the opportunity to take on Haye. 'It was a no-brainer. I'm a prizefighter and money is the prize that drives me. Rankings and titles don't put food in my cupboards and I've a wife and two children to support. If you don't risk, then you don't achieve.'

In July, it was confirmed that Fury and Haye would be fighting in Manchester, on 28 September. Immediately, the war of words started: 'Let's hope he finally agrees and doesn't keep delaying,' said Haye. 'Word is he's looking to duck me and fight Tony "The Tiger" Thompson. Let's hope they're just rumours.'

With just ten days to go before the scheduled fight, Haye boasted that he would knock Fury out in two rounds. But three days later, he postponed, posting a photograph of a deep cut above his left eye. 'Haye's excuses are boring,' responded Fury. 'He doesn't want to fight me.'

When the fight was rescheduled for February 2014, Fury tweeted, 'I'm going to snap @mrdavidhaye's jaw in little bits! If he has the arsehole to fight me.' Seemingly determined to make more friends, Fury went on to tweet, '@LennoxLewis u wouldn't have been any good to me in your hay day never mind now grandad!! Also@Klitschko is a pussy & would never fight me!!'

In November Haye said that he wouldn't be ready for the fight after undergoing surgery on his shoulder. 'I'm absolutely furious but in all honesty this is exactly what I expected,' said Fury. 'Everyone knows I was very suspicious when he pulled out the first time and this confirms to me that he's always been afraid of me and never wanted this fight.'

Instead, Fury would meet thirty-two-year-old American Joey 'Minnesota Ice' Abell at the Copper Box Arena, London, on 15 February 2014. Abell had twenty-eight knockouts in his twenty-nine wins, but he was five inches shorter than Fury and had lost to Kubrat Pulev in December, retiring after four rounds. He was a late replacement for Gonzalo Omar Basile from Argentina, who pulled out due to a lung infection.

Fury would be taking on the fight following a nine-month lay-off. He had been enjoying the good life at a training camp on Palm Beach, Cannes, in the South of France. 'Abell is big and he can punch. Just what I want on my comeback,' said Fury. 'One thing I do respect about him is his power. He's got a great knockout record and in the heavyweights it only takes one shot to turn things around . . . I love these American opponents, they have all the talk. I hope and pray that he does bring it on and comes at me swinging away because it will be one hell of a tear-up and there's one thing I don't come off second-best in and that's a fight.'

Fury claimed his break had not affected his readiness to fight: 'I'm in perfect shape, though, and, even though Abell is a late substitute, there's no way he'll knock me off course for my summer rendezvous with Mr Chisora, who's got his own Yank to deal with in Johnson. I'll do my job and if he's does his then we're all set for a summer settler.'

The Chisora–Johnson fight was to take place on 15 February 2014. The winner would face the victor of the Fury–Abell fight and the winner of that would get a crack as Wladimir Klitschko, then thirty-seven. 'Wladimir Klitschko is a fucking bell-end,' Fury said. 'Whether thirty-seven or twenty-five, I'd still knock him out. Why can I beat him? One, he's never fought anybody of my stature, speed or movement. Two, he specialises in sparring people, beating them up when they're young and then knocking them out when they're men. Three, because his old trainer Emanuel Steward told him to his own face in front of me and a few people, that I'd knock him out when my time was ready – and that was about eighteen months ago. If your mentor tells you you're getting knocked out, you start to believe it. And when your mind's fucked, your boxing's fucked. And you lose. That's why I can beat him.'

There was more abuse to be tweeted about other fighters: '@mrdavidhaye Is a fucking shit house cunt!...' 'If @ LennoxLewis has any balls left at all come fight me & ill have u carried out on a stretcher u fucking pussy! Come & try!!!'

And the idea that Olympic gold medallist Anthony Joshua could knock him out was dismissed: 'Anthony seems a good kid and looks a good fighter. But knocking over some easy touch doesn't mean you can even land a blow on a world-class fighter.'

Meanwhile, Fury was receiving some threatening texts of his own. Then, while he, his wife and kids were away at training camp, there was an arson attack on his home in Morecombe, Lancashire. His £12,000 Volkswagen Passat was torched in his driveway and the vandals tried to set fire to his BMW estate. Uncle Peter said it was a targeted attack. 'Tyson is devastated.'

Fury described the arsonists as 'low-life scum', but vowed they would not put him off his game. 'It's been distressing for me, what's gone on at home,' he said. 'There are some crazy people out there. Someone could have got seriously hurt. It's upsetting to think that someone is going to your house and messing around, burning things. It's just people being silly with jealousy and envy. They know I am away so it is the perfect time to do it. Anybody could have been at home – it's a good job my wife and two kids were with me in France.'

That was not the end of the bad news. In the week before the fight, Fury suffered a cut above his eye while sparring and his wife went into hospital for an emergency operation. Abell said, 'I'm reading that Fury had some trouble recently in his personal life and I'm sorry to hear that, but I've got to say that it's just the start of his problems and he'll have a big one against me on Saturday night.' He predicted he would knockout Fury inside five rounds.

Kevin Johnson, whose fight with Dereck Chisora was topping the bill the night that Fury was to take on Abell, backed his fellow American. 'My main man here, Joey Abell, is hitting so hard, he could well fell that big 'ol oak tree Tyson Fury on Saturday night,' he said. 'It could be timber for Tyson when Joey lands on that big jaw of his.'

Though Abell was described as a journeyman, Fury said he would be no pushover. 'I've got this guy Joey Abell, six-foot-four, southpaw, worst nightmare for me, by the way,' Fury said. 'He knocked down Kubrat Pulev in his last fight . . . and Pulev is the main challenger for Wladimir Klitschko's title.'

But on the night Fury was altogether more casual. He entered the ring to Oasis's 'Wonderwall' at a career-high 19 st 8 lbs, destroying the image of the disciplined fighter he had recently be cultivating. 'Anybody can be Mr Boring and sit in the corner and be nice and quiet,' he had said to the *Daily Mirror*. 'But that's not me. If I'm going somewhere, I'm going to be the life and soul of the place. I'm an all-action man in anything I do. If I'm drinking, I'm drinking until I can't stand up. If I'm going out for Chinese, I'm going to an all-you-can-eat Chinese. If I'm eating cake, I'm eating the whole cake. I don't know what you'd call me – an idiot, maybe? You can never tell what I'm thinking. My wife never knows what we're doing next. She gives me stick because she knows if I go and eat out on a Friday night, I'm coming back at seven in the morning. I'm probably a hard person to live with but it's like-it-or-lump-it. I'm not interested in being a role model for everyone else.'

Out of condition and rusty, Fury still managed to take round 1. It was just like the old days, when he shirked training and got by on size, ability and determination. But early in the second, a big left from Abell connected, catching him with a glancing right hook. Then a straight left rocked his head back. As they came together in a clinch, heads clashed and Abell was warned by referee Jeff Hinds for headbutting.

In round 3, Fury took over and caught Abell with a low blow, giving the American a chance to recover in a neutral corner, but no points were deducted. Then a left jab-right hook combination put Abell down for the first time. Getting to his feet, Abell bravely responded with a left hook that landed flush on Fury's jaw, only for the Brit to respond instantly with a winging right hook, followed by a left hook that put Abell on his knees, only to be saved by the bell.

Abell came out for round 4, throwing everything he had and succeeded in stunning Fury with a right hand, but Fury countered the attack with another combination. He pierced Abell's defence twice with heavy blows that put the American down and after the second count of the round the fight was waved off after 1 min 36 sec.

Speaking to the BoxNation channel after the fight, Fury said, 'I was playing games in there. Joey Abell's not at my level. I'm the best heavyweight on the planet.' Later that night, Chisora beat Johnson with a unanimous points decision. Since losing to Haye in 2012, Chisora had won five fights, four by knockouts, putting him back in contention. Now he was to face Fury, in a fight scheduled for 26 July at the Manchester Arena.

At a televised press conference in a London cinema, Fury launched into a foul-mouthed tirade against Chisora. Asked to moderate his language, Fury replied, 'I don't give a fuck how many women and children are in the audience. We're getting near to the fight and I'm in fight mode; kill mode. If you don't like the station, change the channel, bitch. This is my show, I do what I want. This is boxing, it isn't tap-dancing. If anybody doesn't like that they shouldn't be here.' In the end, the two fighters shook hands on a side bet on the match. The BBBC fined Tyson £15,000 over the outburst and at his next press conference, Fury turned up with a tape over his mouth inscribed with 'BBofC' and a number of question marks. He refused to say a word.

Speaking on his behalf, Mick Hennessy said, 'At the end of the day, you need characters to be able to be themselves whatever they're confronted with. Sometimes you're going to get a gentleman with Tyson and sometimes, if he's rubbed up the wrong way, you'll get another side of him. At the end of the day surely he should be allowed to be himself.'

The fight was cancelled when Chisora pulled out after fracturing a hand in training. Fury tweeted, 'Told you all what would happen find me a real man to fight the furious1, If any1 feels like a fight I'm in Bolton town centre & I feel like a rumble.'

Belarusian Alexander Ustinov was lined up as Chisora's replacement and then it was Fury's turn to pull out after his uncle and former trainer Hughie Fury was taken seriously ill. Fury and Chisora rescheduled the rematch for 29 November 2014, at the ExCeL centre, London.

Chisora had rocked Fury in their first encounter and had returned to form since his defeat by Haye, but on the day Fury had no trouble with him. From the opening bell Fury controlled Chisora with his jab, kept great defensive discipline and maintained a high work rate. Chisora had no answer and his well-meaning sorties were invariably met with a jab, an uppercut or a clinch. He was unable to get inside Fury's reach or make any dent in his defences.

From round 2 onwards, Fury boxed southpaw and it was clear that he could have done *The Times* crossword at the same time for all the trouble Chisora was giving him. There were even boos from the crowd so one-sided was the action, and with Fury on a metaphorical sun lounger referee Marcus McDonnell pulled the fighters together and told them, 'Either we fight or we go home'.

The first two rounds had nevertheless been close, but in the third, as Chisora came rumbling forward, Fury was able to pick him off with jabs and flicks with the back of the glove. As he would say himself, 'Which other heavyweight in the world can box southpaw against a world-class fighter like Dereck, a fighter who will give any other heavyweight a tough fight? I'm very proud of my performance.' For Fury it would be an easier victory than it had been the first time around. It was a relief to everyone when Chisora's corner pulled him out before the start of round 11.

At last, Fury was mandatory challenger for Wladimir Klitschko's titles. In the meantime, it was announced that he would fight the Romanian fighter Christian Hammer at the O2 Arena, on 28 February 2015, the contest billed 'Risky

Business'. 'I've said all along I'm not like these other fighters in the division who pussyfoot around, take soft touches and call themselves fighters,' said Fury. 'I could have taken an easy job at the O2 Arena to keep my position safe for my world title fight against Klitschko, but that's not what Tyson Fury is about or what the public want to see from someone who has promised from day one to win the world heavyweight title. On paper, it's a dangerous job against Hammer, he's highly ranked, he brings a big punch with him, he'll have ambitions of his own to beat me and grab himself a world title shot against Klitschko and I'm sure he'll be full of confidence coming over here.'

Promoter Frank Warren said, 'Fury will have his hands full with Hammer who could create a huge shock if he wins. It's a risky fight for Fury who's within touching distance of Klitschko and the world title. But Fury needs to keep active by fighting until Klitschko gets his fight in April out of the way.' Klitschko was facing Bryant Jennings in Madison Square Garden on 25 April. He would then have thirty days to negotiate his WBO mandatory defence against Fury or the fight would then go to the highest offer at purse bids.

Hammer said, 'I love to fight bigger, taller, men and Fury is perfect for me. It will be a hard fight, but I've got every confidence that I'll surprise everyone with a win in his backyard.'

Fury: 'Hammer will be a spanner by the time I have finished with him. I must have a fight before the Klitschko fight because I can't just wait around. There's many a man who came unstuck on the last hurdle. I'm not going to be one of them . . . I don't believe heavyweight champions should fight easy victims, the best must fight each other in order to keep the division alive.'

On 17 January, Deontay Wilder had won the WBC heavyweight title from Bermane Stiverne on points, the first time he had gone the distance, and he was already talking about defending it against Fury before taking on Wladimir Klitschko. 'I would love to fight Tyson Fury,' said Wilder. 'I think he's doing a good job of what he's doing in boxing. As far as being entertaining, I think he's ahead of his business in the UK in entertaining and I think I'm doing the same in America – and I think that is going to be a big clash down the road. There's nothing like the big guys going at it. It's like a freak show, so I can't wait on that one. I can't wait for it.'

But Fury was already the mandatory challenger for Klitschko's WBO title. He tweeted, 'All this talk stiverne vs wilder?? Stiverne a little fat pudding, wilder a lanky chinless hype gob! Tyson fury the best fighter on da planet.'

There was bad blood between the two of them. Fury told the *Lancaster Guardian*, 'I don't like Deontay Wilder and he doesn't like me. I think he's a big hype-job. We once had a bit of a falling out in Sheffield at one of Mick Hennessy's boxing shows and I told him one day I will get him in the ring and knock him out. That is still my plan. He's got a title now and I'm the mandatory challenger for Wladimir Klitschko. In an ideal world I'd like to fight Klitschko first, because he's got most of the belts and he's the No. 1 in the division, and then I'd like to unify all the titles against Deontay Wilder. Potentially, I'm three or four fights away from being the unified heavyweight champion of the world.'

Nevertheless, the trash talking would help set up a lucrative encounter in the future. 'It would be the biggest selling fight with the greatest smack talk in heavyweight history,' Fury said. 'No other fight could come close to it. It would be pure entertainment. Back in the Ali days, there was only one man doing the talking. The others wouldn't talk. This is different, though. We can both talk, we both play the press and we are both natural-born entertainers. That's why it's the biggest fight out there as far as I'm concerned. It's not just the biggest fight in the heavyweight division, it's the biggest fight in world boxing.'

Frank Warren approached Wilder's advisers, while he and Mick Hennessy also talked to Klitschko's people and found their financial demands unreasonable. 'Mick Hennessy and I had conversations with them and it just broke down as a result of money,' said Warren. 'What they want – like always – you deal with the Klitschkos and you get a crumb off the table. The difference is Tyson is in a mandatory position, so it's a different game.'

The good news for Fury was that his father would be ringside for the Hammer fight. John Fury had been on licence since 2014, having served four of his eleven-year prison sentence, but had been prohibited from attending public events. However, this condition was lifted with his full release on 11 February. He was back in the Team Fury Gym in Bolton, a former public house that carried the legend 'The home of the champions' and alongside Uncle Peter he was assisting in Fury's training. 'We have a close relationship so it's been good and inspiring having him around,' said Tyson. 'It'll mean a lot to me because he started me in the sport and guided me to the British title.'

Even in prison, his father had been a help. 'My dad still analysed a lot of opponents when he was away and always gave me advice on the styles. It will be inspiring to have him back in my corner.'

John Fury said that Tyson had been out of control since he went to prison – losing his temper and swearing. 'Now I'm back, all that is going to change,' he said. 'You're going to see another Tyson Fury from this day on. We don't want any more bad language, no more flipping out, there is no need for it. He's an intelligent fella and, when he's on form, he is a fun guy.'

Believing that Klitschko was continuing to avoid him, Fury laid into Wilder: 'I'll bring it down to a dogfight where it will be a battle of heart and will. If the Wilder fight is put to me I'll take it because it's a world title fight, but I have worked six years to be mandatory for Wladimir.' Still he was pessimistic that the fight would come off. 'If Jesus Christ told me Klitschko was going to fight me, I wouldn't believe it. When I looked in his eyes in Austria he swallowed. I don't think a pack of wild horses can make Klitschko fight me, never mind the money.'

He thought that Klitschko would bottle it and vacate the title rather than fight him. 'So maybe Wilder has the bollocks to take me on, though first time I land one on him it will be goodnight Vienna.' Fury didn't underestimate the importance of the contest. 'Everything is on the line,' he said. 'I'm mandatory to face Wladimir Klitschko next but if I don't win this fight I'll lose that mandatory position and my chance to fight for the world title.'

The run-up to the Hammer fight was notable for the absence of bombast, but Fury was not trying to be good on purpose. 'I've not tried to change anything. I am what I am,' he told the *Independent*. 'I get fined all the time – £20k, £25k, £15k, £10k, £12k. I could have spent that money on sweets and chocolate. Every time I speak out I get fined a lot of money. Couldn't give a fuck, to be honest. Fine me another £20k. It's only money. You can't take it with you, can you?'

Fury preferred being outspoken. 'I'm a gypsy, no education, no schooling, nothing. I don't care what people think of me. I don't care about being a hero, a role model, a champion. I'm doing this for money and money alone. If I didn't box again, who cares?' he said. 'But I can't think of another job that pays me five or six million a year.' For Fury boxing was a business, not a sport. He cared about his family and his kids, but nothing else bothered him. 'I don't care about life, don't care about death. Nothing. That's the kind of man you are dealing with. That's why I can't be beaten. When you don't give a fuck about nothing or nobody you are a hard man to beat. I'm not even scared of the devil. If the devil confronted me I'd confront him as well.'

That did not make him dangerous. 'A dangerous man is a man on the way to jail, so I'm not dangerous, no. I'm a one-off type of a fella.' But he was bad. 'I'm a bad person, a very, very bad man,' he said. 'I'm going to go straight to hell. I've a one-way ticket, unfortunately, and nothing is going to stop me. I've tried to walk with God and all that sort of stuff. I try to tweet about good things. But there is not a lot of good in badness, is there? All filth and dirt. It's all from the devil. Temptation happens and bad takes over good.'

It was also bad that he did not go to the movies any more, but that was because he could not eat sweets and ice cream. 'What's the point of going if you can't do that? My whole life revolves around eating. My idea of a good day out is going for a nice bit of food, going to the movies, stuffing myself full of a load of shit.'

He dismissed the current crop of heavyweights – including himself – as 'crap'. 'The heavyweights of the seventies and early eighties would have destroyed us all,' he said. Riddick Bowe 'would have set about me in seconds – too good for me'. And he would have been flattened by Lennox Lewis. 'Don't get me wrong, I'd have fought any one of them but how long would I have lasted?' he said. He had beaten most of the current Top 10. 'What does that say about the division if a fat gypo can smash them right in?'

Even Wladimir Klitschko, who he rated the best in the division, would be 'an easy fight'. He said, 'I'm not frightened of any man alive or of ghosts, but I scream my head off if ever I see a wild rat, a spider or a snake. If they got too close I'd probably have a heart attack.'

In a last-minute interview in his Bolton gym, Fury now said he felt no deep attachment to his background or community. 'It is not something I'm interested in or care about. You get people saying, "Oh, I fight for my nation," or "I fight for my people". I fight for myself, to pay my bills, because nobody fights for me.'

He clung on to his belief in God, though. 'Without God, what have we got?' he asked. 'All the money, all the women, the drugs, they can't make you happy. Every single day my battle is with myself. My opponents are what they are, just boxers with a pair of gloves on. I'm battling between good and evil within every single day of my life.' And he was troubled, if not tormented. 'Why do we live every day to go to bed and wake up again? What is life about? I'm just a human being, a dirty sinner. I'm not worthy of God's grace.'

On the eve of the fight, Fury began to ramp up the invective against Hammer. 'I should be able to come out of a rave at four in the morning, after drinking ten pints, and still beat a man like that. And if I couldn't, I'd still be ashamed of myself,' he said. 'On a Richter scale of ten, on how concerned I am of Hammer, it'd be minus five. If I can't beat Christian Hammer, I'm useless. He is not a Mike Tyson or a Lennox Lewis or a Holyfield. He's a bum from Romania. I've never met a Romanian who can fight, so he should be no exception. I tried to watch him on YouTube. I turned it off after ten seconds. It was absolute rubbish.' Nevertheless, Fury claimed he was restraining his pre-fight tongue. 'I'm calm because you can't have pre-fight aggression against someone who doesn't speak English,' he said. 'He is a bum. If I can't beat him I might as well pack up.'

So untroubled was he that Fury came into the ring with an Elvis Presley impersonator singing 'Trouble'. The message was that Hammer would soon be entering 'Heartbreak Hotel', but his arrival, and the opening bell, were delayed when a split opened in a glove Fury was wearing. When the bout did begin, Fury started on the front foot, landing an uppercut from a southpaw stance, although many had warned Fury of Hammer's big punch – the Hammer blow. Fury remained elusive, while a series of left hands stirred the crowd. Hammer tried to walk him down to get him within range, but with a seven-inch height advantage, Fury was able to step back to avoid the Hammer blow.

Hammer attempted the big punch in round 2, but missed by a mile, leaving the crowd jeering. While the Romanian was reckless, Fury rediscovered the professionalism that he had taken so long to develop. He dominated the first four rounds, before putting Hammer on the deck in the fifth with a stunning right-hand his opponent did not even see coming. Hammer struggled to his feet, beating referee Marcus McDonnell's count, only to spend the rest of the round on the ropes, soaking up punches.

Although Hammer rallied in the sixth and seventh rounds, he never troubled Fury, who was clearly enjoying himself. A wry smile lit Fury's face as the crowd chanted his name. Sensing victory, he became more aggressive. A combination of shots from Fury at the end of round 8 left Hammer dazed and shaking his head with frustration. When he returned to his corner, they threw in the towel.

While the London crowd left disappointed that there had not been more fireworks, Fury was unapologetic and was left with enough energy to serenade the crowd with 'Walking In Memphis' after the fight. 'I'm here to entertain,' he said. 'I came here to box a very worthy opponent who was very tough. He took a lot of punishment and his corner knew they had to pull him out. I was going through the motions, really. It was a bit of flair and tear. I have come a long, long way in the last three or four years. I went back to basic for this fight, and I'm a much improved fighter. And that's why I'm ready for Klitschko next.'

WORLD CHAMPION

Finally, on 28 November 2015, Tyson Fury's wish came true. He faced Wladimir Klitschko – a.k.a. Dr Steelhammer – for the WBA (Super), WBO, IBF, IBO, *The Ring* magazine and lineal heavyweight titles. It was the fight he had been waiting for his entire professional career. On reflection, he was glad of the delay, saying that had Klitschko accepted his challenge five years earlier, he would have lost.

'I was trying to fight Klitschko after ten fights, but in hindsight was I really ready?' he said. 'Did I have a good fighting chance? Maybe if I'd have caught him with a big punch, but not really. You can't fight a man with sixty-odd fights after ten or eleven professional fights – it's not real. I would've got paid a good lot of money and would've done something else after I'd got chinned.'

But now defeating the Ukraine champion, who had not

lost a fight since 2004, was within the realms of possibility. Fury was convinced that his ability to switch between an orthodox stance and southpaw would give him the edge. 'I believe southpaw is the key because there's not many heavyweights in the world who get southpaw sparring or anything like that,' he told the *Manchester Evening News*. 'The key to beating Klitschko is from a southpaw stance. Corrie Sanders was a southpaw.' The South African Sanders had taken Klitschko's WBO heavyweight title after knocking him out in 2003.

'Tony Thompson gave him problems – both times from a southpaw. Both of those guys were long-range fighters, which I am – but they never had my inside game,' said Fury. 'It makes fights easy. The defence from southpaw is impregnable I believe. I don't think I took a shot at all into the face from his [Hammer's] punches as a southpaw. Sometimes you can get hit over the top from a right-handed stance, but as a southpaw I don't get hit at all – as you saw from the Dereck Chisora fight.'

Negotiations had begun with the fight pencilled in for early September in locations that included Arsenal's Emirates Stadium in London. 'We are looking at Wembley and pending what happens with the football, Arsenal, wherever you can get sixty to seventy thousand people in because it's a huge fight,' said Frank Warren.

First, Klitschko had to get his fight with Bryant Jennings at Madison Square Garden on 25 April out of the way. It was not one of his best performances. Jennings' speed and lateral movement allowed him to land punches on

Klitschko's body and threw the champion off. The referee
Mike Griffins deducted a point from Klitschko for excessive
holding, but he never looked in trouble and won on points
in a unanimous decision.

After the fight, he said, 'I just got the news that I am
obligated to satisfy my mandatories. The way it looks, Tyson
Fury is going to be my next challenger. Obviously, a fight with
Tyson Fury is not going to be in the United States. I think this
fight needs to happen in Europe. I know that he's the WBO
mandatory. It's something that I have to do.'

Clearly, he was not keen. Fury was three inches taller
with a reach four inches longer, but Klitschko would make
the best of it. 'I look forward to it because I like to fight big
men,' he said. 'It is much easier to fight bigger men than
smaller. He is definitely ambitious and I think he is going to
engage in the fight.'

The clash of the Titans also suited Fury. 'Against Jennings it
was the same as usual, a smaller man trying to get inside his
jab with him holding and leaning,' he told the *Sun*. 'Let's see
him try that against someone who's the same size, younger,
stronger, fitter, faster and with a KO punch – me!'

Klitschko, a veteran of sixty-seven professional fights, was
dismissive. 'I think he is more famous for his verbal fighting
than the actual boxing fighting,' he said. 'Obviously he's
had twenty-something fights, but I haven't watched his fights
in particular.'

The fight was rescheduled for 24 October and it was
now to take place in the Esprit Arena in Düsseldorf, with
its capacity of 54,600. Fury could hardly wait. He tweeted,

'The GYPSYKING will come out of this fight as the best heavyweight on the planet, nuffsaid'.

At a press conference in Düsseldorf on 21 July, Fury told Klitschko, 'It's a personal mission for me to rid boxing of a boring person like you. I'm interested in all of them belts you've got on there. I'm interested in breaking your face in. You're boring, I want to rid you out of the heavyweight division. Your jab-and-grab style – surely all of Europe wants to see you get beaten and all of Europe and the rest of the world will see you get beaten. You have about as much charisma as my underpants – zero, none. You go on – you're a sports psychologist, you speak thirty-seven different languages, so what? You're still a robotic person. You're still not exciting and fun to watch. I am the new blood in the division, you are an old man. An old man who is getting knocked out. You have a chin like a piece of glass. I want to hit it and it is going to explode like that glass against a wall.'

Fury told the press that the bout was long overdue. 'I believe he has never faced a challenge like me ever before and I don't think he will face a challenge like me again. I'm a unique fighter, one of a kind, there's never been someone like me before in history. A fighter like me only comes around every thousand years.'

Klitschko refused to get riled, saying that Fury was going to be a tough opponent. 'This guy is so entertaining,' he said. 'He sings, he dances, he is a cool dude. He does different things that people like – or hate. Some people adore you, some people say they can't stand you, which is good.'

Certainly, Fury outpunched Klitschko with the one-liners, telling the audience, 'This Klit is getting licked on 24 October.'

At a second press conference in London on 23 September, Fury made Klitschko wait for fifteen minutes. Then he turned up in a yellow Lamborghini, dressed as Batman, and sent Klitschko's collection of championship belts flying in a mock fight with his cousin, Hughie, who was dressed as the Joker.

'I came as Wladimir Klitschko,' the champion responded. 'I don't need to come as anything else, I don't need to pretend . . . two British fighters rolling around with glasses and threatening to kill each other – that is embarrassing.'

Fury then called Klitschko a 'shithouse' who had only fought 'peasants'.

'I have good friends in the circus who will find a new job for you, buddy,' said Klitschko. 'They can give you a job as a clown. It's tough to make people laugh, but there's a subtle difference between being funny and acting stupid.' Fury feigned indignation, while Klitschko told the press, 'This bipolarity will be well-treated – just let me start the therapy for him by finishing his boxing career. I'll find him a good doctor.'

Uncle Peter found himself agreeing with Klitschko. 'Tyson, at times, is not stable in the mind,' he said. 'That's what makes him such a good fighter because he's unbalanced. It's not a weakness, it's the total opposite. He will come out with all sorts of statements and try to put himself down by saying he doesn't care about this and that, but you'd have to saw his two legs off in the ring before he would suffer a defeat.'

Tyson then lightened the mood again, saying that he was hoping to sing a duet with Rod Stewart who was to perform before the fight. 'I want to sing "Maggie May" with Rod with a minor adjustment to the lyrics,' he said. 'Wake up Klitschko, I think I've got something to say you fool, it's late October and I've really made a mug of you.'

'I've never had such an entertaining press conference,' said Klitschko, possibly with a note of sarcasm, as the abuse continued.

'I can already tell you're afraid because you've got the biggest gloves possible,' Fury shouted. 'You've never fought a Gypsy King before. I cannot wait. Welcome to my city, welcome to my town, UK baby.'

In another exchange, Fury said, 'You will end up on your back on 24 October, you old fool, you idiot, you bum. You've taken too many punches.' After changing out of his Batman costume and into a three-piece suit, Fury continued: 'Don't do your usual jab, punch and run. Let's make it a fight. I want to feel pain. I want you to hurt me. I want broken noses and blood, and bright lights behind the eyes. I don't care if you beat me as long as you do the job properly.'

Klitschko then pledged that Fury would 'receive therapy like David Haye was given', then be sent packing as a clown to Cirque du Soleil.

Tearing off his jacket, a raging Fury said, 'I'll knock you out right here if you call me a clown again.'

Klitschko ignored this, too. 'He was never going to fight me, you could see in the body language. Barking dogs don't bite. This sort of thing doesn't motivate me, it's kind of demotivating because it's a joke. I think there are some screws loose in his mind. Deep inside he is insecure and when you are insecure you put up a wall as cover and act the way he does. What makes him feel comfortable is his experience, but he has never stepped up. It is going to be an interesting challenge for me, but it is going to be really challenging for Tyson Fury. I hope there will be no excuses after the fight.' At thirty-nine, Klitschko was having his twenty-eighth world heavyweight title fight, surpassing the record set by Joe Louis.

'All he does is throw a jab, a right hand or a left hook and jump in and out like a kangaroo,' said Fury. 'It's not about money or belts, it's about destroying that idiot. It will be a very sharp, easy, simple knockout. I just cannot wait for this. I wish it was this weekend. He is getting knocked out.'

Two days later, Klitschko pulled out of the fight due to a torn tendon in his calf. 'Batman worked a treat then, didn't it?' said Fury. He guessed it cost him a £30 million fight. He posted a photo of five pints of Guinness on Twitter with the caption, 'It's safe to say I'm hitting the drink right now. Gutted. Woooop. Woooop #fuckklitschko.' However, Klitschko quickly rescheduled for 28 November, in Düsseldorf, where the fight would be billed as *Kollisionskurs* – German for 'Collision Course'. The delay disrupted Fury's training schedule and presented him with a fresh opportunity to let his mouth get him into trouble.

He gave an interview to the *Mail on Sunday*'s chief sports writer Oliver Holt, which was published on 8 November and led to accusations of being 'offensive and deranged'. He said, 'There are only three things that need to be accomplished before the devil comes home. One of them is homosexuality being legal in countries, one of them is abortion and the other is paedophilia. Who would have thought in the fifties and sixties that those first two would be legalised? When I say paedophiles could be made legal, it sounds crazy. But if I had said to you about the first two being made legal in the fifties, I would have been looked upon as a crazy man. If I would have told you a hundred and twenty years ago that a thousand-ton aeroplane is going to fly through the sky, a piece of steel, that would have been considered ludicrous. People can say, "You are against abortions, you are against paedophilia, you are against homosexuality", but my faith and my culture is based on the Bible.'

Klitschko said that he was shocked by Fury's views, though he was mildly amused by his opponent's further allegations that Klitschko himself was a devil worshipper who practised witchcraft. This confirmed his earlier diagnosis. 'He is bipolar. He has mental issues for sure,' said Dr Steelhammer. 'Some comments that come out of his mouth do not work well with me. I'm not commenting on some of them. I will answer those with my fists in the ring, the way I have done many times before. I have stopped being surprised by Tyson Fury. He is bizarre.'

Fury then claimed that Holt had misquoted him. He posted a clip talking to camera with his entourage, saying, 'See Big Shane there. He's six-foot-six and twenty-five stone. He's going [to] break his [Holt's] jaw completely with one, straight right-hand. I won't do it as I'll get in trouble but the big fella there will annihilate him. Oliver, take a good look at him because that's the face you're going to see before you hit the deck.' Turning the camera on another member of his team, Fury said, 'And that's the face you're going to see when he's jumping on your head.'

The *Mail* stuck by its story and the Sports Journalists' Association (SJA) later withdrew its invitation for Fury to attend an awards ceremony it hosted because of the threat to Holt, an SJA member. But Fury's father made sure the Fury bandwagon stayed on the rails, telling the *Guardian* two days before the fight, 'Tyson is an animal with a cunning, intelligent brain. He's not only here to box but to change the world. And things will change in Düsseldorf on Saturday night. Because I've seen Wladimir's last ten fights and unless he shows something we haven't seen before he can't beat my son.' For him the contest brought particular relish. 'I used to see Tyson on the television. I'd lie on my bed in my cell, nine-foot by six-foot, and I was there with him in spirit and he knew that. I didn't think in my wildest dreams I would be here witnessing this magnificent event.'

But the event was not to be so magnificent. First, there was a dispute over the gloves. Fury found that the Paffen gloves he was forced to wear under his contract with Klitschko's management almost broke his thumbs when he tried them out at his training camp. If they were not altered and delivered to him after the weigh-in on Friday night, the fight would not go ahead. 'They are Paffen Sport gloves, a German brand,' Fury said. His preference was for Reyes gloves, often used by heavier punchers, with less padding in the glove around the knuckles.

'They demanded the gloves,' he said. 'Every rule for this fight was made by them. I don't think we made one. Not about venue, location, ring size, gloves, anything . . . they sent me some gloves over, which Wladimir had asked for, and they had big giant thumbs, which were about two or three inches bigger than normal – so that the thumb is sticking out. Every time I was punching with them my thumb was nearly breaking. No matter how we tried breaking them in, it wasn't working.'

Fury offered his own solution. 'We can always settle it, bare-knuckles, outside now,' he said, explaining, 'Not having the gloves we have agreed on is like asking me to run the hundred metres with no running shoes over shards of glass on the track.'

But new gloves were supplied in time and the dispute was dismissed as 'mind games'. Fury got his own back at a public workout, singing his amended version of Bette Midler's 'Wind Beneath My Wings' to Klitschko who was sitting at ringside. Fury's version included the line, 'You are the one with all the glory, I'm the one with all the strength.' He went on, 'You are the wind beneath my wings. For I am the one with the new gold ring. And I'll be the one with all the belts.'

'Thanks for the song, Tyson,' said Klitschko, 'but it's not a singing contest, it's a boxing match.'

Fury, though, was deadly serious. 'I'm not coming to Germany to win on points, I'm going to do a demolition job on Wladimir. I expect a knockout victory. Klitschko's past opponents came to Germany in the belief they were going to lose. They came for money but money isn't my motivation, winning is my motivation. He's going to wish he'd never met Tyson Fury, but I can't make him more nervous than he already is – he's shaken. Not only am I winning, I'm going to win it in style. I believe this is my destiny. And then I'll sing everybody a victory song.'

John Fury had given his son a final pep talk: 'I've said to him that it's about mental strength, winning fights. I came through the ordeal I've had and I lost my brother, Hughie, who meant the world to me – back-to-back knocks, but I'm still here.' Tyson's uncle and former trainer had died thirteen months earlier, while John was still in jail, when a routine operation to place a pin below his knee went wrong. 'I said, "Bring that into the ring with you and you won't go far wrong". If I'd thought about being in prison, it would have cracked me up . . . it's all about mental strength. This is where he gets it from . . . mental strength – that's what's going to beat Wladimir Klitschko, his strength and my mind.'

There was other, far more joyful, family news. Two days before the fight, Paris announced that she was having another baby. 'I am absolutely delighted,' said Tyson. 'This has taken me up another notch to fight Klitschko. I can't wait for the first bell and I can't wait for the new baby.' Tyson posted a video of him and his brother rapping to Krept and Konan's song 'Freak Of The Week' in his hotel room.

Uncle Peter also believed that it was mental strength that would carry Tyson through. 'If he is losing this fight, Tyson would rather be carried out on his back than lose on points. He will go all out to win. If I say to him, "You're dropping rounds," you will see him kick into another gear altogether. That's his mentality. He's not going to take second best. To beat Tyson, Klitschko will have to knock him out.'

However, there were some who did not rate his chances. 'I only give him a one-in-twenty shot,' said David Haye. 'The best guy on Tyson Fury's record is Dereck Chisora. You look at Klitschko and it's a whole different story.'

Anthony Joshua said, 'I think Fury will come out with nothing to lose. His style is to throw a lot of punches, but ultimately I think Klitschko's class will shine through and he will win.'

Former WBA world champion Brian Magee agreed that the odds were stacked against Fury. 'I think Tyson will give it a go and he is awkward, but for me Klitschko is just too good and too strong. Tyson has been winding him up with all his talking, singing and Batman antics and I think Klitschko will be up for this one and stop Fury with that huge right hand of his.'

Fury did not let others' doubts worry him though. 'I know that ninety-nine point nine per cent expect to see me lose to the great Wladimir Klitschko. I know from looking at him he's got doubts, he's very worried and his trainer is worried. That's what I love to see. I thrive off it.' Besides, he had a lucky charm – a pair of white-and-gold Mizuno boxing boots given to him by the late Emanuel Steward at Klitschko's training camp in 2010 with the name of his famous Kronk Gym in Detroit embroidered on them. 'These shoes have never been beaten. I've had them for most of my big fights and they've never let me down yet. When I've got these on, I feel like

I've got the fastest feet in the world. They might be old and dirty, but I'm sentimental and I'm going to wear them for the biggest fight of my life.'

Anyway, he said, he discounted other people's expectations. 'Nobody can give me advice on boxing. Everyone can have their opinion, but mainly I do what I want to do, basically. I've done my training right. I've eaten right, slept, kept out of the public house, so I should be all right . . . Failing that, it could all go pear-shaped and Tyson could be getting carried off the canvas! We'll find out on Saturday if I'm any good or just hot air.'

Fury was as ready as he was ever going to be. He told the *Lancashire Evening Post*, 'I can't do anything more than I've done. I've been in camp for five months. I've trained, eaten and slept boxing. I've not been out drinking, I've not been taking drugs, I've been doing nothing. If I'm capable of doing it, now will be the time.'

Shortly before the fight, Fury's team inspected the ring and found two extra layers of foam beneath the canvas. 'It was like a trampoline,' said former world champion Johnny Nelson, a pundit for Sky Sports.

'It's more like a wrestling mat than a ring. It's naughty from the Klitschko camp,' said Lennox Lewis.

For fans of Fury, it could be seen as sponging up the canvas in a deliberate attempt to tire the legs of the younger man, slowing him to a plodding pace. Peter Fury objected, threatening to pull out of the fight unless the foam – almost an inch thick – was removed. 'It was like walking through sticky toffee,' said Peter.

The British Boxing Board of Control stepped in and the foam was removed.

Klitschko's hands were bound without a member of Fury's team being present. The wraps had to be cut off and bound again under scrutiny. Klitschko was dispatched to Fury's dressing room to inspect his bandages. Fury could not resist telling him that he was going to beat his brother and take him next.

Tyson then asked Vitali to sign the bandages. 'I'll do better than that,' said Vitali, and inscribed them with love hearts.

As Rod Stewart sang 'Stay With Me', Paris took her place at ringside wearing a jacket with dollar signs on it. Her husband was confident of a million-dollar payout, although he was going into the fight as a four-to-one underdog against a champion who had not been beaten in eleven years.

But Fury thought he knew a secret. He had watched how Klitschko changed his style following his last defeat back in 2004, when he got knocked out by Lamon Brewster. After that he became a master at protecting his chin, under the guidance of Manny Steward, but Fury was confident of finding a way through his defence. 'Chins don't get any better, they just get worse,' said Fury. 'Let's face it, when Wladimir is tagged on the chin, he wobbles all over and he goes down. Let's make no mistake, he's almost made his chin like the city of Troy with the high walls. But even Troy was breached with a bit of brains, wasn't it? I'm the Trojan horse, most definitely.'

He used other colourful analogies. 'It's about winning and beating somebody who "can't be beaten",' Fury said. 'I believe that he's Superman, but I've got the kryptonite and I can handle his special powers with ease.' He also believed that beating Klitschko would make him as big a name as Cristiano Ronaldo or Lionel Messi.

As Fury made his way to the ring on the night there were both cheers and boos, but they were low-key considering his antics in the run-up to the fight. Klitschko then walked in calm to the sound of Ukrainian folk music. After the national anthems, the boxers touched gloves. There were none of the expected fireworks, but Fury continued chatting to Klitschko as he had ever since they got into the ring. As the bell sounded, Fury ran from the corner to confront Klitschko, who seemed surprised by his speed. Nimble on his feet, Fury was all twitch and bluster at first. Neither man landed a blow with a decent punch in the first 90 sec. Fury got the first proper connection with a straight jab to the face. Both men then traded blows to the back of the head. Using head movement to slip Klitschko's jab, Fury taunted the champion by placing his hands behind his back. It was a slow opening, but by the end of the round, Fury had thrown more punches and landed one power punch. He had established the superiority of his jab and, at the bell, he held his arms aloft.

In round 2, Fury drove Klitschko back across the ring with a three-punch combo – jab, cross, jab – put him in a clinch, then patted him on the arse. But Klitschko got a jab to the head and then body. The more aggressive of the two, Fury dominated the centre of the ring, despite fighting off the back foot. And as Klitschko rushed in, Fury caught him with the left hook.

In round 3, Fury continued to outfox his opponent. Full of confidence, he smiled, bounced and chatted, again dropping his hands, inviting the champion in. He then threw Klitschko off by turning southpaw. But Klitschko fell for none of Fury's tricks and maintained his defensive discipline, despite being seemingly clueless about how to launch an attack on the bigger, faster man. Only three punches landed that round, two of them to Fury. Shouting encouragement, Uncle Peter yelled, '*Dance in there! Take this fella to school!*' In the first three rounds, Fury landed seventeen punches to Klitschko's eleven.

Fury reverted to orthodox stance in the fourth. He was active but inaccurate. Fury unleashed a hook that Klitschko fended off before getting his first good right in as the bell sounded. It was the only time Fury looked troubled. Before the round Klitschko's trainer Johnathon Banks told him to be more aggressive and start throwing more power shots. But while Fury had no problem slipping most of these blows, he also could not forget that Klitschko had the power to knock him about with one punch from either hand. 'You've got to go take him now,' Banks had told Klitschko. 'You're playing from behind now.' It was the first round that could be legitimately scored to the champion.

In the fifth an accidental clash of heads caused a cut on Klitschko's right cheek. This was the first physical sign that the champ was struggling in the fight. Fury had a wild swing, turning himself around. He danced away and continued to circle and jab, before landing a solid right that, with 20 sec remaining, won him the round. In a last-ditch attempt to draw even, Klitschko threw a right over the top and missed as the round ended.

During the break, commentator and former boxer Carl Froch told Sky Sports, 'I'm struggling to find scoring punches from Klitschko. He's cocking the right hand and not throwing it.'

Banks told Klitschko, 'Shoot that right hand to the body. That's what's wide open.' During round 6, Fury made choppy irregular movements that left the champion confused and hesitant. Fury again goaded him, holding his hands behind his back. He got two good jabs in. Klitschko did not reply and came into a clinch. Though reluctant to throw punches, Klitschko landed a couple of jabs and, while Fury looked comfortable fighting off the back foot, these probably were enough to give Klitschko the round. Even so Johnathon Banks still wasn't happy.

'You're giving him every opportunity,' he told Klitschko. 'You're just slapping punches now.'

Peter Fury saw the opportunity. He told Tyson, 'Don't let him set because he's waiting, waiting and then in a minute he's gonna start chancing it.'

Now they were at the halfway point and HBO's unofficial ringside scorer Harold Lederman told commentator Jim Lampley, 'This is unbelievable. Wladimir is so inactive it's like he's giving away the heavyweight championship of the world. I got it five rounds to one, 55–59 Tyson Fury.'

Entering the second half of the fight, Fury took back control. He began to dominate Klitschko with his jab and once again showboated with his arms behind his back, drawing boos from the crowd. Again, he patted the champ on his rear. The German crowd looked on in disbelief. No one had ever disrespected Klitschko this way. Also watching the fight was brother Vitali, who punched his fist into his palm in frustration. Wladimir appeared to be waiting, while Fury was more aggressive. He came forward and Klitschko had to duck under a sharp right hook. Then Fury took one good jab to Klitschko's face and a few glancing rights.

'Wladimir Klitschko's lengthy reign atop the heavyweight division seems to be in jeopardy,' said Jim Lampley.

The *Guardian*'s Tom Lutz said, 'Unless the judges are seeing something I'm not, we will have a new champion.'

In round 8, Fury landed another right and more blood seeped from the cut on Klitschko's cheek. But the champion remained tighter and more disciplined. Getting his jab working for the first time, he landed two good blows on Fury. The round was still pretty even – though Klitschko might have finessed it, he hadn't won a single round cleanly yet.

'You have to stay on this guy,' said Banks, though patently his man had not even begun to get on Fury.

Round 9 gave Klitschko the opportunity to let go one of his right crosses for the first time. It connected with Fury's jaw but it did not have the knockout power intended. In the clinch, Fury was warned for a rabbit punch. As the two separated awkwardly Klitschko wound up in a neutral corner with his back to Fury. He was slow to turn back to his opponent, clearly expecting the referee to give him time to compose himself. Fury did not give him the chance. Immediately he landed a massive left hook, catching the champ off balance. It was the biggest punch of the fight so far. Klitschko did not seem to know where he was as Fury continued the attack, opening another cut on his forehead. Back in the corner, Vitali talked earnestly to his brother in Ukrainian, while all Banks could find to say was, 'If you want it you got to go take it.'

Lederman summed up: 'I got it seven rounds to two, 88–83 Tyson Fury. You know Jim, Wladimir Klitschko will land one good shot in a round and do nothing else. He gives the round away. For example, in that round 9, he landed a nice right hand, he could have just stepped on it, jumped all over Fury and he let Fury take the round away from him. Fury keeps touching him, touching him, touching him – piling up points with that left jab, that wild right hand and Wladimir keeps doing nothing.'

In round 10, the old Fury re-emerged. He was wild while Klitschko remained tame. The contender looked the fresher and stronger. Fury was keener to come in on the champ now, working him with a few jabs to the body when all the significant shots had gone to the head until then. Klitschko brushed Fury with a jab, but the challenger returned fire with some glancing body blows.

Fury exchanged words with the weary champion at the end of the round and they barged each other as they walked to their corners. Banks then told Klitschko, almost in desperation, 'You got to dig down. You got to get this motherfucker. You're better than him. Stay low and fight this motherfucker.' Clearly, the only way Klitschko was going to win this was with a knockout. His corner told him to work the challenger to the body, then to the head. Taking the hint Klitschko stepped up in the eleventh, yet still continued leaning on Fury in the clinches as if he was dealing with a smaller man.

'He's the shorter guy – why isn't he punching on the inside?' asked HBO analyst Roy Jones Jr.

In the closing stages of the round, Klitschko wound up a left hook but Fury beat him to the punch and landed a hook of his own. Referee Tony Weeks deducted a point from Fury for another rabbit punch to the back of the head. Roy Jones Jrsaid of Klitschko, 'He's not used to getting hit upside the head this much.'

As he came out for the final round, Klitschko was under no illusions. Banks told him, 'The only way you can win this is to knock him out.' But Fury was after a knockout, too. A left hook hurt Klitschko as chants of 'Fury! Fury!' rang out. The two men fearlessly traded blows for the first minute of the round. But Klitschko always favoured clinches over coming forward. At last, there was a big right from Klitschko. It rocked Fury, but he stayed up.

'Where was all this aggression from Klitschko earlier in the fight when it might have made a difference?' asked Jim Lampley.

With all guns blazing, Fury caught the weary champion with a left hook and left uppercut in quick succession. But Fury was tired, too. He delivered a right but Klitschko swayed out of the way. Klitschko hurt Fury with another right, but he held on. At the final bell, both fighters held their arms aloft, but Fury's celebrations looked the more convincing. Back in his corner, he jumped up on the ropes and shouted, '*And the new* . . . *!'* Then he was smothered in hugs from his father, Uncle Peter and Cousin Hughie.

Lederman scored the fight 116–111, taking into account Fury's one point deduction. On the web, fans unanimously agreed. On camera, Fury prayed, 'Now Jesus, don't rob me in this country.' German boxing judges were notoriously fickle and Klitschko, who regularly fought there, was considered one of their own. After what seemed like an age, MC Michael Buffer stepped up to announce the verdict: 'Cesar Ramos scores it 115–112; the same score from Raul Caiz Sr, 115–112, and Ramon Cerdan scores it 116–111. All three scores for the winner by unanimous decision . . . from the United Kingdom, the new unified heavyweight champion of the world: TYSOOOOOOON FUUUUUUUURRRRY!'

The stats told the whole story: punches thrown – Klitschko 69, Fury 202; punches landed – Klitschko 52, Fury 86; power blows – Klitschko 18, Fury 48.

Amid the ensuing pandemonium, Fury found time to kneel in prayer and display a T-shirt tribute to his former trainer, his late Uncle Hughie. He thanked Jesus – 'my rock, my salvation'. Addressing Klitschko, Fury said, 'You're a great champion Wlad, thanks very much for having me. It was all fun and games in the build-up, I just wanted to be confident, young and brash.'

He told Lennox Lewis, 'It's hard to come to a foreign country and win. When I got that point deduction I thought I had lost.' Then Fury handed him his water bottle, saying, 'Here Lennox, hold this.' From the ring he serenaded Paris and the crowd with Aerosmith's 'I Don't Want to Miss a Thing', dedicating the song to his fans in Ireland, the UK, the US and Germany. After the song, Fury addressed the crowd.

'What more can I say? I always said what I would do and I delivered tonight. I didn't have this confidence for nothing. I knew all along I could win the fight. I saw in his eyes that he was going to lose this fight. It was a tough task coming here, that's why he's avoided me for the last five years. People can say what they want about me, he was hanging on for dear life in that fight all the way through. I've got to give the judges their fair dues as well. I thought I had to get a knockout but they showed me that love in Germany. He's been a great champion, but every good dog has its day. Tonight is that start of a new era. I'll be the most charismatic champion since Muhammad Ali.'

Speaking on BBC Radio 5 Live, he said, 'I knew I could come here and upset the apple cart. I knew all along I could win the fight. Wladimir knew, his full team knew tonight. I saw in his eyes tonight he was going to lose the fight and he saw the new, hungry champion in me. I never took my eyes off him during the stare-off. I wasn't fazed by the crowd or nothing because I knew I was going to be the new heavyweight champion of the world. God gave me the ability to do like I've done and I want Him to thank him for that. With God, anything is possible. Thanks very much and happy Christmas.'

With his face cut and bruised, Klitschko stared blankly into the middle distance not knowing what to do. He and Vitali looked dejected, but even David Haye was delighted. 'That's the best thing to happen to heavyweight division in years,' he tweeted, 'What a great ending. Justice prevailed, the better man won. Fury can bin matalan belt, as he now has world title belts. #KlitschkoFury.'

Lennox Lewis also addressed Twitter: 'Maximum respect to @Tyson_Fury and team on the big win. We've now buried the hatchet. Welcome to the club champ!'

Other boxers took to social media in order to stake their claim for a future title shot. Among them was Deontay Wilder.

BREAKDOWN

Tyson Fury had always been a controversial figure. While not taking performance-enhancing drugs himself, he argued that they should be permitted in boxing, after Barry McGuigan said that anyone caught taking drugs should be banned from the sport for life.

In an interview with BBC Radio 5 Live before his world title fight, he said, 'Why don't they just make drugs totally legal in sports, then everybody would be taking drugs. Then it would be fully fair, then, wouldn't it? It's none of my concern really but if the governing bodies want to do that then I think it would be a bit fairer because you've got all them people taking drugs and when you face a man who is not taking drugs it becomes unfair doesn't it? It's a disadvantage. So this is why it's a big scene, but if everyone was taking drugs then it would be fairer I think because you can't tell me that ninety-nine per cent of these sports people ain't taking drugs when they've got bodies like Greek gods. I know because I've trained all my life, I'm fighting for the heavyweight championship of the world. But my body is like jelly, it's a natural body you see.'

Indeed, a roll of fat could be seen above his shorts. British boxers Kid Galahad, Enzo Maccarinelli and Dillian Whyte had all failed drug tests, while American and continental European boxing had also seen several high-profile doping cases recently. 'I would say boxing's got a big problem with drugs,' said Fury. 'It doesn't bother me because at the end of the day it's determination over drugs any time. If a man wants to pump himself full of drugs it's only shortening his life isn't it? That's why you see a lot of these bodybuilders and weightlifters have heart attacks young because they're pumped up so much and the heart can't take the pressure.'

After the Klitschko fight, Fury alleged his opponent's team were crooked and said he had refused to drink any water in the changing rooms after the fight, fearing it might be drugged. 'I went home dehydrated before I even touched anything. I was so frightened of being drug-tested and failing the drug test. They are cheats, they are extremely good at cheating. There were all these little things they thought might affect me, as it has with fighters in the past, but not one of them did.'

The Klitschko camp had made accusations of its own in 2004, after Wladimir was defeated by Lamon Brewster in Las Vegas. Team Klitschko claimed the fighter's water bottle was poisoned, leading to the fifth-round TKO. It was not proved and Klitschko defeated Brewster in a rematch in 2007.

After his own fight, Fury was asked about women in boxing and said, 'I think they're very nice when they're walking around that ring, holding them cards. I like them actually.

They give me inspiration when I'm tired. I'm all for it. I'm not sexist. I believe a woman's best place is in the kitchen and on her back. That's my personal belief. Making me a good cup of tea, that's what I believe.' Fury was summoned by the BBBC to defend his controversial comments.

Fellow Mancunian boxer Ricky Hatton commented, 'I know Tyson personally and he's a really nice guy. But sometimes he puts his mouth into gear before his brain and when someone puts a camera in front of him he feels he has to say something outrageous.'

When Fury appeared on the shortlist for the BBC Sports Personality of the Year (SPOTY), an online petition called for him to be stripped of his nomination, citing his 'homophobic and misogynistic comments'. He was challenged on BBC Radio 2 about the views he had expressed in Oliver Holt's interview in the *Mail on Sunday*. Fury said, 'Homosexuality, abortion and paedophilia – them three things need to be accomplished before the world finishes. That's what the Bible tells me.'

After the clip was played on Victoria Derbyshire's BBC Two current affairs programme, Fury was reported for a hate crime. The Greater Manchester police investigated. His trainer Peter told Derbyshire that his nephew should not be removed from the award nominations but should apologise for airing his controversial views. 'He gives his opinions,' said Uncle Peter. 'He's not a robot. There is freedom of speech – we're in 2015. If he's offensive he needs to explain his actions and move on from there but he's entitled to his opinion just like everybody else.'

Fury stirred up more controversy by saying of another contender for SPOTY, world champion heptathlete Jessica Ennis-Hill, 'She's good, she's won quite a few medals, she slaps up good as well. When she's got a dress on she looks quite fit.' Fury responded to criticism on Twitter: 'Hopefully, I don't win @BBCSPOTY as I'm not the best roll [*sic*] model in the world for the kids, give it to someone who would appreciate it.'

Paris leapt to her husband's defence, telling the *Sunday Mirror*, 'Sometimes in interviews, he sounds terrible and he sounds brash but he's not like that. He has a show side to him. He's a loud personality person, but there's no harm in him. If you sit back and smile you don't get anywhere in boxing. Tyson is loud and brash and, yes, it is a side of his personality but that's just to make himself more known.' At home, he was a new man. 'There's no pig-headed arrogant man there,' she said. 'He helps round the house – he's not one of those that goes, "I'm a man, I won't put my hands in the washing up bowl". He's a modern man and does his own washing. He'll help with the kids, take them to school, pick them up. He may be stone-faced, but he's definitely not stone-hearted. He'll watch a movie and cry. We watched *Marley & Me* and I was fine, but I looked at him and he was crying his eyes out.'

But Fury undid much of the good she had done by saying of his wife, 'Sometimes she needs an uppercut, but other times she doesn't.' With Paris standing alongside him, he said, 'I'm a little bit backward. I didn't really go to school. Which part of "a woman looks good in a dress" is sexist? Or was it about the cooking and cleaning? I stand up for my beliefs. My wife's there. Her job is cooking and cleaning and looking after these kids. That's it.'

He emphatically denied being sexist. 'It's up to everybody what they want to do,' he said. 'I'm all for it. I'm not a sexist. I believe if a man can go to work all his life, a woman can. Who am I to say, "Don't do that 'cos you're a girl"?'

Asked if he was homophobic, he said, 'No. Definitely not. I wouldn't be a very good Christian if I hated anybody. If Jesus loves the world, I love the world.' Nor was he racist. 'I can actually say I haven't got any hate for anybody. I have no enemies. I don't hate any race, colour, creed, generation, nobody. My team is one of the most diverse teams in the world of boxing. We've got Jamaicans in there, Pakistanis, Indians, Christians, Muslims. We are all united. Why don't they broadcast that – "Tyson Fury is uniting the world – uniting Christians and Muslims in a time when everything is up in the air"? We don't hear about that, do we? We don't hear about the good things I'm doing. We just hear about the comments that people want to twist and try to make it sound like I hate people and I hate the world. I love all of God's children, we are all God's children. No matter what somebody does, it's not up to me to judge them, it's not up to you to judge them. God will judge them.'

On top of that, he was not worried one way or the other about his SPOTY nomination. 'I can honestly say I'm not really interested in winning BBC Sports Personality of the Year,' he said on a YouTube video. 'I know for a million per cent I've got more personality in the end of my little finger than the whole of the nomination group put together.'

Those who signed the petition did not concern him either. 'Fifty thousand wankers. That's what I say about them,' he said. 'They can say what they want about me but they can't knock my achievement. I beat the man who nobody can beat. So until someone can go in and beat him again then they can suck my balls. I am Tyson Fury, Gypsy King, 'nuff said.'

Olympic gold-medal long-jumper Greg Rutherford, another nominee, threatened to pull out, but was persuaded to stay on. Fury could not help tweeting, 'All this talk of @ Greg Rutherford – who is he exactly?????'

In the event, Fury came fourth in SPOTY with Rutherford five places below him. At the ceremony, Fury apologised, saying, 'I've said a lot of stuff in the past and none of it is with intentions to hurt anybody. It's all a bit of tongue-in-cheek and if I've said anything in the past that's hurt anybody, I apologise to anyone that's been hurt by it.'

But that was not the end of his involvement in making controversial comments. In May 2016, he posted an hour-long video rant on bestiality, paedophilia and women, concluding with an outburst, claiming, 'Zionist, Jewish people . . . own all the banks, all the papers, all the TV stations.' The Campaign Against Antisemitism called for him to banned by the British Boxing Board of Control. Fury responded by tweeting, 'I see all the Zionist media outlets are on my back, because I speak the truth! U will all see the truth soon enuf, they killed my lord jesus.'

Once more, Fury apologised. In a 57-minute clip on YouTube, he said, 'I said some things which may have hurt some people – which as a Christian man is not something I would ever want to do. I apologise to anyone who may have taken offence at any of my comments. Though it is not an excuse, sometimes the heightened media scrutiny has caused me to act out in public. I know more is expected of me as an ambassador of British boxing and I promise in future to hold myself up to the highest possible standard. Anyone who knows me personally knows that I am in no way a racist or bigot and I hope the public accept this apology.'

Meanwhile, back in the world of his sport, Fury had been stripped of his IBF title as his contract with Klitschko included a rematch clause that precluded him facing the IBF's mandatory challenger, thirty-one-year-old Ukrainian Vyacheslav Glazkov who had won twenty-one of his twenty-two professional fights. Fury had held the IBF belt for only ten days.

But he had to have a rematch and Fury wanted it to be staged in his home town. He had in mind Old Trafford as the venue, the home of his beloved Manchester United. In the end the fight was scheduled for 9 July at the 20,000 capacity Manchester Arena. At the press conference to announce the contest, Klitschko said, 'I'm not OK with what comes out of Fury's mouth, his statements. For example – that all homosexual men and women and paedophiles belong in the same place, in jail basically. That all women belong in the kitchen and on their back. So that is basically where he sees Elton John and the Queen. To all people who say the same and think the same way out there, and to you Fury – I want to say fuck off.'

Fury turned up to the press conference with five

cheerleaders with a letter on each of their shirts that spelled out 'TYSON'. He stripped off his own T-shirt, grabbed his gut and said to Klitschko, 'Shame on you – you let a fat man beat you!' His fitness showed, he said, that he didn't care about his sport. 'Boxing doesn't mean a lot to me. If it did, I wouldn't have gone into camp four stone overweight and eaten every pie in Lancashire and drunk every pint of beer in the UK. I hate every second of it, and I wish I wasn't a boxer, but I'm in this position. I hate the training, the boxing, speaking to all you idiots, the whole lot. I'd rather be at home with the kids watching television. I hate boxing, but I'm just too good at it and making too much money to stop.'

Nevertheless, he was going to beat Klitschko again in the rematch. 'You will need to be about a thousand times better. You landed about four shots in twelve rounds,' he said. 'You might be going down as a Hall of Fame fighter, but you are [a] Hall of Dogshit fighter in my eyes. If the super champion can't land on a big, fat, lazy gypsy with a loud mouth, what kind of super champion is he? I'm going to knock him out inside a round.'

Fury then claimed that he was moving to Los Angeles where he felt he would be appreciated. 'I am not accepted in this country. I am a gypsy and that's it. I will always be a gypsy, I'll never change. I will always be fat and white and that's it. I am the champion yet I am thought of as a bum. The Americans enjoy the kind of brash talking I do, so what's the point in staying somewhere where they don't like what you are doing?'

In June, Fury had to postpone the Klitshcko rematch until

29 October after spraining his ankle in training. That same day, Fury was suspended by UK Anti-Doping (UKAD) after traces of the banned substance nandrolone were found in a urine sample taken from Fury in February 2015. His cousin Hughie was also charged with the same finding. Fury appealed and the suspension was lifted until a hearing could take place before the National Anti-Doping Panel (NADP).

In September, the fight was put off again by Fury because he was 'medically unfit'. The NADP hearing was scheduled for November. By that time, he had brought further trouble on himself. In October, he told *Rolling Stone* magazine that, for the past four months, he had been taking drugs, drinking every day and getting as fat as a pig. 'I'm going through a lot of personal demons, trying to shake them off,' he said when interviewed on 3 October. He said that he had been sober for three days. 'This has got nothing to do with my fighting – what I'm going through right now is my personal life.' And his life was a mess. 'I can't do nothing in my life that's any good to the general people because I'll never be accepted for who I am and what I am. They say I've got a version of bipolar. I'm a manic-depressive. I just hope someone kills me before I kill myself.' He revealed that he had quit training in May. 'From that day forward, I've never done any training. I've been out drinking, Monday to Friday to Sunday, and taking cocaine. I can't deal with it and the only thing that helps me is when I get drunk out of me mind.'

Among his profane tweets and impromptu videos, he posted a photoshopped image of himself sitting behind a mountain of coke, as drug kingpin Tony Montana – played by Al Pacino in the 1983 crime classic *Scarface*. He then announced his retirement before retracting it just three hours later with a tweet: 'Hahahaha u think you will get rid of the GYPSYKING that easy!!! I'm here to stay.'

Fury was on the verge of a nervous breakdown. During the summer in 2016 he had been driving his new red Ferrari F12 down the motorway when he realised that he wanted to kill himself. At the end of a five-mile straight, there was a bridge across the carriageway. He wound the car up to 190 mph and drove straight at it. 'I didn't care what anybody was thinking. I didn't care about hurting my family, friends, anybody. I didn't care about nothing. I just wanted to die. So bad. I had given up on life,' he said.

But he heard a voice saying, 'No, don't do this, Tyson. Think about your kids. Think about your family. Think about your little boys and girls growing up with no father, and everybody saying their dad was a weak man who left you and took the easy way out.'

He pulled over, shaking, and decided that he would never try – or even think about – killing himself again. After driving home safely, he got in touch with counsellors and began to deal with his clinical depression. Back in the gym he shed over 130 lbs. He prayed to God and swore that he would never parade his private opinions in public again.

On 12 October Fury relinquished his WBO and WBA titles, figuring he would have been stripped of them anyway after pulling out of the 29 October Klitschko rematch. The BBBC also temporarily revoked his licence, 'pending further investigation into anti-doping and medical issues', they said.

In a statement, Fury said, 'I feel that it is only fair and right and for the good of boxing to keep the titles active and allow the other contenders to fight for the vacant belts that I proudly won and held as the undefeated heavyweight champion of the world when I defeated the long-standing champion Wladimir Klitschko. I won the titles in the ring and I believe that they should be lost in the ring, but I'm unable to defend at this time and I have taken the hard and emotional decision to now officially vacate my treasured world titles and wish the next-in-line contenders all the very best as I now enter another big challenge in my life which I know, like against Klitschko, I will conquer.'

Mick Hennessy added, 'Tyson will still be the linear world heavyweight champion in everyone's eyes. He beat the most dominant champion in the modern era of boxing on an amazing night in Germany to earn that accolade and that will never change. Whilst it's heartbreaking to see Tyson vacate the world titles that he worked so long and hard for all his life, what's paramount now is that he receives the medical treatment along with the love of his family and friends and the support of the boxing world to make a full recovery.' Fury was suffering from severe depression. This was being addressed and the early signs were good. 'If he gets himself together, he is an incredible fighter, an incredible athlete and he will be impossible to beat in the heavyweight division.'

No matter who picked up the vacant titles, Peter Fury insisted that Tyson would regain his belts when he returned to the ring. 'I'm very proud of my nephew's achievements and Tyson will be back stronger from this,' he said. 'I will make sure, no matter what we have to deal with, Tyson not only comes back but will reclaim what's rightfully his.' He believed that, once he was well again, the world of boxing would welcome Tyson back with open arms and the BBBC would have no option but to restore his licence. 'This is a guy that's needed medical treatment. Once the powers that be say he's fit to box, then there's no reason why he can't be reinstated. He's at the pinnacle of his career. He's only twenty-eight. He's got a massive future.' Tyson was being treated for bipolar disorder and Peter thought his suspension might be a blessing in disguise. 'How many young people do you hear about who have committed suicide down to depression? Depression is an illness.'

Even so, Fury was determined not to stay out of the fight game for too long. On 23 December, he tweeted, 'Merry Christmas, guys. I've had a nightmare 2016, done a lot of stuff I'm not proud of, but my promise to you is I'll return in 2017.'

Uncle Peter said they were looking for a fight against WBC champion Deontay Wilder in April or May of the new year. In March, Fury said he would make his comeback on 13 May, tweeting, 'I'm taking on all bums. Keep my belts warm guys as they belong to the king – who ever got my belts I'm coming for you! Big or small.'

However, the British Boxing Board of Control pointed out that he was still suspended. 'He has anti-doping issues and other medical issues which all have to be considered,' said general secretary Robert Smith. 'What we're more concerned about is that he looks after himself and gets himself in a fit and proper state of mind to carry on with his career, if he does.' A legal battle over loss of earnings ensued and looked like it could bankrupt UKAD, who eventually backed down. They issued a statement: 'Taking into account the delays in results management that meant charges were not brought in respect of the nandrolone findings until June 2016, and the provisional suspensions that Tyson and Hughie Fury have already effectively served, the two-year period of ineligibility is backdated to 13 December 2015 and therefore expires at midnight on 12 December 2017.'

The BBBC agreed. After interviewing Fury on 19 January 2018, they lifted his suspension, subject to receipt of his latest medical records. Fury could not wait. On 31 March 2018, IBF and WBA champion Anthony Joshua was due to face the WBO title holder Joseph Parker, a New Zealander, in a unification bout. Fury immediately tweeted Parker: 'If you want I'll come spar you when in the UK training for the fight. It will help both me and you. You won't find better sparring than me I promise you. Let me know pal?'

Fury then signed with Frank Warren, who announced that Fury's comeback would be on 9 June, in the Manchester Arena. He had already gone back into training at Ricky Hatton's gym in Hyde and began posting pictures on social media, showing himself slimmer. He was also taunting Joshua who, by then, had the WBA, IBF and WBO titles. But a showdown with Joshua was at least three fights away.

COMEBACK

Fury's comeback fight would be against thirty-nine-year-old Sefer Seferi, an Albanian born in Macedonia. He was a cruiserweight with twenty-one knockouts in his twenty-three victories. Just six-foot-two with a reach of seventy-five inches, he was 66 lbs lighter than Fury at the weigh-in. In his one bout in the heavyweight division, he had lost to the Syrian Manuel 'Diamond Boy' Charr for the vacant WBA international heavyweight title in September 2016. However, he had been significantly more active than Fury, fighting four times since Fury faced Klitschko two-and-a-half years earlier.

Resident in Switzerland, Seferi told local magazine, *20 Minutes*, 'This would make a dream come true. I never thought I'd have the chance to stand against Fury – my idol. Fury is a boxing legend of the twenty-first century. He is tall, has weight and strength, moves to it quite easily, and he has dethroned Wladimir Klitschko. Fury is a bear.' Nevertheless, he was confident that he could cause an upset. 'I will not make it easy for Fury. I will try to put pressure on him. Someone has to stand up to him in the build-up.'

Fury had shed 7 stone for the fight and had found his old form, turning up to the press conference in Manchester wearing a loud shirt, filming Frank Warren on his phone and shouting, *'You're live on Instagram!'* Explaining his comeback, he gave thanks to the WBC champ. 'It was Deontay Wilder who gave me inspiration do it because he said I was done. I was walking along a canal at the time and I felt like jumping in. I'm going to turn it around and knock him out. I believe I can tie one arm behind my back and beat Wilder and Joshua. They can pick which one they want, left hand, right hand. That's how confident I am in my own ability.'

There was real venom, too. 'I'm going to come back and knock him out for what he said and for what he said about Mike Tyson.'

This was a comment Wilder had made about Fury's namesake back in January, when he said, 'Me versus Tyson in '86 – I'd kick the hell outta that guy. Listen, I've got to keep it real. I know people always go back to the old school or look at the new school and there's no school where I'm not No. 1 on Earth.'

Fury said, 'Mike Tyson is a legendary person and he said he would have knocked him out in a round. To speak about someone that you can never fight from a different era in a disrespectful manner is distasteful.'

But there had been times, Fury admitted, when he had

second thoughts about returning to boxing at all. 'I didn't want to fight. I almost didn't make it to the training camp in Marbella. It was a 1,700-mile drive and there were about five or six times along the road that I almost turned round. I was making excuses. But I'm here, I'm back. The fire is back now.'

Warren pointed out that Fury was still the lineal world champion, as he had never lost his titles in the ring. 'Until Wilder and Joshua beat Tyson [Fury], they are not the true champions.'

Fury said that he did not need to fight for the money. He wanted to inspire others. 'There are a lot of people out there with mental health problems, so if I can come back, they can, too.'

Unbeaten heavyweight Alex Dickinson, who was fighting on Fury's undercard on 9 June, had been sparring with the former unified heavyweight champ during training. 'It was a pleasure to share the ring with him, he's flying,' said Dickinson.

'He beat the shit out of me!' Fury joked. He was convinced that they had chosen the right opponent for his comeback. 'Seferi is a fighter with a big punch, but I intend to show the world I still have the best skills and movement in the heavyweight division,' Fury told the *Daily Telegraph*. 'I want to be very active this year and get myself into the position to get all my belts back . . . I'm fitter, stronger and faster than the Fury of 2015.'

Warren thought that the fight would shake off Fury's ring rust. 'Seferi is no pushover, he's gone the distance with a world-class fighter in Manuel Charr. He has spent the majority of his career at cruiserweight, but so had Tony Bellew and David Haye before stepping up to the heavyweight division.'

In fact, it was later revealed that Fury had wanted to face Joshua on his comeback, but promoter Eddie Hearn had prevented it. 'Frank Warren picked Seferi because the other ones won't fight me,' said Fury.

By this point he had stopped working with his Uncle Peter as his trainer and taken on younger coach Ben Davison. 'I went down to Marbella and saw Ben training some boxers,' Fury told the *Sunday Times*. 'I was impressed with the way he worked and told him that he would be one of the world's best trainers within five years.' Before taking him on, Fury wanted to test Davison's confidence and see if he was game. 'If you're going to train somebody like me you have the confidence,' and he came up with an interesting trial. 'I was having coffee with Ben down at Puerto Banus and there were two very attractive girls walking down the front in bikinis. So I said, "Ben, if you go up to those girls and ask for their number, if you get it, you can be my trainer." He was straight up and after them. Two minutes later, he was back, waving a piece of paper, saying, "Here, I've got their number."

'I said, "Deal done, you're my trainer."'

Davison told the *Daily Telegraph*, 'With Tyson, I've had to be a trainer, psychologist, physiologist, nutritionist, and a friend . . . when I finish a session, I assess where Tyson is, to see how he is mentally. I've got to make sure he's not eating this or that. It's a twenty-four seven job.' On one occasion, Tyson sat down with him and said, 'You've saved my life and I never could have done this without you.'

Davison brought into the team conditioning coach Kristian Blacklock and nutritionist Greg Marriott, who put Fury on a ketogenic diet – minimal carbohydrates, high levels of fats and some protein. 'My goal at the beginning was to get his love back for the sport,' Davison said. 'His father, John, and his brother, Shane, have been a brilliant support. Sometimes I ask their advice about him as they know how his brain works . . . John has said the only person who can beat Tyson is himself.'

Fury was now a man of limitless ambition – outside boxing. He told the *Sun* that he wanted to host a TV weight-loss boot camp. As a Man U fan, he wanted to meet then-manager José Mourinho, as his training schedule did not let him get to Old Trafford very often. And he wanted to sing like Johnny Cash. But most of all, he wanted to be a doctor. 'After boxing, I am going to be a doctor and I'm going to help people,' he said. 'When I have finished in a few years, I'll still only be in my early thirties. Then I'll study for the next seven years to be a doctor. If I'm forty and a qualified doctor, I'm still a young doctor.' This was not a new plan. 'I made that decision a few years ago. I studied very hard at school but I turned to sport because that was my calling.' After all, everyone in his family – 'except for my mum' – had been a prizefighter.

Fury's whole attitude was now different. He did not even want to be the bad guy in the clash. 'Now I don't have to play-act to sell tickets,' he said. 'I'm just enjoying every day in the gym. Every day is Christmas, every day is a bank holiday.' Before boxing had not meant much. It had been strictly business. 'This time it will be fun for me and entertainment for everyone. Everything you love that becomes business always ends up shit, basically. When it is about making money it can become monotonous. It was crap, it was just a job, something I didn't enjoy.'

In the *Sun*, he said he was in no mood for baiting Joshua and called him a 'top bloke'. Nor was he concerned about the fifteen belts he had given away. 'I can't really fit any more belts in my house. It was a long time ago, I've moved on and those belts have new owners,' he said.

He insisted that Seferi would be no pushover, telling the *Daily Telegraph* that he was 'a distant relative of a barbarian who was a Macedonian king'. Fury also said that he himself needed to put in some rounds in the ring because he had been away from fighting for so long. 'I don't need a knockout after ten seconds. These Albanian fellas are very, very tough. That's why I picked him . . . Any man who's had twenty-four fights and only lost once on points and never been knocked out can't be a pushover. Even if he's fought Romanian road-sweepers, they all take knocking out. Try punching someone and knocking them out. It's quite hard.'

And he was taking the fight very seriously. 'This is a world title fight for me,' Fury said. 'Every one of these people who come to fight me are challenging me for my lineal heavyweight status, which goes back over two hundred years.'

Fury compared himself to Sugar Ray Leonard, who came back after three years in 1987 to fight one of the greatest middleweights in Marvin Hagler – and beat him. Davison added, 'Muhammad Ali had great wins after he came back, even though he lost the first big fight against Joe Frazier in 1971, which was down to tactics. Wladimir Klitschko and his brother Vitali both had great wins as heavyweight champions after they had suffered defeats. Lots of fighters have come back. And Tyson is still undefeated.'

Still never short of confidence, Fury said, 'If I can't wipe the floor with the whole of the current heavyweight division, I will get on my knees in front of whoever beats me and kiss their feet . . . if I can't win against Anthony Joshua, Deontay Wilder, Sefer Seferi and whoever else wants to fight, then I will say I never was any good and I should never have been boxing.'

With a week to go to the fight, Fury was as ebullient as ever. 'I am the greatest heavyweight of all time, I've not got to be modest. I am the best ever – me, Tyson Fury, the Gypsy King, the one and only. When has there ever been somebody like me? There have been plenty of come-forward aggressors, there have been plenty of boxers off the back foot. But when has there ever been a six-foot-nine switch-hitter with the confidence of Muhammad Ali and Floyd Mayweather rolled into one? I'm unbeaten, I'm fast, I'm brash, I'm young, I'm good-looking, I'm tanned – I've even got white teeth. What more could I have?' That was a question he would answer in the ring. 'I'm a fighter, I'm a boxer, I'm a sportsman, I'm a showman, I am the greatest of my time. I've already beaten the lineal champion, I've already beaten the legendary champion Wladimir Klitschko, and guess what, I did it easily. So, put me in the ring with these bums and I will tell you how to put them down – easy-peasy lemon-squeezy.'

He could not wait to get at them. 'I'm so serious I can't sleep at night thinking about bums all the time. I'm thinking about putting my fist through the side of A. J.'s [Anthony Joshua] jaw, I'm thinking about knocking Wilder spark out, all fifteen stone of him. Putting him upside down on a heap in the floor.' Fury had his sights firmly set on both Joshua and Wilder. 'I have nightmares about these guys. The nightmares consist of me looking at them and wanting to smash their faces right in, but not having the opportunity to do so. When I do get the opportunity to do so, I will annihilate them both.' What was more, he knew they would have to face him sooner or later. 'I have to beat both of them in order for my career to be defined, and to be looked back at as a legendary champion. Whatever they bring, I can adapt. I don't think they'll land on me.'

Frank Warren agreed. 'Joshua would have a big problem against him because he is easy to hit. His defence is not good enough. Wilder wouldn't even lay a glove on Fury. In their hearts, they know it, too,' he said. 'But if Tyson and Joshua ever meet in a world title fight, it would be one of the biggest events in British sporting history. Right up there with the 1966 World Cup Final.'

Fury made it clear that his mental problems were behind him. 'I'm in the prime of my life. I have never felt fitter, stronger or better. Rome wasn't built in a day. This is my second career now and I'm coming back after nearly a thousand days,' he said. 'I needed the rest. I felt tired of boxing and was drained. I needed to be rejuvenated, so a hundred per cent the break benefited me. I woke up every day wishing I would not wake up any more, but I am living proof anyone can come back from the brink. There are a lot of people out there suffering with mental health problems who think all their days will be grey, but life can improve again and you will start to enjoy the little things again.

'There are challenges out there that I want to take on. I want to achieve more. I was at the top and didn't feel there was more to do, but now new champions have risen. A structured routine in life is key – such as having short-term and long-term goals. I advise living a healthy, clean life. There is nothing better than getting in the gym and getting the endorphins going.' He likened himself to a goldfish that had been trapped and was now being released back into the river where he belonged. He still had a craving for fast food, though. After a public workout at the National Football Museum in Manchester, he headed to Nandos where he treated all fifty-two people in the restaurant to their evening meal. It cost him £700.

Fury weighed in at 19 st 10 lbs, having lost almost 8 stone in training, while Seferi tipped the scales at 15 st 1 lb. To emphasise the difference, Fury lifted his opponent off the ground and cradled him in his arms.

Before the fight, Fury was visited by ring legend Roy Jones Jr, only the second fighter after Bob Fitzsimmons to win both the middleweight and heavyweight world titles. The American boxer was doing a few shows in the UK and drove from Newcastle to Manchester to have lunch with Tyson.

'He said it's unnatural for someone so big to have so much movement, talent and skill,' said Fury. 'He said he has never seen it ever before. He's been around boxing all his life and never seen anything like me.' At the pre-fight press conference,

Fury concurred with Jones' assessment. 'There ain't been no one like me – ever. There ain't been a six-foot-nine southpaw-orthodox counter-punching puncher, who has got the brain and movement of a middleweight. I am a freak of nature.'

He was wearing another loud shirt with animals printed on it, the '"King of the Jungle" shirt – with no lion, because that's me.' He did not want to talk about Klitschko, who he dismissed as 'a bum, useless'. As for Anthony Joshua or Deontay Wilder: 'Give them bats and hammers, I am ready. I don't need any warm-up fights. Put them up now and I will whup them all . . . I will fight Wilder and Joshua on the same night. People haven't seen the best Tyson Fury yet. They think the Klitschko performance was my best. That was nowhere near, it was about fifty per cent.' And his dark days? 'Forget about it. Move on. Chapter two.'

He also said it was great for him to be back fighting in Manchester. It was the seventh time that he had a fight scheduled to take place at the Manchester Arena, but all of the previous six failed to take place. 'I'm looking very much forward to fighting in Manchester, putting on a show and going home. I've been away from my kids for eight weeks and it's been hard. The youngest two, I've never been away from them ever and they don't know what it's like. It is hard being a boxer and a dad. The sacrifices have to be made, if you want to be the best you have to do the best.'

On 9 June 2018, Fury walked out to the ring to a medley including Afroman's 'Because I Got High' while the Mancunian crowd roared. He was so glad to be back in the ring that as the two fighters touched gloves he leant over and kissed Seferi on the lips. Fury went on to dominate his opponent completely and began playing to the 15,000-strong crowd, at one pointed doing the Ali shuffle and firing off a big right hand on the bell. During round 2, Fury was warned by referee Phil Edwards for gurning and showboating and in the meantime Seferi tried in vain to reach Fury's head with his right uppercuts. A huge fight broke out at ringside with dozens turning away from the ring to join in. At one stage, Fury even stopped fighting and appeared to have a laugh with Seferi. He then switched stance to southpaw.

The pair fought in earnest in the third, with stewards in yellow T-shirts in the background trying to break up the brawl in the crowd. Fury rocked Seferi with a long straight right. Later in the round, he landed a right uppercut and cuffing right hook. An unexpected attack from Seferi followed in which he landed a right hook on Fury's midriff, but it surprised rather than hurt him and Fury controlled the rest of the round with his jab. It looked like Fury had dropped the Macedonian with a body shot but the referee judged it to be a slip. In the fourth, Fury caught Seferi with a big right, putting him on the back foot. An uppercut sounded like it had done a lot of damage towards the end of the fourth and Seferi's corner retired him. There were boos, and drinks bottles and beer cascaded down from the upper tiers.

'It felt fantastic, thank you to the fans. Manchester, you're beautiful,' Fury said on BT Sport after the fight. 'It meant miracles to me. Sefer is a tough guy, he's quite awkward, I wanted to have a fight with him. Congratulations to Sefer, God bless him.'

Later he dismissed the fight 'a little dance under the lights' and 'a loosener'. 'If I am brutally honest, I could have done him in the first ten seconds,' he said. 'But what good would that have done me?' He compared the fight to his debut, having been so long out of the ring. 'I learnt two and a half years is a long time to be out and now I am back I want to enjoy every moment.' It wasn't his fault, he said, that Seferi had pulled out after just four rounds and he promised to have a world title back by the end of the year.

Frank Warren said he would have to lose more weight first. 'At the weigh-in he wore those pants for the testicular cancer charity. He put them on and I'm surprised he never got testicular cancer because they were so tight. They made him look a bit bigger than he was. He's still got a stone, stone-and-a-half to get off and when he does it will make him more mobile.' Warren blamed nerves for Fury showing off so much to a star-studded crowd, including former footballer Paul Gascoigne and celebrity chef Gordon Ramsay. 'I get pissed off with that, but that's what he does. He's a spontaneous guy,' said Warren. 'He plays to the crowd, he's always done that. I think that's the last we'll see of that. I think that was all about him being pleased to be in the ring.'

Tony Bellew also watched the fight. Having beaten David Haye for a second time, he was looking for a new opponent, and tweeted, 'I will knock the big man @Tyson_Fury out!! Simple as that! #LetsDoThis'.

'It's up to Tony Bellew,' said Warren. 'We could do Tony Bellew before the end of the year.'

In fact, Fury's next fight would be against Italy's Francesco

Pianeta in Windsor Park, Belfast, on 18 August, on a bill topped by local superstar, WBO interim featherweight champion Carl Frampton, who faced Australian challenger Luke Jackson. The venue was also the National Football Stadium and when Fury made his appearance it would be the first time he would fight outdoors. Pianeta had twice challenged for the world title – once against Wladimir Klitschko – with twenty-one knockouts in his thirty-five wins.

When the fight was announced on 12 July, Frank Warren said, 'I don't believe we will have him playing up to the crowd on this occasion because he will need to be more business-like in a riskier fight and also because of his desire to start putting a marker down once again in the heavyweight division.'

At 18 st 6 lbs, Fury was 18 lbs lighter than when he had fought Seferi. Pianeta weighed in at 18 st 3 lbs. The thirty-four-year-old Italian was four inches shorter than Fury with a reach that was five inches shorter.

'Tyson had a short rest after Seferi, but is back in full-time camp ready for this challenge in Belfast,' said Warren. 'He needs rounds under his belt before moving on to the next level and this fight will do that and make him work for his win.'

Ben Davison also wanted Fury to be serious in the ring. Fury acknowledged, 'We saw the joker in the last camp, we saw the showman, the entertainer. Ben wants a serious approach this time and that is what he'll get. All business in Belfast! Everything is great, but if he wants me to be serious about this fight, then I will be serious.' It was not in his character to be like that. 'I'm not serious about anything in my whole life, everything is like fun and games – even for Klitschko I wasn't serious. I was doing all dance moves, everything. But listen, if Ben wants serious, Ben will get serious. I'll go in there and do my job and that's it. I won't even smile once.'

Meanwhile, negotiations were underway for the Wilder fight now scheduled for December. After performing an open workout in cow-print underpants, Fury said the deal was very close to being done. First, there was Pianeta to deal with. 'I've got to flatten him first, then Wilder, let's dance,' he said, putting the WBC title-holder on notice. 'You've been dealing with shithouses in the past, Eddie Hearn and Anthony Joshua. I am a man of my word, if I say I'll fight you, I'll fight you. I'll knock Francesco Pianeta into next week. Then I'll knock you spark out, too. Good luck.'

Fury reckoned that Joshua and Hearn were running scared of scheduling their own fight with Wilder. 'They've no bottle, no heart and no guts,' he said. 'When you've got no nuts, you won't fight people. I'm taking this fight to prove to the British public what they are – shithouses.' Elsewhere he called Joshua 'an idiot . . . chiselled out of stone who is afraid of his own shadow' and suggested he had 'made a laughing stock of British boxing' for failing to sign a unification fight with Wilder in 2018, putting his WBA, IBF and WBO belts up against the American's WBC crown.

Fury said he had come out of retirement to put British boxing back on the map. In fact, *Daily Telegraph* boxing correspondent Gareth Davies pointed out that British boxing was already enjoying a golden age with Fury joined by the likes of Anthony Joshua, Dillian Whyte, Dereck Chisora,

Tony Bellew and Hughie Fury all staging mega-money fights. Davies also pointed out that Fury was sitting pretty because he knew that Wilder had to come after if he wanted to be the lineal heavyweight champion of the world.

'I believe I am the best in the world by a mile and my three years out of the ring can have only given them a quarter of a mile. I am still three quarters ahead,' Fury said. 'I will prove it by knocking out Pianeta, I will prove it by going to Las Vegas and knocking out Wilder, and then I will outbox all the bums over here.'

Joshua's promoter Eddie Hearn dismissed the idea that Fury would face Wilder later that year as hype. 'What? When he's just fought Sefer Seferi? And now he's fighting "Andrea Pizza-netta",' Hearn said. 'Don't be ridiculous. Listen, you can be bluffed out by what you want.'

Meanwhile, Wilder announced that he would be coming to Belfast to see the Fury–Pianeta fight. Fury, as always, knew that even the easiest fight could end in disaster, but was willing to risk it all. 'There is a target on my back,' he said. 'Pianeta is just one win away from being back right there among the best. I sparred with him in Germany when he was 26–0. He was tough, strong and he is a good opponent – very good. It was before he went on to fight Klitschko and [Ruslan] Chagaev for world titles, but I was impressed.'

Consequently, after a two-day break following the Seferi fight, Fury had been training in Ricky Hatton's gym every day, although he took time out to dismiss Wilder as 'a dosser who's never fought anybody . . . when you look at Wilder's record, who's he fought?' he said. He then reeled off a list to show why Wilder's wins scarcely counted: Bermane Stiverne was an easy win – 'a powerful hand, but we can all avoid that'; Johann Duhaupas – 'a French journeyman beaten by everybody'; Eric Molina, a Mexican schoolteacher 'who is relatively a bum, too'; Gerald Washington – 'the lad with no guts on him, the tall fella, a novice who was afraid of getting hit . . . Luis Ortiz is the best man he fought, but Ortiz is George Foreman's age. Ortiz was a very good win, but Ortiz is a very old man in sports terms. Even Ortiz nearly had him out of there . . . if I can't beat Wilder and Joshua on the same night, I'm a bum, too.' This, he felt, was not the case. 'Not only am I the best boxer, I'm the best talker, mover, puncher, dancer, singer and the best-looking, too. Have that in your pipe and smoke it.'

He claimed his forthcoming fight with Wilder would be 'on like *Donkey Kong*' and goaded the WBC heavyweight champion by calling him 'Beyonce Wilder'. Fury knew that Wilder would be at ringside for his Pianeta fight, doing commentary for BT, but he said it wouldn't put him off: 'I will deal with him when I'm done with the fight.'

Four days before the fight, Fury turned his guns on Pianeta. 'I've eaten, slept and drunk boxing – I've done nothing else but box since November,' he told the pre-fight press conference. 'So if I can't beat Pianeta I might as well get on my knees and kiss his two feet because I'm clearly shot to pieces. But if I'm half the man I was a few years ago I will write Pianeta off like a good 'un, put a face on him like the Elephant Man . . . I'm going to smash him to pieces, make Italian sausage out of him.' And he was ready to take the next step. 'I'm feeling healthy as a trout, fit as a flea. Sparring is going fantastically well. I've had some great sparring with southpaws. I've had two Americans over, a Scandinavian and a Yorkshireman, and the one I couldn't understand was the Yorkshireman. He had the worst accent of everybody.'

Wilder gatecrashed the weigh-in at the Europa Hotel in Belfast. The Bronze Bomber came in yelling his trademark 'Bomb squad!' Fury's father took exception to this. Following attempts to shout each other down, fifty-four-year-old John aggressively approached Wilder before he was restrained by a security guard and Ben Davison. Further shouting ensued. Fury initially remained cool, even shaking hands. But as the atmosphere grew heated Wilder had to be separated from Tyson himself.

Wilder said, 'Fury's going to win, then I'm going to knock him out.' Of John Fury, he added, 'I'll get my grandfather out of the grave to knock him out.'

Tyson responded, 'I'll butcher Wilder, you watch.' Wilder would end up fighting him because he was a boxing legend. And it would be Fury who would be the draw in what would be a £10 million fight. 'Make no mistake, Wilder is not a pay-per-view fighter in his home country. He's never ever done a pay-per-view fight. I am the draw on this side of the fight – without me, he goes back to fighting some bum for a million dollars.' Fury did not need any more belts to add to his collection. 'Like Mike Tyson said, as a kid, these belts are of some use and you think they're something. But when you've actually got them, you realise they are just a bit of metal with some leather welded on them.'

Just before the Fury bout began, Wilder faced his own fight, albeit of a less powerful variety, as he was at ringside. He was talking to Paul Gascoigne when the footballer caught him off-guard with a playful left jab to the side of the face, followed up with a right-hand punch. Gazza then gave the WBC champion a kiss on the cheek before taking his seat. However, some of the fans were not so sanguine and gave the Bronze Bomber a hostile reception. One threw a pint of beer over him. Wilder reacted angrily and had to be led away by security before he put on a brave face for the TV cameras. That had not been the only confrontation out of the ring that evening. Earlier, middleweight boxer and fellow traveller Billy Joe Saunders threw half a chicken at Wilder in a branch of Nando's. Tables and chairs were knocked over as Wilder gave chase.

Finally, it was time for the scheduled boxing entertainment to begin. Pianeta walked to the ring to 'We Will Rock You' by Queen. Fury came out to 'Live Your Life' by Rihanna, but as he approached the ring it changed to Lynyrd Skynyrd's 'Sweet Home Alabama' – Wilder's home state.

From the first bell, Pianeta went on the offensive, forcing Fury to move in and out of range. But the Italian failed to land a power punch, while Fury moved behind his jabs. The Gypsy King began putting together punches in bunches, dancing off the ropes to elude the Italian and bank some valuable points. With Ricky Hatton, Billy Joe Saunders and young Ben Davison in his corner, Fury moved through the gears, looking agile, flashing out the jab and showing the deft footwork that belied his height and weight. As a southpaw, Pianeta looked to counter with sneaky left hands, behind a high guard.

Fury was light on his feet and Pianeta could not catch him in round 2. Tyson could see the Italian's punches a mile off. In round 3, Fury began to put together some useful combinations, but took a right from Pianeta against the ropes at the close. In round 4, Fury landed a left hook. He was both agile and accurate.

Despite a minor lapse in the fifth, Fury showed that he was the better fighter. His focus never wavered. Time and again he tied Pianeta up, looking to release his best shots. It began to rain on those sections of the crowd who Q. had not? got seats under cover.

In round 6, Fury began leaning on Pianeta, occasionally dropping his hands, though Davison warned him not to do anything silly. Then, in round 7, Fury caught Pianeta with a low blow and the Italian was given some time to recover. A right hand from Fury then began the unravelling of his opponent. Fury hurt Pianeta with a clubbing left, forcing him to tuck up to survive the remaining seconds.

In round 8, Fury landed a solid left to Pianeta's head. While in complete control, he made no effort to move in and finish his man off. Fury switched to southpaw in the ninth and caught Pianeta again in the dying seconds. Then he cruised through the last 3 minutes, keeping Pianeta at arm's length. His shots were sparing – perhaps, with Wilder watching every move at ringside, he did not want to give away his whole box of tricks. It was an easy victory with referee Steve Gray scoring the fight 100–90.

After the fight, Frank Warren confirmed that Fury's next contest would indeed be with Deontay Wilder. Fury gave the news to the 25,000 fans at Windsor Park: 'We are two men that will fight anybody. Wilder has been trying to make a big fight with the other chump' – referring to Joshua – 'they called, I answered. I said, "Send me the contract", I said, "Yes." Now he gets his chance to fight the lineal heavyweight champion of the world. Believe me, I will go to Las Vegas and I will bring home the belt. I will knock this man out.'

Wilder climbed into the ring and told Tyson, 'We are ready now. The best fighting the best is what the world wants to see, and they will get it. I will knock you out, Tyson Fury, in devastating fashion.'

Addressing the crowd, he said, 'It is one thing that Tyson Fury has never had. He had many belts, but he's never had the WBC belt. And if he ever thinks about having this belt, he better wake up and apologise to me because he'll never have this.' Turning back to his future opponent, he said, 'I can't wait to fight you because I am going to knock you out. I promise you. You've never been knocked out but you're going to feel the experience, what it feels to get hit by the Bronze Bomber.'

'Listen, you can't knock out what you can't hit,' said Fury, indicating Pianeta. 'This man couldn't land a blow on me tonight.'

SHOWDOWN AT THE STAPLES CENTER

Fury always knew that Deontay Wilder was the man to beat. The month after defeating Klitschko to become world heavyweight champion, Fury flew to New York to watch Wilder take on Poland's Artur Szpilka in January 2016.

'It wasn't a set-up job, when I went over to New York they wouldn't even let me in the building, I barged my way right through,' said Fury. 'I said, "The first man touches me gets their jaw broke." As soon as the fight was done, I was in the ring. I was on him.' His camp had warned him against taking the trip at all. 'I was advised by Mick Hennessy and Peter not to go to America, as that was giving him relevance. But I said I'm trying to make a multi-million-dollar fight. I know how to promote boxing. I paid for my own ticket, my own hotel. It was all paid for by me setting this up years ago. It is written in the stars I will knock him spark out.'

Deontay Wilder was born in Tuscaloosa, Alabama, on 22

October 1985, making him nearly three years older than Fury. Originally his sports were American football and basketball and it was only when he was in college, about to make the basketball team, that everything changed when his girlfriend called to say that a child was on the way. The doctors told them that their newborn daughter Naieya had spina bifida and Wilder realised that he needed lots of money to pay the hospital bills.

'I had to grow up fast and it was the scariest thing of my life,' he said. 'I thought that every fighter that stepped in the ring made a pile of money.' At the age of twenty Wilder began to attend the Skyy Boxing Gym in Northport, Alabama, to train under former US Olympic boxing coach and promoter Jay Deas. Wilder supported himself by working on a truck delivering Budweiser. He was assistant to delivery driver Robbie Hallman, and from the first day of his training told his boss, 'I'm going to be world heavyweight champion.' His job also helped to promote his strength. He would walk into bars carrying two 60-lb kegs of beer. Later, he would carry a 165-lb barrel on his shoulders.

As an amateur boxer, he won the national Golden Gloves championship and a bronze at the 2008 Olympics in Bejing – that was where the nickname Bronze Bomber came from. It was also a tribute to Joe Louis – the Brown Bomber – another Alabama boy. That November, Wilder turned professional. In December 2012, he knocked out the unbeaten Kelvin Price in Los Angeles with his signature shot, a straight right to the jaw, to take the vacant WBC Continental Americas heavyweight title. The following April, he knocked out former European heavyweight champion and 2000 Olympic gold medallist Audley Harrison in Sheffield a minute into round 1. Harrison retired after the fight.

Tyson Fury was not impressed by any of his achievements. 'You're a skinny guy, a basketball player,' he told Wilder. 'You only started boxing when you were twenty. I've been doing this all my life. I beat guys like you every day.'

But Wilder was a puncher. None of his first nine fights went past round 2. Only four of his first thirty-two contests reached round 4. His thirty-third fight did go the distance, against the Canadian Bermane Stiverne in January 2015. Wilder won with a unanimous decision to take the WBC heavyweight title. At a rematch in November 2017, he knocked out Stiverne 3 minutes into round 1.

The fight against Szpilka, watched by Tyson Fury, was not so straightforward for him. The Pole took the first three rounds. Wilder changed tactics and took the next five with the jab. Realising that he could not win on points, Szpilka rushed out in the ninth and launched a big swing. Wilder anticipated this and Szpilka ran into a right hook that knocked him to the canvas. He had to be stretchered from the ring and ended up in hospital.

Tyson Fury climbed into the ring and called Wilder out, telling him he couldn't fight. As they stood face to face shouting at each other, the six-foot-seven Wilder found himself in an unusual position. He had to look up at Fury. Ever the showman, Fury started the soccer-style chant, 'There's only one Tyson Fury' and eventually security pushed him out. His parting words to Wilder were, 'Anytime you want – anywhere. Fury's coming for you.' But then came Tyson Fury's lengthy boxing hiatus. While he was out of the ring, Wilder made five defences of his title, winning them all with a stoppage.

Now it was time for the two men to meet and both were unbeaten – Wilder had forty victories with thirty-nine knockouts, nineteen in round 1. Fury had twenty-seven wins with nineteen knockouts, only three in round 1.

On 27 September, it was announced that the fight would take place on 1 December at the Staples Center, Los Angeles, which had a capacity of over 20,000. According to the California State Athletic Commission, Wilder would earn a guaranteed base purse of $4 million and Fury would take home a guaranteed $3 million. Revenues would be split, with Wilder estimated to make up to $14 million and Fury said to earn around $10.25 million. Both boxers would see this increase to their base purses after receiving their percentages from pay-per-view revenue.

First, the publicity was pumped up: 'It's on baby! I'm gonna knock @BronzeBomber out he never fought a puncher like me. That I promise,' Fury tweeted, while Wilder went on Instagram to say: 'This fight is definitely on and I can't wait – it's going to be explosive. The two best heavyweights competing against each other, the best fighting the best, giving the people what they want.'

Fury responded, 'Shit just got serious. Deontay Wilder, you're going to get it mate.'

During a media tour that took in London, New York and Los Angeles, the two rivals engaged in a battle of words.

Fury maintained he had 'the psychological edge' because Wilder's nickname, the Bronze Bomber, meant he'd be a 'third-placed man'.

'I want this to be one of the greatest comebacks in boxing history, similar to George Foreman, Muhammad Ali and the other great comeback fighters,' Fury said. 'If I can win this belt they'll put me amongst the greats of the comebacks. All the controversy and stuff I've been through, adds to the flavour.' Victory was assured. 'I know for a fact, deep down in my soul. It's written in the stars for me to come back and wipe you out, in style, in America. And everyone is going to say, "How did he do that?" And I'm going to say, "I told you so." I'm back. I'm beating you one million per cent. I have no doubts, even after all the time off – you cannot beat me. I know deep in my heart you can't beat me. I know no one can – I'll retire unbeaten heavyweight champion of the world, like Rocky Marciano, the second man to do it in history. You can't beat me and ten more like you can't beat me.'

Wilder's response was, 'It's not your time. This is my time. It will for ever be my time – until I retire. Because I speak it, believe it, receive it.' He told the *Sunday Times* that he underwent a transformation in the ring. 'Sometimes I frighten myself when I'm like that,' he said. 'It's scary.' In his forty fights, when he once failed to knock his opponent out, he then knocked him out on the rematch. 'When I hit them with the right hand, I feel their bone structure, the bone structure of their face, on my hand. Then I know it's over.'

Fury and Wilder's final press conference in Los Angeles had to be abandoned after their rival entourages came to blows on stage. At first there had been laughter from the crowd when Fury said, 'He tried to make it in American football and basketball, but he was not good enough. I did not want to do anything else but be a fighting man. That is all I have ever done. I even had the opportunity to come to the United States once to be a basketball player, but I said, "No, thank you, I am going to be the heavyweight champion of the world."' Wilder began screaming obscenities in Fury's face. He accused Frank Warren of pushing him, before appearing to accidentally poke Fury in the eye. Fury then pushed Wilder. Fury's brother Shane, who was on crutches, mounted the stage to join the argument, while Fury removed his shirt. Numerous security guards intervened, struggling to regain control of the situation before the stage was cleared.

Fury put the altercation down to nerves on Wilder's behalf. It was a sign of weakness, he believed. 'He's definitely rattled,' Fury said. 'He's nervous and he's on edge. I'm going to make him look like the clown he is. He knows he's going to lose. I keep saying it, "Let the fighters talk" – and he's got his family to jump in.' The fracas was Wilder's fault, he insisted. 'He looked very nervous, I didn't instigate that, he did. He was shouting, screaming and everything. That was exciting, wasn't it? He knows he can't outbox me, so he was trying to get personal. He's trying to psych himself up for the fight, but I'm relaxed. I'm a born fighter.' Fury said he did not need to psych himself up, nor did he need any monetary incentive. Before the fight, he said, he would donate £8 million of what he made from the fight to the homeless and needy. He said he was not interested in becoming a millionaire or a billionaire.

'I don't really have much use for it. When I go home I'm going to build some homes for the homeless and set up some funds for drug addicts and alcoholics.' Los Angeles had opened his eyes to their plight. He was staying downtown where he saw thousands of homeless people.

Numerous VIPs from boxing, other sports and film stars came to watch the fight. William H. Macy, Floyd Mayweather, Michael Strahan, Zlatan Ibrahimovic, Dominic West, Joshua Jackson, Gennady Golovkin, Evander Holyfield and Maura Tierney were seen at a pre-fight party. Reality TV star Telli Swift – Deontay Wilder's fiancée – stole the show with a risqué thigh-split silver sequin dress, worn over a nude bodysuit.

In round 1, Wilder came out swinging to push Fury back on the ropes, but missed. Nodding his head, Fury put his hands behind his back to egg on his opponent. He landed a couple of good punches on Wilder's body, but the champ responded with a left hook. Fury came back with a right hand and a left hook to take the round. The crowd were already on their feet and a smiling Fury went back to his corner with his hands in the air.

In round 2, Fury continued goading Wilder, holding his hands in the air and telling Wilder to show him what he had got. By then the rival fans were chanting the boxers' names. Fury used his speed to avoid punches, while landing some of his own. Towards the end of the round Wilder landed a big punch, but Fury raised his arms and called the champ 'a bum'.

In round 3, Fury avoided Wilder's punches, drawing him on to the ropes before delivering a strong right hand to the face, while the crowd chanted, 'Fury! Fury!' Wilder fans responded with a chant of 'USA! USA!' during round 4. The champ found his mark with the jab but missed with the bigger shots. Nevertheless Fury, ending the round with a small cut over the eye, pumped his fist at the bell, convinced he'd won the round.

Fury continued to evade Wilder in the fifth, hoping to tire him out. Then Wilder had to cover up as Fury pummelled him with body shots and ended the round with bruising to his face. Wilder's eye continued to swell up during round 6 as Fury's fans got louder. Again he outpointed the champion, slipping and sliding and looking for openings.

In the seventh, Wilder either missed or his punches bounced off Fury, while the Gypsy King connected, landing two great right-hand punches. They clinched for the first time. Another two big right hands in the eighth slowed Wilder down but, on the instructions of Davison, Fury did not try to get greedy with a KO finish, content to stay ahead on points. He ended the round with a little showboating, punching his own head to indicate that Wilder was not making enough clean shots.

Then in the ninth, Wilder kicked off, downing Fury with a right. Taking a count from referee Jack Reiss, Fury got to his feet and rode out the storm, while Wilder threw everything he had at him. He could not close Fury's mouth though. Fury kept on goading him as Wilder began to tire. Wilder kept on swinging in the tenth, but his punches had lost some of their power. Avoiding high-arching punches, Fury rocked Wilder with his right, taking another round. In round 11, Wilder looked tired and continued missing, while Fury remained fresh, ducking, weaving and jabbing.

Then in the final round, it all came crashing down for Fury. He had outboxed the Bronze Bomber, who then suddenly landed a massive combination and Fury hit the canvas, out cold. Wilder leant over him, yelling, '*It's over!*' He drew his glove across his neck in a throat-cutting gesture. 'That's it!' he shouted. But his jubilation was premature. Referee Jack Reiss could not start the count until Wilder had stepped away. To everyone's amazement, Fury picked himself up and beat the count. What's more, he still had fight in him. While Wilder was unable to land another shot, Fury caught him with a massive hook to the body.

Those at ringside were convinced that Fury had won. The punch stats showed that Fury was the more accurate over the match, landing eighty-four of his 327 shots, for a 26 per cent success rate. Wilder converted just seventy-one of his 430 shots, for a 17 per cent success rate. However, Wilder had put Fury down twice and the judges had scored the bout a draw.

After the fight, Fury spoke to the media: 'I'm not going to cry over split milk.' He launched into a rendition of Don McLean's 'American Pie'. A week later, talks of a rematch began.

13

JOSTLING FOR POSITION

Following the Wilder fight, Tyson Fury got rid of his red Ferrari, along with his Rolls-Royce with the number plate TLF 1. Instead, he used a classic 1970 Rolls-Royce Silver Shadow left to him in his grandfather's will to pull his 1895 gypsy caravan. He planned to tour Italy in it.

Meanwhile, he was in training in Spain accompanied by Paris and their four children (with another on the way). The Ferrari had been given to a friend who was one of his trainers. The two-seater had been replaced with a nine-seater Ford Transit minibus to carry the kids about.

Leaving America two days after the Wilder fight, Fury had gone straight back into training twice a day, only taking four days off over Christmas because he had the flu. 'I need boxing and training as my medication,' he said. 'Without it I get ill, so I must train every day.'

By mid-January, he was ready to fight again. He had already sent a text to Wilder suggesting a rematch in April. Fury was also keen to meet Joshua in the ring to unify the titles. He also outlined his even more ambitions plans for the Tyson Fury Roadshow to the *Sunday Times*. He said he would go on tour and stage twelve fights in twelve countries, one a month. 'Let's do something that's never been done before. Let's leave a legacy. I'm serious. It's my dream. I've done everything else, I may as well follow my dream. Why not?'

It didn't work out like that.

There was talk of Fury signing for a fight with Anthony Joshua on 13 April 2019, but Fury's promoter Frank Warren dismissed the offer of a near 60/40 purse split as 'derisory'. There was more talk of a rematch with Wilder in Las Vegas in late April or early May and the WBC gave Fury the go-ahead to find neutral judges. Meanwhile, Joshua was trying to arrange a fight against Wilder, and Joshua's promoter, Eddie Hearn, bemoaned the fact that the Wilder camp would not even pick up the phone.

In February, Fury signed an £80 million, five-bout deal with US sports broadcasting giant ESPN through US promoters Top Rank. The two-and-a-half-year package – the biggest in British boxing history – put in jeopardy a rematch with Wilder, because he was signed to Showtime. Nevertheless, Fury insisted that the rematch with Wilder, which had been set for 18 May in Las Vegas, was still on the cards and that the new deal simply made it easier for him to negotiate a fight against Joshua.

'I want Wilder, I still want a Wilder, but I would also take

Joshua and I have more chance of getting them with this deal,' Fury said at a press conference. 'If you're watching, Deontay, I'm coming for you and this time you can't rip me off. As far as I'm concerned, the fight is more makeable now than ever because we have the biggest boys in the game behind us and I'm only a fighter. I can only fight who they put in front of me. I want the biggest fights, the Joshuas, the Wilders of the world and everyone else out there too.'

Fury's promoter Frank Warren said of the Wilder match: 'Tyson wants it, we all want it, and now we've got to make it happen. It's up to us now to sit down and get it over the line. We want to fight Joshua, too. We tried to make the fight, it's a fifty–fifty fight and they did not want to make it.'

Fury had proved a huge hit with American viewers in his thrilling draw with Wilder in Los Angeles, which aired on Showtime. And his fighting style, coupled with his personality, convinced ESPN they could make him the biggest British sports star the US had ever known. Warren said: 'This is a massive and historic deal which blows out of the water anything seen before in British boxing and can make Tyson a huge star in America and across the world.' However, Joshua was teamed up with the new US sports streaming service DAZN and they and ESPN could not come together to set up a bout between Fury and Joshua.

When Fury pulled out of the Wilder rematch, deciding to take an interim fight first, the WBC champ tweeted: 'You sorry muthafucka. We knew you only said this bec[ause] you knew you wasn't fighting me next. #CloutChaser you requested a warm-up fight first. I don't blame you though, I probably would too if I saw my brains splashed all over the canvas.'

But Fury insisted that the rematch would go ahead, eventually, tweeting: 'I will fight anyone in world boxing, don't use boxing politics as an excuse not to challenge me the lineal heavyweight champ.' He taunted, 'Get yourself a bit more well known in America first kid & then I'll give you another chance! I already beat you & the world knows it & so do you.'

Frank Warren said that he was disappointed that the rematch would have to be postponed. 'It's not our doing. ESPN/Top Rank, they're insisting they want to give Tyson an exposure fight in the States first,' he told TalkSport. 'I'm very disappointed we're not going straight to it, but it is actually beyond our control.'

Meanwhile, Fury toured the UK with 'An Evening with Tyson Fury,' where he spoke to sell-out crowds about his battles both in and out of the ring, and occasionally sang. He and Paris then had their fifth child, Prince Adonis Amaziah, and he had a racehorse named after him.

First in the frame to fight Fury was British boxer Dillian Whyte, who had lost the WBC International title to Joshua in 2015 but won it back by beating Óscar Rivas in 2019 – beating Dereck Chisora twice along the way. Fury joked that he was going to face a welterweight first, saying: 'Yeah, I think I'm fighting Amir Khan, he's moving up to heavyweight.'

Khan did not get the joke. 'I find that quite strange really,' he said. 'I don't want to be in the ring with Tyson Fury, he's huge compared to me. Maybe he's trying to say that I'm looking big, I'm looking strong. I don't know why he would mention my name.'

But Fury was serious about getting back into the ring as training kept his depression at bay. 'I'll just fight anybody, the local binman, anyone as long as I can keep active and keep busy,' he said. 'It's not the boxing that drives me, it's the training. When the boxing's done, I will always continue to train and that will keep me well, mentally and physically. It took me twenty years to figure that out.'

He was not clear why the negotiations between ESPN and Showtime over the Wilder rematch had broken down. 'I did text him just after Christmas to say "Let's get the fight arranged",' said Fury. 'Didn't get a reply – usually not a good sign! Maybe he's a little bitter.' Fury later dubbed Wilder a 'big dosser' in a tweet, saying that the American fighter would be nothing without him.

In an interview in the April edition of *GQ* magazine, Fury was still adamant that he had won the bout with Wilder in Los Angeles in December. 'I won the fight quite clearly, ten rounds to two,' he said. 'If you're not going to win on ten rounds to two, then it's highly impossible that you're going to win overseas. Maybe if I win twelve out of twelve, I might get another draw. Who knows? Wilder needs to improve drastically.'

Fury insisted his first clash with Wilder was 'fun', even though Wilder had put him down twice. Speaking of his resurrection after being flattened in round 12, he said: 'If that's hell, it's not a very scary place. Yeah, he's the hardest puncher in the world, but you don't really feel the punches when you're in a boxing fight. Getting hit is part of the job.'

Fury continued his charity work, speaking about mental health. He and Joshua made a video to raise money for a terminally ill nine-year-old girl. Tapes of Fury's interview were also used to bring fan Chris Griffin out of a coma after a pub fight.

Meanwhile, Wilder dropped plans to fight Joshua, instead taking on Dominic Breazeale, who had been defeated by Joshua in 2016. The following year, Breazeale had beaten former world title challenger Eric Molina, on the undercard of the rematch between Wilder and Bermane Stiverne. For his part, Fury announced that his next fight would be against German contender Tom Schwarz, ranked second by the WBO, but outside the top fifteen with both the WBA and the WBC and ninth with the IBF. However, Schwarz was undefeated in twenty-four professional bouts with sixteen knockouts. That meant Fury's rematch with Wilder would have to be put back to 2020. Fury blamed Wilder for this, saying his pleas for a rematch earlier had fallen on deaf ears.

'I have to take care of Schwarz, Wilder has to take care of Dominic Breazeale and then I say we get it on,' he said. 'He has gone quiet; I send him messages and he doesn't reply any more.' Fury was looking forward to his first fight in Las Vegas as it would increase his profile in the US. Nor did he write Schwarz off as a place-holder. 'I'm very fit and ready, so I can't wait,' he said. 'Tom Schwarz is a young, fresh and ambitious fighter, but I'm going to put on a good show as usual.'

He told BT Sport: 'Deontay's a nobody; let's face it. He was nobody before he fought me, he lost to me, he's still a nobody.

No interest in talking about the bum. Big bum dosser, that's all he is.' Joshua was dismissed in similar terms. 'I'll tell you what I can do with them two, I can give them a job carrying my boots and bags. So when they've all been busted very soon, when they fight each other and knock lumps off each other and they get beat up and they lose and their careers [are] over, they can come to the Gypsy King and I'll employ them. Because let's face it, they've not got the most brains in the world. So I'll give them a job when they've spent all their money because it's coming. When they're all skint, I'll employ you boys, don't worry. I'll bring you over, you can brush up the drive. Carry my bags, clean my pool, feed my animals and pick up the dog shit. Because that's all you'll be good for sooner or later.'

Wilder responded by warning Fury that, by dodging a rematch, he risked losing his American fans. 'He will have to suffer the backlash from the people. The one thing Americans don't like is when you say you want to fight nothing but the best, then when it is a controversial fight you get the rematch and you run.' He ramped up the criticism. 'Tyson Fury doesn't have an exciting style, he can easily stink out a place with his style. People don't want to see you just boxing and being boring. They want to see excitement, they want to see knockouts. Him dodging me and not taking that rematch is going to mess up his profile. If I don't give Tyson Fury the rematch ever again in his life, that will be his problem. ESPN is going to be shitting bricks and so will he. By him not taking the rematch and facing someone at the bottom of the list, it's not going to work out for him. Everything he gained in our fight, he lost. I hope he is aware of that.'

Wilder said he was king of the heavyweights in American and warned Joshua and Fury that they had to beat him to take the throne. 'America has been wanting a heavyweight king for a very long time, someone they can look up to and be happy about,' said the Bronze Bomber. 'I give America that pride and joy of having their own superstar and heavyweight champion they can call their own "baddest man on the planet." Since the last few fights, I've got the world's attention like I wanted it. This is just the beginning for Deontay Wilder – the things that I can do from now are incredible. Those guys have a chance. If they do the right things, make the right fights, have the right fights, then America will love them. We like to be cocky, we like to talk old school, we like to see aggressiveness, the fighters fighting the best. I am the king here. Everyone in the sport looks up to me because I'm the monster in the heavyweight division. They can't look over me.'

In the run-up to his fight with Schwarz, Fury began filming a reality TV series. He was going to use Freddie Roach's Wild Card Gym in Los Angeles, preparing for the Schwarz fight. He had used it before the Wilder fight and used Roach as his cuts man. However, Roach rated Joshua over Fury. 'Joshua, I like a lot,' he said. 'He is the best heavyweight in the world, ahead of Wilder and Fury.'

Meanwhile, Fury took time off from training to be photographed on a night out with the sixteen members of the Mana Cheerleaders Dance Team, a London-based company who performed at events around the world. His wife Paris tweeted, 'Good pic babe', with a string of emojis.

Before his fight against Breazeale on 18 May, Wilder claimed that Fury was dodging a rematch because of their last fight. 'I hurt Tyson Fury very badly,' Wilder said. 'I gave him a concussion. Like I said, this man had memory loss, and that's not healthy. That's not healthy for you. And as a man, as a man with a family, hey, if you need a warm-up or tune-up to make sure your marbles are back in place, go do that. Take as many warm-ups as you need. We understand. He said he got three more fights and then he out of here. We all know why he's gonna be out of here – because one of those fights leads up to me. And I'm gonna finish it.'

Meanwhile, Fury turned his trash-talking on Joshua, saying: 'He needs to grow a set of nuts and step up to the plate – instead of *talking* about fighting the heavyweights – and actually *fight* some. People are sick of hearing all the same stuff with him – grow up and step up to the plate and fight somebody. You have to prove yourself in the boxing ring, that's how boxing works. I've had to prove myself time and time again.' Fury's language continued to be colourful as he told Joshua to 'get his nuts out of Eddie Hearn's handbag and use them to gain respect in the heavy-weight division'.

Fury also claimed he was already above Wilder and Anthony Joshua in the heavyweight pecking order. 'Let's rewind a few years to November 2015: there's no doubt in anybody's minds that Wladimir Klitschko was the undisputed heavyweight champion. When I kicked his ass, I became the undisputed heavyweight king.'

On 18 May 2019, in the Barclays Center in Brooklyn, Wilder knocked out Breazeale just 2 min 17 sec into round 1. Afterwards, Wilder said he would 'fight anyone'. Fury then said that he would face Wilder again the following spring, even challenging him to a bare-knuckle fight on the streets of New York.

'He is a big dosser, bum-city, hashtag anytime, any place, anywhere. When we fight again, I promise he'll be looking at the stars,' said Fury. 'Deontay Wilder, go suck my nuts. If you want to do anything about it, come and fight me. If he's got anything to say, come see me. We'll have a bare-knuckle fight in Times Square this evening.'

Wilder responded: 'That's typical Tyson Fury. The only highlight from our whole fight is him getting dropped on his back. The same Tyson Fury that I gave a concussion to, I gave him memory loss to the point where he doesn't know how he got on the ground or how he got up.'

He then said he would put a fight with Fury before one with Joshua. This prompted another expletive-ridden rant from Fury, 'Punch his face in, he's a big, bum dosser. Joshua is not a great fighter. He's just a mediocre, average heavyweight from the seventies and, if he was in the seventies, he wouldn't even be a world champion. You need nuts to fight me and nuts he doesn't have. Cojones, bollocks, testicles, whatever you wanna call them; Joshua don't have any.'

But before Wilder took either of them on, he signed for a rematch with Cuban fighter Luis Ortiz, who he beat with a tenth-round knockout in March 2018. After that, he confirmed he would take on Fury again.

Unable to fight Fury, Joshua planned a US debut at New York's Madison Square Garden, which was altered after contender Jarrell Miller failed a drugs test. Mexican-American heavyweight Andy Ruiz Jr took Miller's place. Joshua's plans were upset when he was knocked down four times by Ruiz. In an electrifying round 3, it was Joshua who knocked Ruiz down, only for the portly Mexican-American to come right back and use an overhand right that rocked the champ and sent him to the canvas. Joshua recovered only to get pummelled in the corner. Ruiz knocked him down again in the final second of the round as fans in Madison Square Garden screamed: 'Oh my God!' Again, Joshua beat the count then was saved by the bell. If it hadn't been a championship fight, the bout might have been stopped right there. Ruiz took victory in a TKO to claim his unified WBA (Super), IBF, WBO, and IBO titles.

In the post-fight press conference, Joshua said he still wanted to fight Fury and Wilder, but faced a rematch with Ruiz first. He judged his defeat, generally considered one of the biggest world heavyweight title upsets ever, a 'minor setback'. Frank Warren warned Fury that Ruiz's victory might provide Tom Schwarz with inspiration. Meanwhile, Fury tweeted his support to the defeated heavyweight: 'We have our back and forths but Anthony Joshua changed his stars through life. Heavyweight boxing, these things happen, rest up, recover, regroup and come again.'

However, he was less sympathetic when interviewed by ESPN radio. 'He'll never live it down,' Fury said. 'Can you imagine? You're built like an Adonis, you're six-foot-six, you're ripped, carved in stone, and a little fat man who has eaten every Snickers and Mars bar in California comes in there and bladders you all over. What a disgrace. If that was me, I would never show my face in public ever again.'

He also predicted that Ruiz would beat Joshua in any rematch, while in *Ring* magazine Joshua slipped from No. 1 heavyweight in the world to No. 4, putting Fury back on the top spot.

'If I can't beat Tom Schwarz then what is the point in boxing anymore? I must be shot,' said Fury. 'We won't know until we get in there. A lot of people say I might be chinny after the Deontay Wilder fight. We don't know. It's exciting times.' Assessing his twenty-five-year-old opponent who had won all twenty-four of his fights, Fury said: 'He's 6 ft 6 in, weighs 250 lbs, he's unbeaten, ranked No. 2 by the WBO and is in the Top 10 of the IBF. Not a pretender by any shadow of the imagination. Schwarz has boxed limited opposition. He's never been on the big stage before. Never fought a lineal champion before. Has a lot to work on. Leaky defence, not the best footwork in the world and looks quite fragile. He carries his left hand low, hasn't got the fastest feet, defence ain't great, doesn't box on the move – typical German style. I should beat this guy, but many worse things have happened at sea.' Again, Fury said he should retire if he could not beat Schwarz.

His trainer, Ben Davison, said they would not make the same mistake as Joshua made in his defeat to Ruiz. They had prepared for the fight with Schwarz in Las Vegas 'professionally'. Davison offered an analysis of Joshua's tactics, saying the former world heavyweight champion lacked variety and the ability to change patterns, which might lead to his downfall to Ruiz for a second time if they were to rematch. He had lived with Fury for eighteen months to help him shed 140 lbs, battle depression and return from the boxing abyss.

'We always prepare professionally, no matter who we're boxing or where we're boxing,' said Davison. 'At this level, it all boils down to game plans. If you go in there with the wrong game plan, it can make an easy fight a tough fight . . . I am a young trainer and sometimes you want to go and do things, but it's my job to be a wise head. People talk about punchers, but in the heavyweight division they can all punch. At the minute I don't look at Deontay Wilder at all, because we've got Tom Schwarz first. What I care about is that Tyson's in a good place – psychically and emotionally – he's back to normal thriving boxing in Las Vegas.'

Fury was staying in a lavish mansion the size of a small castle in the southern suburbs of Las Vegas and training just across the freeway from the Vegas Strip, while his face bedecked the frontage of the MGM Grand Hotel Resort where he was to fight Schwarz in the Grand Garden Arena. Ricky Hatton warned him to stay away from the hotels and casinos because of the air-conditioning, which he believed had been responsible for his own poor performance against Juan Urango in 2007.

Fury was getting £10 million for his Las Vegas debut and was 50/1 on with bookmakers. Promoter Bob Arum's plan was for Fury to make a connection with the American people and build his fanbase. 'For the first Wilder fight, they just saw Fury as the opponent,' said Arum. 'They didn't see him as the attraction. Our goal is to make him the attraction. I have worked with Muhammad Ali and George Foreman. Let me tell you, Tyson is a chip off the old block.'

Fury was enjoying himself too. 'I got a warm welcome in Las Vegas, I have been all over the city and seeing people,' he said. 'Seeing my name up in lights has been an amazing experience. I can't wait to get in there and put on a show on Saturday.' Despite the Joshua upset just two weeks earlier, he was brimming with confidence: 'The fact is I'm going to knock him out. Unfortunately for Tom Schwarz I'm going to break his jaw, break his ribs and leave him in Las Vegas. Then we are going to go party. The drinks are on the Gypsy King.'

Schwarz was confident too. 'I have big balls and a big heart, I am a surprise package,' he said.

But Fury reckoned he could take anything Schwarz threw at him. 'I hope he chins me a couple of times. I hope I have to get up off the floor three or four times and slug a win out. I hope it's the toughest fight of my career, that's what I've trained for.'

It was Mike Tyson who had made MGM Grand an iconic boxing venue. Fury was just seven when his namesake made his first appearance at the arena in the bowels of the famous hotel. 'It's great to follow in Tyson's footsteps. It's my opportunity to be here, make this my venue and fight here on a big night. This is a massive stage. I cannot wait. I came here to set precedents and be different, because that's what I am. I'm a much different person from your average Joe. The average boxers want to come here, be all serious and look at each other in the face, all that sort of stuff, but I don't.'

The fight brought in a crowd of 6,676, with just over 1,000 tickets given away. After Schwarz's ring-walk to Bob Marley, Fury appeared in red, white and blue gear – including a top hat – as he stepped through a cordon of showgirls. With a broad grin, he took to the ring to James Brown's 'Living in America', the entire entrance in homage to Apollo Creed's entrance at the MGM Grand in *Rocky IV*.

Unlike Creed, Fury survived and won. He made short work of Schwarz, dominating round 1 with his jab. Fury then switched to a southpaw stance late in round 2, when Schwarz caught him with a shot. Fury got mad, battering Schwarz with a combination and dropping him to a knee with a huge right hand to the head. Schwarz got up with a badly bloodied face, and Fury teed off, peppering his turtling opponent with big shots. Referee Kenny Bayless stepped in at roughly the same moment Schwarz's corner threw the white towel into the ring before the bell.

'I used the jab,' said Fury. 'I was slipping and sliding. I caught him with the straight left. It was a good shot. It could put anybody away. I put on an extra twelve pounds, and I could really feel it.'

After the fight, holding the microphone in his boxing glove, Fury serenaded his wife, Paris, with Aerosmith's 'I Don't Want to Miss a Thing'. 'I came here to enjoy myself and put on a show for Las Vegas,' Fury said. 'I hope everybody enjoyed it as much as I did.'

'There is no heavyweight in the world that can beat him,

now that he's in shape,' Arum said. 'Deontay Wilder is not going five rounds with him. We will have another fight, then we will fight Wilder.'

After the fight, Fury visited Schwarz's dressing room and told the twenty-five-year-old: 'I want you to come to England and train with me for a bit. Hopefully, we'll try and get you on my next card, and that's a promise. I don't say things that I don't back up. I'd like to invite you to come and train with me, and you'll come back better.'

Fury also admitted that, during the fight, he had defied Davison. 'Ben wanted me to go out and box for six or seven rounds and let him tire; I didn't, I didn't want to. I wanted a knockout in America. If I've ever gone out to look for a knockout in my mind, I've never not got one. But for some reason I wanted to knock Schwarz out and make a statement in America, and put on a show because that's what they like. I said it's going to be him or me because this is America and everyone wants an explosive performance.'

There was talk of Fury moving to the US in the wake of the success. Paris said: 'We're going to be in America a lot and we have even talked about moving. If we did, I'm sure it would only be for a few years – maybe ten.'

After confirming new plans for a rematch with Wilder, Fury celebrated by showing off his new £300,000 Ferrari GTC supercar. The outcome of the rematch was going to be different, he insisted. 'This time, I haven't been out of the ring for three years,' he said. 'This time, I haven't been abusing too much alcohol. And this time, I'm going to knock him the fuck out.'

The rematch was scheduled for 22 February 2020. In the meantime, Fury named Jarrell Miller and Trevor Bryan as two possible opponents for a fight in October, before it was announced that his opponent would be twenty-eight-year-old Swede Otto Wallin, a southpaw who was unbeaten in twenty-one fights with twenty wins and thirteen knockouts. His last outing, against Nick Kisner, had been ruled a no-contest because of a clash of heads in round 1. The bout would take place in the T-Mobile Arena, Las Vegas, on 14 September.

According to Fury, four other fighters had turned him down before Wallin accepted. 'Alexander Povetkin was offered the fight and he said, "No", and took a fight with [Fury's cousin] Hughie instead,' he told online boxing channel Behind The Gloves although, after Povetkin beat Hughie in London on points, he asked for a shot at Tyson, who was still looking elsewhere: 'Kubrat Pulev was offered the fight and said "No"; Charles Martin, no; Trevor Bryan, no. "Big Baby" [Jarrell] Miller, popped for a drug test and Dillian Whyte popped for a drugs test. Wilder is fighting [Luis] Ortiz. Ruiz is fighting Joshua – who the fuck else is there? I could have fought Chris Arreola or someone who's been knocked out five times but what am I gaining by that? This guy Wallin was the highest-ranked opponent who was willing to step up – there's nobody else.'

The fight against Wallin would have a new belt on the line – the WBC 'Mayan', a special title created to celebrate Mayan culture. According to the WBC, 'The Mayan belt is not a championship but a trophy and recognition to the winner of the fight.' Meanwhile, Wilder wanted Fury to stand aside so he could fight the winner of the Joshua–Ruiz bout and unify the heavyweight belts. Fury said: 'I've heard about Wilder saying he wants to pay me some step-aside money, but I wouldn't take fifty million pounds to step aside because it doesn't mean that much to me. I only care about winning and victory. The truth is, Wilder doesn't want to fight me. He couldn't beat me when I'd had three years out the ring and he couldn't beat me when he knocked me down twice. So he hasn't got a chance of beating me now. I don't care if he's got 104 belts. Belts are lovely things to have, to hold, to win. But it's about more than a belt between me and Deontay Wilder, I want to beat the man himself.'

The Wallin fight was to take place on the same weekend as Mexico's Independence Day and Fury said, 'I've got the Mexican shorts, the Mexican gloves, the Mexican mask, the Mexican flag. I don't know how much more respect I can show.' He donned them for a public workout when he also took a swipe at Donald Trump. 'Isn't it a great thing that a total outsider from this country is showing so much love, passion and respect for the Mexican people? They are being oppressed by the people here – building a wall, chucking 'em all out, and treating them terrible. Every Mexican person I've met has shown love, respect and honour. I don't know what is going on, but it is nice to see a total stranger, heavyweight champion of the world, coming here and respecting people and paying homage to their beliefs and special days. I know what it is like to be on the outside. I've grown up around it, I've been brought up around it.'

Ben Davison said that he had stopped Fury from over-training. His aim was to keep Fury in good condition until he made Wilder 'look silly' in their rematch. 'I know there will be a better version of Deontay Wilder than from the first fight but I also know there will be a better version of Tyson Fury as well,' he said. 'With Deontay Wilder you can't be reckless, you have to be smart, calculated. It is a big risk but there is big reward.'

Fury himself promised to be a good boy, stay healthy and stay out of trouble, although he could not resist sending Wallin a picture of some sweets called Swedish Fish via Instagram. 'He was smiling and he had that, but I never got back to him!' Wallin told BT Sport.

However, the Wallin fight did not prove popular. Only 1,500 tickets were sold for the fight at the 20,000-capacity arena. In all some 8,249 fans turned up after 3,898 tickets were given away. The arena was not even half-full, although Fury still looked set to take home £12 million. And he used the pre-bout press conference to show off his language skills, saying: 'Well yes, I am the Gypsy King, *El Rey Gitano.*'

Fury walked to the ring behind a mariachi band, wearing a poncho and a sombrero. He quickly found himself in a rough-and-tumble battle with Wallin, who had his moments in the fight, but never seemed to really hurt Fury. However, in round 3, Fury was cut over the right eye. 'I couldn't see out of my eye,' Fury later said. 'I got cut over my eye and it changed the fight completely.' He struggled to keep going. 'It's all heart and determination. If I can keep going, I keep going. Otto is a great Swede, a Viking warrior.'

The injury clearly bothered him as the fight went on. Blood flowed down the right side of his face and stained his trunks, and Fury kept wiping at the cut to try and keep the blood out of his eye. The referee stopped the fight briefly in round 6 for the ringside doctor to look at the cut. When the fight resumed, Fury fought at a quicker pace, chasing Wallin around the ring in search of a knockdown that never came. Fury's cutman, Jorge Capetillo, said: 'That was probably the worst I've seen in my years of doing cuts. But I knew the capacity of Tyson, I knew his experience and his will to fight so I knew I had to get it right, put my job on the line and get the work done so he could continue fighting and not get stopped. I was surprised that the doctor didn't stop it because it got really bad. But I was just doing my best to keep it clean and try to prevent the blood from pouring into his eyes.'

The Swede rubbed up against Fury's open wound with his head and glove but Fury did not let his frustrations boil over. Unable to see half of Wallin's shots coming, Fury had to dig in and get up close to protect his cut. The gash had been caused by a punch, rather than a clash of heads, and if the fight were to have been stopped, Wallin would have won by a TKO. In the event, he connected with a cracking left in round 12. Fury was rocked, reeling back into the ropes and went back into survival mode. He survived the round and won on a unanimous points decision: 116–112, 117–111 and 118–110. Despite the cut, he enjoyed the fight. During a round break he had told trainer Ben Davison: 'I live for this shit.'

After the fight, Fury did not sing – instead he was taken to the University Medical Center of Southern Nevada, Las Vegas, with one gaping gash over his right eye and another, smaller one on the eyelid. In characteristically ebullient mood, he told BBC Sport before leaving Las Vegas: 'I went to the hospital, had a few stitches, went home and had an early night. Then I've got up, gone to the casino, won five grand, had a few beers and now I'm going to have a few more beers.'

In fact, he had forty-seven stitches and his father feared that the cut might end his career. He advised his son to sack his whole team, including Davison, who he believed was responsible. Fury senior said his son was like a 'kitten' against Wallin. But Davison responded: 'Listen, if Tyson was a kitten, he wouldn't have been able to do twelve rounds like that. John is Tyson's dad so, of course, you have to respect him but Tyson was fully prepared and you can't do anything about sustaining a bad cut.'

Frank Warren was also sanguine: 'The doctor said it was a clean cut so it doesn't need microsurgery inside and he said it would stitch well. Fingers crossed it will be all right.' He said that there was five months before the scheduled Wilder rematch and Fury needed to rest. 'If it doesn't heal well the fight may have to be pushed back. Hopefully, that will not be the case. It depends how it heals. If it's OK, it won't be a problem. It's not just the fight, it's the training and sparring. He has to be a hundred per cent right.'

As was standard practice in such cases, the Nevada State Athletic Commission gave Fury a two-month suspension on medical grounds. 'Listen I'm all right. It's boxing,' Fury commented. 'You can't go swimming and not get wet. It's the fight game.' He appeared wearing dark glasses to hide the wound and was happy to pose for photographs with fans as he walked through Las Vegas's McCarran International Airport on his way home to Manchester.

Warren had a Harley Street plastic surgeon on standby in case a surgical incision was required to ensure the cut healed properly. Jorge Capetillo was rewarded for his work with a bonus. Wilder then said he was going to open the cut back open again. 'He better be ready, but the way I hit, I'm gonna cut him back open, period,' he said. 'No matter what they do – he can have plastic surgery, whatever. I'm gonna cut that back open, period. It's over with. I got Fury's number.' But he was happy that Fury won, otherwise he would have lost his lucrative rematch. 'See, that fight was supposed to be stopped. Everybody knows that. But, of course, they don't want this man to lose because of me. They want the big fight. We understand that. People are not dumb.'

Fury had the stitches taken out after just nine days and Frank Warren said, 'As much as the cuts looked horrific and there was a lot of blood, the cuts were quite straight lacerations, they were not jagged and they did not tear into the muscle. But the only way we will know if Tyson will be ready for 22 February is in six or seven weeks' time when we will see how they have healed. And even then, the issue will be whether it has healed enough to start sparring. If he starts sparring just before or after Christmas, then he has seven or eight weeks in camp. We will see.'

In the meantime, Fury did not sit down and relax. In early October, he was seen backstage at the WWE Smackdown at the Staples Center, Los Angeles, for his son Prince John James' eighth birthday. He posted pictures of himself with The Rock, Hulk Hogan, Vince McMahon, Triple H and Ric Flair, in an eccentric white suit. Then it turned unpleasant. WWE champion Braun Strowman spotted Fury sitting in the front row and pretended to square up to him. It all seemed light-hearted to begin with, as Fury played along, standing up to face Strowman and putting up his fists. But then chaos ensued after Dolph Ziggler attacked Strowman from behind.

'Monster Among Men' Strowman spun around and threw Ziggler into the ring-post behind him, then back the other way into the barricade, hitting Fury and knocking him back down to his seat. Fury got up, looking less than impressed at Strowman, who appeared to hope the Gypsy King would see the funny side. But Fury wasn't laughing along and Strowman was soon back in the safety of the ring. Fury jumped the barricade, shouting and pointing at Strowman, but was held back by at least eight security staff as Strowman carried on laughing in the ring.

In a video posted on Instagram, Fury said: 'I was insulted in front of my whole family by Braun Strowman. It got a little bit heated and we saw what happened. I have been invited to an open-mic session at *RAW* [WWE TV programme] on Monday night. I accept and I will be there. If Braun Strowman doesn't behave himself, he will get some of these hands, the big dosser.' Fury's children then chanted, 'You big dosser' along with their father as they aimed jibes at Strowman.

At the WWE *Monday Night RAW*, Fury demanded an apology from Strowman. When this was not forthcoming, Fury pushed Strowman against the ropes. Security men tried to restrain the two of them as a brawl broke out, with Fury knocking several of the guards to the floor before the WWE locker room emptied to pull them apart. There were some four million views of the spectacle on social media.

Fury agreed to meet Strowman in a wrestling match, WWE's Crown Jewel, Saudi Arabia, on 31 October, earning himself another £11.9 million. 'His profile gets bigger every time and he's doing us promoters a real favour by going on WWE,' said Frank Warren. 'But, truthfully, I don't like the risk of his cut opening up. Tyson's a law unto himself. It's risky though, no doubt about that.'

Fury also realised that the bout risked his rematch with Wilder, but told a press conference: 'I'm a lifelong WWE fan and this is a fantastic opportunity for me. I'd like to say how excited I am to be fighting the Monster Among Men, Braun Strowman. But me, being the undefeated lineal boxing champion, I fear no one. When I go to Saudi, I am still going to be undefeated, I am going to knock Braun Strowman out. He is messing with a guy with the best hands in boxing. He don't want none of them hands.'

Another altercation during a training session with Stowman left Fury limping. He told *Good Morning Britain*: 'I was training in the ring, minding my own business and he came out of nowhere and my neck is still killing me now. I hurt my ankle but it wasn't too damaging. It was more annoying because he came out of nowhere and I didn't see him coming. I didn't know he was going to turn up. I am an athletic person and a very quick learner. I have been in the gym for the last two weeks. Everything has been practised.' He also took the opportunity to plug the track 'Bad Sharon', a Christmas single he had recorded with Robbie Williams that he predicted would go to No. 1.

For his WWE debut, Fury walked to the ring to the Isley Brothers' 'It's Your Thing' and wore traditional Arabic dress, the *thawb*, and a *keffiyeh* headdress as the waiting Strowman glared at him. Fury displayed his boxing skills by turning around Strowman on the ropes and letting go with a couple of punches to the body. Strowman, who weighed in nine stones heavier than his opponent, floored Fury with a drop-kick and started to dish out plenty of punishment in the form of kicks, elbows and headbutts. Fury responded with a big right hand and a boot to the face, with Strowman narrowly surviving a two-count.

Then Fury was knocked down by the veteran wrestler and lay motionless on the canvas, before rising to his feet, as he had in his controversial fight against Wilder in Los Angeles, ten months earlier. Fury went on to weather the storm before delivering a right-hand that left Strowman crumpled in a heap. Strowman was unable to beat the count and Fury celebrated his victory, lifting both hands in the air. Strowman did not take too kindly to the defeat and surprised Fury by climbing back into the ring and body-slamming him to the canvas, before storming off backstage. Nevertheless, Fury remained unbeaten. He did not rule out returning to the WWE after the Wilder fight.

'I've got a big fella called Deontay Wilder to see to, 22 February, and then we see where we go from there,' he said. 'It was absolutely fantastic, a great experience. Braun is the Monster Among Men. When I hit him with that piledriving right hand, I cannot believe he got back up and slammed me to the floor. It was a bit of a cheap shot after the bell, but what can we do? It's WWE.'

A week later, Fury and Strowman met up again in Manchester. This time they teamed up together, against the B-Team duo of Curtis Axel and Bo Dallas. Strowman knocked the pair off the ring apron before smashing them with a running attack at ringside, then throwing Dallas into the ring. Fury knocked Dallas out, before Strowman landed a power slam on Axel to bring the curtain down on the show.

Fury's showmanship did not go unnoticed. 'It's mad for me at the moment,' he said. 'I'm doing a Christmas song with Robbie Williams, I'm releasing my autobiography, I've also got an ITV documentary as well. But I've also had an offer from Sylvester Stallone to do a movie. It's not another *Rocky*. Apparently, it's an action movie. They are looking for a villain, maybe someone to be beat up by him. I think it might be at the same time I'll be training for the Wilder fight, so not sure what's going to happen yet.'

At the same time, Fury was exchanging trash-talk with Wilder, who met Luis Ortiz in Las Vegas on 23 November. In a lacklustre fight, Wilder was cautious for six rounds – two judges giving him just one of the six, the third giving him two rounds. Then in round 7, a vicious right-hand seemingly came out of nowhere. It landed flush on the face of Ortiz, who crumpled to the canvas and was unable to get up at the count of ten. The rematch with Fury was on.

Joshua went the distance with Ruiz in Saudi Arabia on 7 December, winning back his belts in a unanimous decision, with scores of 118–110 on two scorecards and 119–109 on the other. Joshua was now back in contention, but he would have to wait.

REMATCH

With less than two months to go before the rematch with Deontay Wilder, Tyson Fury split from Ben Davison, who had been his trainer since his comeback in 2018.

He returned to the famous Kronk Gym and teamed up with Javan 'SugarHill' Steward, nephew of the legendary trainer Emanuel Steward, who had previously worked with Fury. He was, he said, 'getting the old team back up and running'. Davison said they remained friends while Wilder claimed that Fury had made the switch because he was nervous.

SugarHill explained Fury's thinking behind the change: 'He wanted a trainer who was technical. He wants to be very technical. We will work on his technique. These are the characteristics he was looking for when he called me, and I fit the description. It all happened so fast. Initially, he spoke to me about coming into camp, then I heard Ben Davison

is gone and I'm the head trainer.' The idea was to finish the
fight with a knockout. 'This is the heavyweight division. Both
guys are big punchers but Wilder is bigger, he is a beast of a
puncher. But one punch changes a fight and this is why the
heavyweights are the big daddies of them all. A knockout is
always the plan. Why think anything less?'

And SugarHill was confident that he could supply it in a
way that would make his late uncle proud. 'It's the Kronk
style, so it's not hard to figure out,' he said. 'What did
Emanuel like the most? If you know that answer, you know
the plan Tyson spoke about. It's so simple, you could miss it.'
SugarHill remembered Fury well from the old days. 'We lived
together for one month – me, Tyson and Emanuel,' he said.
'We had good and memorable times. Now, the boys are back.
Emanuel would be proud. He probably saw this coming.'

He had a great deal of time for Fury both as a boxer and a
man. 'You don't forget a person like him. Big, loud, funny and
could back it up in the ring. His athleticism was crazy and his
spirit was beautiful. He wasn't arrogant, he was appreciative.
What did I see in Tyson? How he thinks, how he treats other
people, his character, what kind of person he is. It's not just
about training a fighter's skills. He has qualities you only see
in people every so often.'

Fury told ESPN: 'We're gonna go back to basics. I trained
with SugarHill Steward back in 2010, we got on like a house
on fire. I was going a little bit stale, repetitive, doing the same
things day in, day out for years. I needed a change.'

Joshua offered to spar with Fury at his training camp in
Las Vegas. He told Sky Sports News: 'Fury, if you need me,

if you need me for sparring – we're going to fight one day, I've sparred Tyson Fury when we were kids anyway. I'll go out to America to spar Tyson Fury to get him ready for this Wilder fight.'

He likened Fury to Muhammad Ali and tipped him to win the rematch against Wilder. 'In terms of skill, I rate him highly. He's a real boxing connoisseur, he studies his boxing like I do and he's around a lot of boxing people. Also, he has some resemblances with his movement and style to Muhammad Ali, and the way he talks and stuff. If you listen to what he says, you can see one of his role models is Muhammad Ali.' There was more than a little self-interest in Joshua's offer. 'Fury is a world-class fighter and I'm a world-class fighter that is still trying to improve so I can become like an elite-level fighter when I'm fighting,' he said. 'Sparring Fury is only going to do me good, in my opinion. So, I'm never too big for my boots where I can't learn anymore. So, that opportunity, for me to spar Fury, is for my own benefit as well.

'And the reason why I thought about it and the reason why it came to fruition for me is because I feel like, if Fury was to win that fight I think he would be more inclined to fight me next and quicker than Wilder would. So, how long I've been waiting to fight for the championship belt, I think if Fury had it, me and him would have got a deal done already now. So that's why I was rooting for Fury to win because I just want to fight and collect my last belt . . . Imagine that fight on British soil.'

Fury replied on Instagram, saying: 'I just saw a video of Joshua on Sky Sports saying he'd love to come and help me in camp and that I'd fight him quicker than Wilder – that's for sure. When I beat Wilder I will fight you A. J., no problem. I'd really love to have you in camp to work out for this fight and give Wilder a proper beating . . . Thanks very much and well done in your last fight, congratulations.'

Joshua would have to wait to get to Fury as Bulgarian bruiser Kubrat Pulev was Joshua's next IBF mandatory challenger, while the WBO ordered him to fight Ukrainian Oleksandr Usyk, who had recently stepped up from cruiserweight. In addition, Frank Warren was planning a third fight between Fury and Wilder in the summer, irrespective of who won in February. Warren said that there would only be a fight with golden boy Joshua in 2020 after Fury completed a trilogy against the Bronze Bomber.

'To make that fight, it's a fifty-fifty split now,' he said. 'Tyson is the bigger star after the Wilder fight. His two recent US wins and stint on WWE also mean Tyson now has a bigger US profile than Anthony, but we will forgive him for that . . . If we both have deals with broadcasters, we just put it on both channels. On our side, there is not a single stumbling block to making that fight.' He told the *Sun*: 'Fury versus Joshua would be the biggest fight in my time in boxing, bar none. It would be one of the biggest moments in British sport since England won the home World Cup in 1966. It would transcend boxing.'

Joshua agreed to the split and Fury did not need the money. Tyson Fury Ltd, the firm that channels his sporting earnings, was worth £6.6 million, earning £5.66 million the previous year. In the meantime, Warren urged Joshua to stay out of the ring, even if it cost him one of his belts. He was vulnerable to a knockout by a lesser opponent, risking the biggest payday of his career. Warren was also against Joshua sparring with Fury.

'Who wants to see Fury sparring with Anthony Joshua? What a load of b.,' he said. 'We want to see him fight Anthony Joshua, forget about the sparring. The real deal counts. The public want to see it. I believe he will come through his fight with Deontay Wilder and let's see the Anthony Joshua fight.'

Eddie Hearn was against it too, but could do nothing to stop him. 'It's a bit weird because he might fight the winner. Josh is his own boss: if he fancies it, he'll just go,' he said. 'Doesn't matter what I or Rob McCracken, trainer, will say, he'll just go.'

Fury himself was concentrating on the face-off with Wilder. In a video on Instagram, Fury said: 'This is a special message for Deontay Wilder, the big dosser. I'll put everything down on beating you next time. I'm not afraid of you, I ain't bothered about you, bum. I wasn't bothered about you back then and I certainly ain't bothered about you now. You big dosser, you're getting it. You know you lost – your trainer, your manager, your wife, your kids know. They all know the Gypsy King beat you – I'm coming for you. He's going round saying he fights all the best heavyweights. But Dominic Breazeale isn't the best heavyweight and nor is Luis Ortiz. They're average at best. You've only fought one good man in your career – that's me, and I beat you. Everybody in the world knows you lost to the Gypsy King. The Gypsy King that was out of the ring for three years on fifty per cent. You'll get bust next time.'

While Fury began the media build-up for the rematch in the US at the end of December, he called Wilder a 'big pussy, for not turning up. In a message to his rival on social media, Fury said: 'This is Tyson Fury AKA the Gypsy King this is a message to Deontay the Bronze Bomber the big pussy Wilder. He's not turned up to any of the media events today, blagging he's got the flu because he doesn't want to be in the same room as me because I'll take him to school. His management team and his full team are afraid to put Deontay Wilder in the same room as Tyson Fury, facts. Keep him away Al, keep him away Shelly, keep him away his wife. Deontay, what a little bitch you've become. You can't even come and see me and be face-to-face with me as you know you'll be taken to school... '

Fury also said that fighting mixed martial arts could be his next career move. UFC star Conor McGregor had offered to train him should he make the switch from the boxing ring after three more fights – two against Wilder then, if victorious, a fight against Joshua. He was already working with Conor McGregor's nutritionist, George Lockhart, a former US Marine. Fury had previously worked with nutritionist Greg Marriott, when he lost ten stone before making his successful comeback. By contrast, Lockhart considered his job was to bulk Fury up.

'Each day I try to give Tyson a diverse group of food,' he told Sky Sports. 'He has a different type of meat with every meal. From what I've heard in other camps he ate chicken and rice. Now we make crazy meals. He's had the same meal just twice in the entire camp – a jambalaya that I made. He eats six times per day and, apart from that, hasn't had the same meal twice. I would never make him something that he doesn't like because I can find something similar in texture and taste which would fit their palate. If he doesn't like something, he wouldn't eat it.'

Fury ate a bowl of fruit with Greek yoghurt for breakfast with an emphasis on berries. These provided antioxidants to help with recovery. He also had at least one portion of salmon and a curry each day, although Fury ate red meat only every other day.

'There should be no reason to even want to cheat,' said Lockhart. 'People think healthy food is not tasty. But he's not hungry, he's not craving anything because he has a diverse diet. He has dark chocolate, honey, sweets and spices, salts – his palate gets everything that it wants. There haven't been any issues. He has a strict regimen and is perfect to the schedule. He wakes up, eats, works out, comes back to eat, works out, eats, works out, eats again. Same thing every day. My job is to increase performance whether you're a heavyweight or a welterweight. The point of a fight camp is not to make weight, it's to get better at fighting.'

Fury was putting on weight. He topped 19 stone when he posed for pre-fight photos in Las Vegas and said he would weigh in at 270 lbs, a stone heavier than he did for the first fight. He also revealed that he dipped his fists in petrol to toughen up his knuckles.

Fighters David Adeleye and George Fox were flown to Las Vegas to help prepare Fury. Adeleye had TKOed Dmitrij Kalinovskij at the Copper Box in just 2 min 25 sec, while Fox had two points wins in 2018. Fury also had American heavyweight Jared Anderson in the training camp. Then came Mancunian Jordan Thompson, said to be a 'Wilder clone'. 'I've always thought that, for anyone who is fighting Wilder, I am literally a carbon copy of the man,' Thompson told *British Boxing News*. 'I am 6 ft 6-7 in, fifteen-and-a-half stone when I am walking around, so I am a replica. I mentioned it to my management and then I got a text on the Monday before I came out asking if I wanted sparring with Fury.' Thompson – nicknamed 'Troublesome' – fought at cruiserweight, but felt his frame matched up with the unbeaten Wilder, and believed he had a technical edge.

'I like to think I am a bit sharper and a better boxer than Wilder,' he said. 'In terms of physical attributes, we are similar, but I'd like to think I've got better legs than him because his are skinny! I'd like to think I've got a right hand like him though.' According to Thompson, Fury was in tip-top shape.

Fury also hired a new cutman for the fight – Jacob 'Stitch' Duran. Meanwhile, he insisted he was putting in the hard work. 'On Instagram it may seem like I'm living the dream in Las Vegas, with blue skies and palm trees. But in reality I'm in a gruelling training camp and it's repetitive every day. Instagram would make you believe it's a whale of a time and I'm enjoying myself and everything is fantastic. In reality I'm being worked to the bone every single day. I'm being smashed, session after session, and I'm in the recovery pool because my joints are smashed and I need the recovery. Anything good in life comes from hard work.'

In January, Fury again explained why he had changed trainer for the Wilder rematch: 'The consensus is: either he knocks me out or I win on points, but when people say that it usually goes the other way. I'm not looking for herky-jerky. I want him to meet me dead centre in the ring and have a slugfest. I didn't come here again to get a bad decision. I know I won't get a decision in the United States, that's clear. That's why I hired SugarHill. If I didn't want a knockout, I wouldn't hire the Kronk trainer who specialises on sitting on your punches, landing the right hand. He knows I rocked him three or four times, but I didn't have the gas to finish him off. Just look out for the right hand because you're going to sleep in two rounds. I keep having the same dream about knocking him out in round 2. I play poker all the time and I keep getting dealt number two. He is getting knocked out in round 2, a hundred per cent. What is going to happen is that I am going to get what I won last time. I am going to get that green belt, I am also going to get the *Ring* magazine, and I am also going to keep my lineal championship, too.'

Fury's game plan depended on a knockout, to avoid a repeat of what happened in the previous encounter: 'They had to rob a man who had been out of the ring for three years and they still couldn't beat him. I'm not coming here for a points decision, I've had too many of them – nine of them. I'm coming here for a knockout, I've had twenty-one of them and, from the heart, that's what I'm looking to do.' He was also employing that unusual training routine. 'I'm doing a lot of things I didn't before. I'm eating five or six meals a day, drinking eight litres of water. If it's gonna give me an edge, I'm willing to try it. I'm masturbating seven times a day, keep my testosterone pumping.'

'Enjoy yourself,' said Wilder. 'Just use the proper lotion.'

Columnist Carol Midgley commented on his workout in *The Times*: 'Presuming he is asleep for eight hours a day and has other stuff to do, such as boxing, that surely means he performs the "flute solo" roughly once every two hours. Which requires quite some dedicated fist-work. It's a blessing that the gloves will hide his hairy palms. This week Fury suggested that he would cash in on the interest around his "wanky-panky" by releasing his own lotion. Or better still, why not a candle, Tyson? If Gwyneth Paltrow can flog one inspired by her vagina, I'm sure fans would buy one based on your happy sock. Incidentally, do you know how boxers enter the ring to a personal theme tune? If Fury is a Beatles fan, may I suggest "We Can Jerk it Out"?'

It was only two months since Wilder's fight with Luis Ortiz, but he was ready for the rematch. He was confident because he had two knockouts in the two fights he had had since he faced Fury: 'I can't wait, it's been a quick turnaround but I'm still coming in shape,' he said. 'We all know I'm in shape for rematches because I've been in there before. I knocked him out before . . . I told Fury two years ago I was going to baptise him and I did that. This time around, it's unfinished business; he won't be able to get up. Since he's in the WWE I'm going to make sure he goes right out of the ring.' For Wilder too, victory depended on a knockout. 'Rising up is part of the baptism. I told him he was going to go "Timber!" and he did just that . . . I am going to knock him out. I am the lion. I am the king of the jungle and, come 22 February. I am going to rip his head off his body. I am going to knock him out of those ropes . . .

'He goes around talking he has the lineal title, something that is make-believe and fake. He has no belt except the one that holds his pants up now. That's the only thing he has. Come 22 February, that lineal bullshit, it ends. It ends with him. All that talk before, it dies, it's dead. This is a new beginning, this is unfinished business – that I will finish. I will do exactly what I said I would do, I will knock him out.'

He claimed that, in their last bout, he gave Fury concussion. 'When you've got power, there ain't no way around that,' said the Bronze Bomber. 'You can't prepare for power. The only thing you can do is hope that when it lands, it doesn't do that much damage. I gave this man a concussion the first time. He don't even know how he got on the ground or how he got up and, ladies and gentleman, that is a concussion.' And he mocked Fury's change of trainer. 'Why so many new trainers? Why so many rotations? He rotates trainers like he does his drawers, every day changing, hiring, firing. I'm sat here with the same old trainers and still to this day I have the same people. You don't see me firing anyone. You don't see me bringing anyone in, yet you're supposed to be this great fighter.'

Meanwhile, Fury defended his lineal title. 'Anyone who knows boxing knows its lineage goes back to the days of John L. Sullivan right up to me today,' said the undefeated Fury. 'If he beats me, he'll be beating the lineal heavyweight champion of the world, which means he will be the best of his era.'

SugarHill said he believed that Fury's dancing feet would win him the rematch and compared him to basketball legend LeBron James. He told MTK Global: 'Tyson loves to dance.

He's very creative. He's so athletic and co-ordinated for such a big man. He's like LeBron James! You can group Anthony Joshua and Deontay Wilder being one-punch guys. They don't have some of the other things Tyson does, but Tyson can also get you out there with one punch. Tyson has character and charisma and that strong desire to win. This is going to be a huge year for Tyson. I want him to be undisputed heavyweight champion. I'm not a big talker, really. Me and Tyson are on the same page. We speak about things we're going to work on. We're in agreement. We're satisfied and I think he can do the job. It's a perfect combination. All this positive energy is going to put us in the right place.'

Fury warned Wilder and Joshua about their 'undisputed' titles. He had had those titles and gave them up. 'Undisputed heavyweight champion means fuck all, it means nothing. I am already the main man,' said Fury. 'When I beat Klitschko he was the main man – no ifs, buts or maybes. When I beat him I became the main man. I have done that and am the only active heavyweight around who can say he beat the main man in the division, the top guy, the rest haven't. Wilder beat Bermane Stiverne, on his first defence of the belt, not that good. Joshua beat Charles Martin, who won his title on a default and should probably never have been a world champion. I became champion by beating a guy with twenty-six world title defences, who had gone unbeaten for eleven years, in his own country and backyard. I am the man to beat and none of these guys can claim to be the man until they beat me.'

Nevertheless, Fury insisted that he had great respect for

Wilder ahead of their rematch. He said: 'You're looking at a man here who's knocked out forty-three opponents in a row: now, even if I hate this guy, I've got to respect that – that's awesome. I never met anybody before who knocked out everyone they ever fought. Deontay's got amazing power and no matter what it comes to, verbal blows or anything, you always have to respect him. He's ten defences, beaten Lennox Lewis and Mike Tyson and all these guys' records defending the belt and he's done a fantastic job here in the United States, holding his title and defending it regularly so congratulations to the guy.'

He posted: 'I've got nothing – I can't take anything from him. He's a great puncher and he gets the job done. That's what he does but I don't believe anyone can match me with heart and determination. I will put my iron will on Deontay Wilder and we'll see.'

Eventually, Fury did admit that he had doubts about changing trainers with just weeks to go before the fight. 'To train with someone and feel like an absolute novice is exciting,' he told BT Sport. 'Me and SugarHill have not worked together for a long time and even before I only had a week with the guy. Everything is different; I feel like I'm learning again. Before, we were polishing stuff I did good and it was a winning formula. Now we're working on stuff I don't do so well and that's new to me, and that's the challenge. I thought if there is anyone who is going to be a good heavyweight trainer it's SugarHill and I believe the switch is a good thing. I wasn't so sure at the beginning, you never know what you're going to get with a new trainer and your whole team is separated, but after three weeks together I knew it was going to be a fantastic choice.'

SugarHill confirmed that he wanted to take the rematch decision from the judges. 'That was a risk that Tyson took in the first fight, in not stepping on the gas, and trying to win on points,' he told iFL TV. 'He doesn't want that again. I don't want it. I wasn't raised that way. Emanuel [Steward] always taught me, "Get the knockout." That's the only one hundred per cent way you know you won the fight – by taking it out of the hands of the judges. I thought Tyson did enough to win the fight, even though he was knocked down twice. I'm not mad at the decision because I was always taught, "Don't leave it in the hands of the judges".' As for the cut above the eye Fury had sustained in the fight against Otto Wallin, that would not be a problem. 'Everything is OK as far as I can see from the cut. It's been healed and it's been stitched up. I haven't seen anything that would make me believe it'll open up.'

Fury himself was not so sure. 'Is there any risk? I don't know because I am not a surgeon. I am sure there will be. There is nothing much I can do about that. If it opens up, it opens up. It's out of my control. There is nothing I can do about that eye opening in a fight.'

According to SugarHill, Fury's comeback proved he was one of boxing's best. 'It reminds me of how Muhammad Ali came back and no one believed he would do what he did in his career after being laid off for such a time,' he said. He also expressed admiration for Wilder. 'I've been around a lot of heavyweights that have been dominant throughout the years and he's been making his way and being dominant. He's been a champion for five years, and that's a long time in any division, especially the heavyweight division. Wladimir Klitschko almost broke Joe Louis' record for the longest-reigning heavyweight champion. To do what Wilder has done for five years, it's a big accomplishment. You have to put him up there with the great heavyweights. Wilder is knocking everybody out. I don't know of any other heavyweight that has knocked anybody out like that.'

Even Wilder joined the love-in, saying of Fury: 'He's a funny guy, he's a skilful fighter, a good fighter. And for me, in my opinion, he's a breath of fresh air, being in the heavyweight division, being able to have great fights with a person that can help me promote a fight. Because I've come up and so many guys don't talk, or they don't want to say what they want to do, or hype the crowd. It's always been me promoting.'

Asked whether he would target Fury's cut in the rematch, he said: 'I mean, that's what you do. If it opens it all depends on how good his plastic surgeon was, how fast it opens. Because the power that I have, I know how to cut a man open. It was longer than his eyebrow itself. Two inches wide. Bro, that was automatic stop, but we all know there's so much money involved.'

Fury's Uncle Peter told Sky Sports: 'It can go either way. Definitely you can't underestimate Wilder's power. He has got that one-punch, knockout ability, so that's clear. If he does it educated, we know Wilder can very easily be out-boxed. He does rely on that power. He pins his feet to the floor and that's the way he goes about it. I think Tyson's got to take the fight to him, maul him around a bit. Take him out of his comfort zone . . . I don't do predictions. I think it's a fifty-fifty fight.'

Wilder's trainer Jay Deas was confident that his man would win. 'The last time he fought against Tyson Fury, Deontay had an arm injury,' he told World Boxing News. 'Even though it was healed by fight-time, the timing on it was still off. Deontay was also very light and wasn't eating as much as he should. This time he's very healthy and firing on all cylinders. Things are good. The sparring is going well and we are looking forward to the fight.' He dismissed SugarHill's new tactics. 'Tyson Fury can say what he wants about how the fight will go. But whatever their game plan is we will be well-prepared for it. In regards to the weight, he's a big guy anyway. Heavyweights shouldn't let the scale dictate anything. As long as a heavyweight is training hard and eating well, the weight is the weight. I think Tyson will always be able to move well, regardless of whether he weighs 270 lbs.'

Wilder was not worried either. 'I'm not worried about his game plan, how much weight he gained. How many times he jerks off. I ain't worried about none of that stuff.' Asked about the titles on the line during the rematch, he added: 'I ain't worried about that either . . . I want you to remember greatness. I want you to remember something that you could only see in a Wilder event.'

Greatness was the furthest thing from Fury's mind when his reality show *Tyson Fury: The Gypsy King* aired on ITV in February. The boxer was seen carrying out menial household tasks while decked out in flamboyant designer clothes worth thousands. He headed to his local dump where he rifled through the bins and went home with some cast-off Manchester United posters he thought would go well in his Morecambe home. He and his wife, Paris, were seen grappling with their five kids and looking back over their eighteen-year relationship as they went through a box of gifts they had given one another.

Talking about his breakdown in 2015, he said: 'I always knew I was unwell. But I always put it to the back of my mind because I had a job to do – to become heavyweight champion of the world. So you put all your eggs in one basket and you've an addictive personality, so it's all or nothing in everything you do and you've achieved your dream. And, when there's no further you can go in your career, that was Everest and that's it – it all came crashing down.'

And the failed drugs test in 2016: 'You're looking at the man who has everything – acclaim, glory, fame, many achievements, a family and everything that goes with it, the trimmings, the gravy and still he isn't happy. We're made to believe success is happiness, but that's very untrue.'

His father said: 'There's never been a gypsy like Tyson. What he has you can't teach, it's a gift from God. Tyson will always be a gypsy, no matter what he does. He'll live fancy, he'll live better than a lot of gypsies, but he's still a gypsy.'

Fury added that he was on the way to recover his heavyweight title. 'I haven't defeated mental health,' he said. 'I still have bad days and good days, everybody does. It never goes away. But I learn to maintain and that's it. Thinking positive and being around positive people.'

Of his marriage, he said: 'Me and Paris are like soulmates.

When God married us and two became one, let no man tear apart what God has put together.'

Paris said: 'From being sixteen years old I've loved this man. Even during the bad times when I think: I really hate you, but I love you. That's how we get through things.' Paris also spoke out about his battles with mental health.

Wilder smelt a rat when he heard Fury talk about his life. He told ThaBoxingVoice.com: 'A lot of stuff that he's doing is making me feel like he's setting up an excuse for when he loses. The weight thing – I don't wanna hear nothing about being out of shape or, "He didn't have enough time to get in shape." All these trainers around – I don't wanna hear when I knock him out that, "If he had Ben it would've been better." Don't wanna hear no excuses. I already feel like all this stuff that's going on is going to be bent around as excuses. We'll see what happens.'

When asked if he thought that new trainer SugarHill Steward would help Fury when the pair clashed, Wilder replied, 'I don't. It's similarities to the Dominic Breazeale camp when they added Virgil [Hunter]. When you have bad habits, it's hard to correct. Sometimes it takes years to correct bad habits. And it takes even longer when you ain't used to that, when you ain't worked with that person.' Fury had doubts, he concluded. 'I feel he's nervous deep down in his heart. I feel he is very, very nervous from the first time, what happened. When you knock someone down and give them a concussion, you don't forget that. You never forget who did it and how they do it. When you're going in the ring with them for a second time, to relive that moment all over again, then it has to be stressful. You definitely can't sleep at night and I understand why he is changing up a lot of things in his team.'

The Bronze Bomber said that Fury would not have made such sweeping changes if he genuinely believed he had won their last fight. 'For me, I just think that's nervous energy from the first fight. He can go and say he beat me by a wide margin, but he doesn't believe that. That's why he's changed up a lot of things. If you really believe that, you would not change so much. I don't think he's confident in his head because he understands how I left him. I gave that man a concussion. It could easily happen again because the head is not meant to be hit, especially by the power of someone like Deontay Wilder.'

Wilder said that in their previous fight there were no rounds during which he felt threatened by Fury and he mocked his opponent's power. 'Like I said before, he has pillow fists. That's how soft they were in that fight. Maybe my adrenalin was too high to even feel anything. But even after the fight, I didn't feel anything. I took all his punches, the ones he's landed, and I walked right through them. So I don't respect none of his power he has. He's just a tall, big man, who can move around the ring. That's about it.'

Just seven weeks with a new trainer would solve nothing. 'For his power, there's none there and I don't think he can develop it no matter what trainer he brings in,' Wilder said. 'You just don't develop power in a couple of weeks, just in a month, just because this trainer comes in. I don't see his trainer develop a fighter with power, what fighter has he developed power with? So, if he's never developed a fighter into a power-puncher then how in the hell is he going to make Tyson Fury into that, in this short amount of time he has? It's impossible, it's impossible. I know these things, I'm an expert in them.'

Wilder also claimed that he himself had not been at full power in their previous encounter, as he had suffered a broken arm in the build-up. 'I was probably fifty per cent or less,' he said. 'I didn't fight my normal fight and I could pinpoint so many things.'

As the pre-fight barney ramped up, Fury said he was going to dethrone Wilder – 'rip his heart out and feed it to him'. He said, 'I look at Wilder and I don't see a tough fight. I see a long-legged pussy that I'm going to break in. I am going to give him his first loss. That's what I'm going to do to Deontay Wilder.'

Wilder responded: 'People go on about his knockout power and him being the biggest puncher in heavyweight history, but who you have fought counts. Honestly, over here in America they call his level of opposition "tomato cans". He has only had probably seven competitive fights, where people have actually tried to fight back. The rest were duck-egg dummies, only there to fall over.'

Stirring controversy, Fury told the news website Daily Caller: 'After this fight I'm going to binge on cocaine and hookers. Is there anything better than cocaine and hookers? I go to the cheap, thirty-dollar ones. Always give yourself a shot of penicillin before shagging them.' He advised anyone doing likewise to 'double-bag up'. Fury then explained the training he was doing to counter Wilder's knockout punch: 'I have got confidence in my chin but I've been doing a lot of pussy-licking to strengthen my jaw up.' He declared 'fucking war' on Wilder. If these comments in the media did not annoy his wife enough, he said he also was banning her from the Las Vegas mansion where he stayed while making his final preparations for the fight.

'I've been barred from the house,' said Paris. 'I don't quite understand. The boys are all there and they've all said it's a serious fight. But I don't think they realise that I've been here for eleven years and I understand all the rules and regulations of nights before fights, so I'm just going along with it.' However, she would be there at ringside, as ever.

The two fighters also slugged it out on the fashion front as well at the pre-fight press conference, Fury wearing a dark suit emblazoned with pictures of his own face and gold-leather slippers, while Wilder wore a fur-collared leather coat with a gold chain and medallion hanging around his neck, a gold ring and jazzy, spiky footwear to prove he truly was the King of Bling.

Fury's attire had a deeper purpose. 'The idea of the suit is to throw Deontay Wilder off his game,' said his tailor, Navid Salimian. 'All of our suits incorporate a storytelling element. They will have moments of history and moments that are potentially yet to come depicted on the shirts. Most of them have Tyson's face on the shirt, by his choice . . . We're there to give Tyson that extra five-per-cent confidence. At this first press conference, we noticed Deontay Wilder came in a tracksuit and Tyson was in a three-piece. Then at the next

press conference, Tyson is wearing a shirt with World War
Two Spitfires on with a tweed suit, almost like a general and
then the next one, Wilder turns up in a golden Versace shirt.
And that's when we realised, we're making a difference here.'

Fury had clearly learnt from his experience with the WWE,
according to *Sports Illustrated*, who said that the face-off at
a weigh-in was straight out of the pro-wrestling playbook.
'Maybe that's why Fury looked so comfortable when he and
Wilder engaged in some extremely fake pushing and shoving,'
said the magazine. 'Wilder and Fury just went through the
motions. They looked like two guys trying to emulate what
they've seen at other weigh-ins.'

But the Nevada State Athletic Commission took it more
seriously, banning the two champions from facing off at the
final weigh-in on the day before the fight. NSAC executive
director Bob Bennett told CBS Sports: 'The actions of the two
fighters pushing each other – which was not staged – is not
indicative of the image of our sport as a major league sport,
thus having a face-off is not in the best interest in the health
and safety of the fighters, the public and the event.'

Fury admitted that things were legitimately heated, saying,
'We were almost at blows' as he and Wilder exchanged insults
throughout the event. 'He shoved me and I shoved him.
When a man raises his hand to you, it's an automatic instinct
to defend yourself. If someone laid hands on me, I've got to
protect myself.'

But Wilder could spin too. 'Don't you ever forget that,
when I found you, you were strung out on coke. You were
like a big house, contemplating killing yourself. Don't you

ever forget who brought you to big-time boxing. I brought you back, dragged you back. I laid him out and he will be laid out again. All 6 ft 9 in of him, like a murder scene. I put food on your table for your family to eat and I'm doing it again for a second time. I'm the one who sells the pay per view and tickets. They come to see me.'

Fury, as always, was up for a retort: 'I was the man who beat Wladimir Klitschko. I gave you your biggest payday. You're a bum – nobody even knows you in your own country . . . And that's the man you take on. A man thinking about killing himself. You thought you were getting an easy victory, didn't you? Well, it didn't work out. I came back and kicked your arse all over.'

Weighing in at 231 lbs, Wilder was heavier than expected, 18.5 lbs heavier than at their first fight. Fury had also put on weight for the rematch, weighing in at 273 lbs, just three pounds short of his heaviest ever and 16.5 lbs heavier than at their first fight. 'The weight's not a problem,' Fury said. 'It's 273 pounds of pure British beef.'

'At the end of the day, we're heavyweights,' said Wilder. 'So it doesn't really matter about the weight.'

It did matter in the ring though. Fury's extra weight gave him more punching power, while Wilder's made him slow and leaden-footed. As soon as the bell sounded, Fury bounded across the ring and threw close to a dozen big right-hands and lead left-hooks. Wilder fended him off with a nice right, followed by a jab. Fury tried a right over the top but Wilder blocked his jab. Fury caught Wilder with a decent shot, then made a double feint to score with a jab. Throughout, Fury was the aggressor. From the beginning Wilder was on the back foot and uncomfortable with it. At the bell Fury raised a glove. There was no doubt who had won the round.

As soon as round 2 started, Fury delivered a stiff jab to Wilder's head, jolting it back. The crowd roared Fury's name and taunted Wilder, shouting: 'You big dosser!' But Wilder found his right hand and that's not what Fury wanted to see. Wilder then set him up with the jab and unloaded a massive right, but Fury slipped it. Fury cracked him back with a right and Wilder froze. For a moment, he was stunned and blinking, but then landed one of his own. Fury took it and span him. The round ended with Fury barrelling Wilder into the corner and wrestling with him.

In round 3, a looping ring hook from Fury got the crowd fired up again. Wilder was not able to land his jab, which meant that he could not tee up the big right. His bottom lip had swelled up. A jab and right hand to the temple dropped Wilder to the canvas with 30 sec to go. He had only ever been knocked down once before in his pro career, back in 2010 when he got up to destroy Harold Sconiers in four rounds. But this time, his senses were scrambled. No sooner was he up than he hit the canvas again. The referee, Kenny Bayless, judged this a slip, but it was clear Wilder was stunned by Fury's onslaught. The AP had Fury ahead 30–26 after three rounds.

At the beginning of round 4, Fury delivered a right uppercut on the side, before the ref split them. A blow on the back of the head sent Wilder down again. Bayless judged this to be another slip, but it was clear that Wilder was rudderless: blood was coming from his ear. Nevertheless, he got in a right-hand, reminding Fury how dangerous he was, even when groggy. But Wilder was off-balance and the blow was more of a lunge than his trademark, knockout punch.

In round 5, Fury roared out of his corner again to land a big right-hand. Wilder had nothing to counter this. A left hook to the body put him on the canvas once more. He beat the count, but he was now defenceless. Fury pummelled him freely and Bayless had to warn Fury about holding and using his extra height to lean over his prey. He had a point docked, but it seemed unlikely that he was going to need it, though it made this one round even.

Fury got Wilder up against the ropes in round 6 and mauled him relentlessly. Another left hook left Wilder clinging to the ropes. Fury was covered in blood – but not his own. He even appeared to be licking fresh blood off Wilder who was, by then, a mess. Wilder looked all in, but clung on bravely.

The one-sided hammering continued in round 7. Fury scored early with a left, then a jab. Wilder looked a bit clearer than he had in previous rounds. Fury landed another left. Wilder fired off a right that grazed Fury's shaved head, but it had no power. Fury then trapped Wilder in the corner while he smashed him in the face with a straight right. Bayless was about to stop the fight when Wilder's corner threw in the blood-stained towel after 1 min 39 sec, while Wilder himself protested the stoppage. But he knew it was all done and dusted.

After the fight, Fury gave a gracious speech.

'Thank you to my lord and saviour Jesus Christ,' he said. 'I told everyone the Gypsy King has returned to his throne. Last fight I was underweight and over-trained. This time, how about pillow fists, eh? I told Deontay I am going for a knockout. Everyone said, "Oh, stick to your boxing.' I was knocking a 250 bag off his hooks every day, not padding around. Deontay is a hell of performer, dynamite in his fists and he will always be dangerous. People look at my fat belly and my bald head and they think I cannot fight. I had my mental problems and issues and I was out of the ring three years. But he was fighting the real Gypsy King this time. I expect he will want a rematch and I will have that. Great fights should have trilogies. And I want it here, just across the road, at the Raiders Stadium outdoors, in front of seventy-thousand.'

He showed respect to the defeated champion, saying: 'A big shout-out to Deontay Wilder. He came here tonight and he manned up and he really did show the heart of a champion. I hit him with a clean right that dropped him and he got back up. He is a warrior. He will be back. He will be champion again. But I will say, the king has returned to the top of the throne!'

Wilder also had some words to say: 'The best man won tonight, but my corner threw in the towel and I was ready to go out on my shield. I had a lot of things going on heading into this fight. It is what it is, but I make no excuses tonight. I just wish my corner would have let me go out on my shield. I'm a warrior. He had a great performance and we will be back stronger. Even the greatest have lost and came back, that is just part of it. I can make no excuses tonight. I had a lot of complications. But we'll come back stronger next time around. This is what big-time boxing is all about, the best must fight the best. I appreciate all the fans that came out and supported the show, and I hope that everyone gets home safely.'

But Fury was not going home. 'Were you not entertained?' cried Fury before heading off to a nightclub to celebrate his victory wearing one of his 'Gypsy King' suits. The answer was: 'Yes, we were.' It was one of the greatest victories in British boxing history. And there would be more to come.